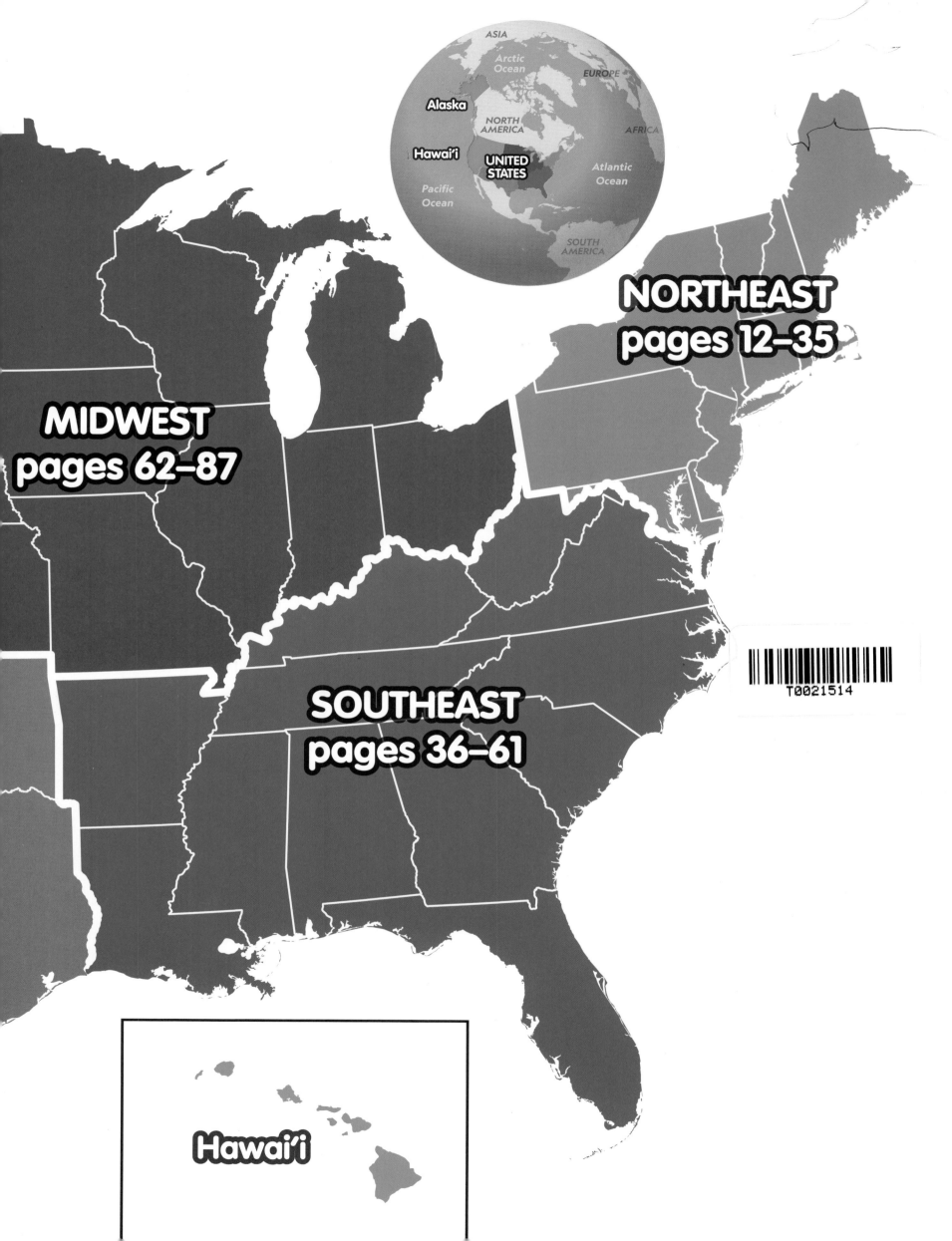

ASIA
Arctic Ocean
EUROPE
Alaska
NORTH AMERICA
AFRICA
Hawai'i
UNITED STATES
Atlantic Ocean
Pacific Ocean
SOUTH AMERICA

NORTHEAST
pages 12–35

MIDWEST
pages 62–87

SOUTHEAST
pages 36–61

T0021514

Hawai'i

NATIONAL GEOGRAPHIC
KiDS

BEGINNER'S
UNITED STATES
ATLAS

NATIONAL GEOGRAPHIC
WASHINGTON, D.C.

Contents

Learning the Basics

This atlas uses maps and photographs to show the many differences in the people, animals, and places that make up the United States. The atlas divides the country into five regions, each indicated by a different color, as shown on the map above. The introduction to each region includes a locator map that highlights the states of the region in yellow.

What Is a Map?

An atlas is a collection of maps and pictures. A map is a drawing of a place as it looks from above. It is flat, and it is smaller than the place it shows. Learning to read a map can help you find where you are and where you want to go. Maps in this atlas are simplified to help you read them.

Mapping your home ...

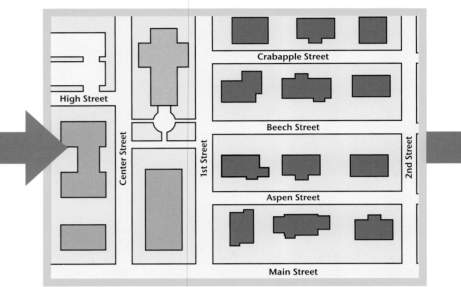

From a bird's-eye view ...
you would see only the tops of things, just as a bird flying directly overhead would. You wouldn't see walls, tree trunks, tires, or feet.

On a large-scale map ...
you see places from a bird's-eye view. But a map uses drawings called symbols to show things on the ground, such as houses or streets. The map of the National Mall in Washington, D.C., on pages 10–11 is an example of a large-scale map.

Finding places on the map

A map can help you get where you want to go.
A map includes a compass rose, a scale,
and a key to help you read the map.

A compass rose helps you travel in the right direction. It tells you where north (N), south (S), east (E), and west (W) are on your map.

Often only a north arrow is used.

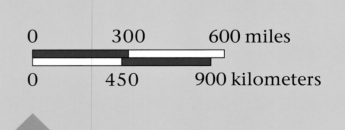

A scale tells you about distance on a map. The scale shows what length on the map represents the labeled distance on the ground.

On an intermediate-scale map …

you see a place from much higher up. A town appears as a tiny dot. You can't see houses, but you can see more of the land around the town. Most maps in this atlas show a whole state with its towns and cities and other special features.

On a small-scale map …

you can see much more of the country around a state, including other states. But on a small-scale map there is much less detail. You can no longer see most features within the state. Two states—Alaska and Hawai'i—are often shown in separate boxes or on a map of the whole continent, as on pages 6–7.

A map key helps you understand the symbols used by the mapmaker to show things like cities, rivers, boundaries, forests, and points of interest on the map.

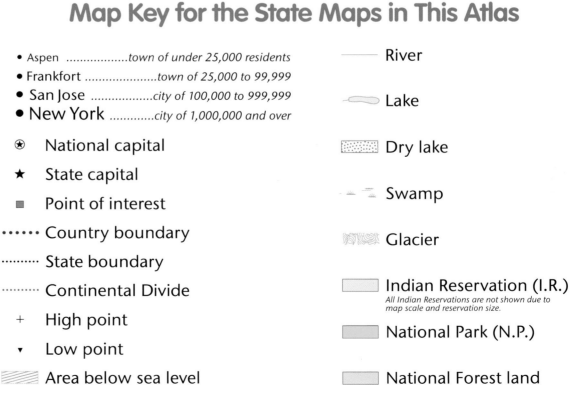

Map Key for the State Maps in This Atlas

- Aspen ....town of under 25,000 residents
- Frankfort ....town of 25,000 to 99,999
- San Jose ....city of 100,000 to 999,999
- New York ....city of 1,000,000 and over

⊛ National capital

★ State capital

■ Point of interest

••••• Country boundary

········· State boundary

········· Continental Divide

+ High point

▾ Low point

⧄ Area below sea level

—— River

◯ Lake

▦ Dry lake

🗻 Swamp

🗻 Glacier

▭ Indian Reservation (I.R.)
All Indian Reservations are not shown due to map scale and reservation size.

▭ National Park (N.P.)

▭ National Forest land

THE LAND
The Physical United States

LAND REGIONS The rugged Sierra Nevada and Rocky Mountains run north to south through the western United States. Between these mountains are dry lands with little vegetation. East of the Rockies are wide, grassy plains and the older, lower Appalachian Mountains.

WATER Together, the Mississippi and the Missouri form the longest river system in the United States. The Great Lakes are the largest freshwater lakes in the country.

CLIMATE The United States has many climate types—from cold Alaska to tropical Hawai'i, with milder climates in the other 48 states.

PLANTS The United States has forests where there is plenty of rain. Grasslands cover drier areas.

ANIMALS There are many kinds of animals—everything from bears and deer to songbirds large and small.

North America is famous for its deciduous forests. Leaves turn fiery colors each fall.

The majestic bald eagle is the national bird of the United States. It is found throughout the country, but about half live in Alaska.

Deserts are found in the southwestern part of the United States. This large rock formation is in Monument Valley in Utah.

H a w a i'i

PACIFIC OCEAN

Moloka'i

Hawai'i

Waves off the Pacific Ocean roll onto a beach along the shore of Moloka'i, one of the islands that make up the state of Hawai'i.

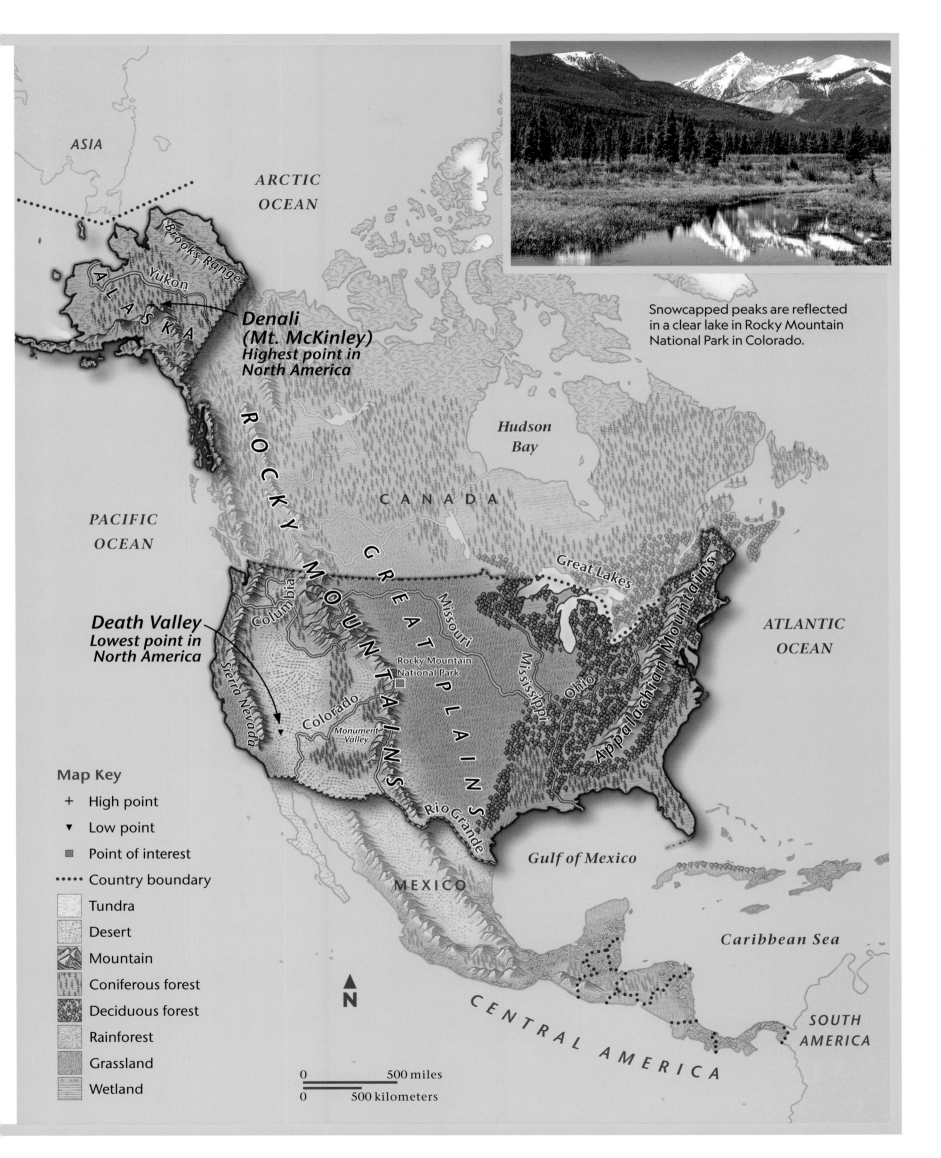

ASIA

ARCTIC
OCEAN

Brooks Range

ALASKA

Yukon

Denali
(Mt. McKinley)
Highest point in
North America

PACIFIC
OCEAN

Death Valley
Lowest point in
North America

Columbia

Sierra Nevada

Colorado

Monument
Valley

Rio Grande

MEXICO

CANADA

Hudson
Bay

ROCKY MOUNTAINS

GREAT PLAINS

Rocky Mountain
National Park

Missouri

Mississippi

Ohio

Great Lakes

Appalachian Mountains

ATLANTIC
OCEAN

Gulf of Mexico

Caribbean Sea

CENTRAL AMERICA

SOUTH
AMERICA

Snowcapped peaks are reflected
in a clear lake in Rocky Mountain
National Park in Colorado.

Map Key

+ High point

▼ Low point

■ Point of interest

•••• Country boundary

Tundra

Desert

Mountain

Coniferous forest

Deciduous forest

Rainforest

Grassland

Wetland

0   500 miles

0   500 kilometers

N

THE PEOPLE
The Political United States

 STATES The United States is made up of 50 states. Alaska and Hawai'i are separated from the rest of the country. So you can see them close up, they are shown here in the Pacific Ocean south of the state of California.

CITIES Washington, D.C., is the national capital. Each state has its own capital. New York City has the most people of any U.S. city.

PEOPLE The United States is made up of people from all over the world and descendants of the native people who first lived on this land. Most live and work in and around cities. In this atlas, city proper and state population figures are from 2018 unless otherwise noted.

LANGUAGES English is the main language, followed by Spanish.

Baseball is a popular sport in the United States, along with soccer, basketball, and football.

Chinese New Year is a big celebration in San Francisco. Many Chinese Americans live in this California city.

WASHINGTON
Seattle
Olympia ★
Portland
★ Salem
OREGON
Columbia
I D A H O
Helena ★
M O
Boise ★
C A L I F O R N I A
Carson City
Sacramento
San Francisco
San Jose
NEVADA
Salt Lake City ★
U T A H
Colorado
Las Vegas
Los Angeles
San Diego
Phoenix ★
A R I Z O N A
Tucson

PACIFIC OCEAN

ALASKA
Juneau ★

PACIFIC OCEAN

0   400 miles
0   400 kilometers

PACIFIC OCEAN

HAWAI'I
Honolulu ★

0   150 miles
0   150 kilometers

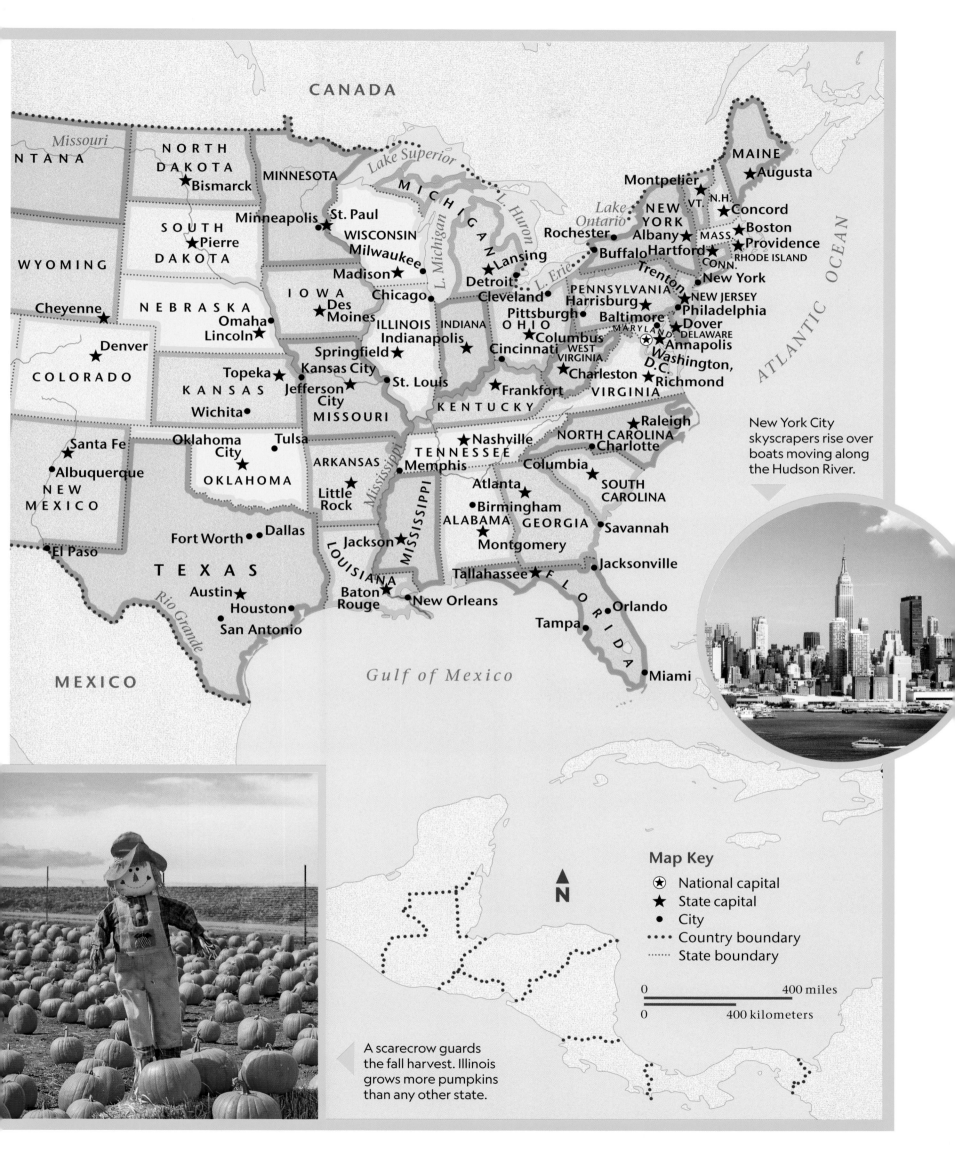

CANADA

Missouri

MONTANA

NORTH DAKOTA
★ Bismarck

SOUTH DAKOTA
★ Pierre

WYOMING

MINNESOTA
Minneapolis ● ★ St. Paul

WISCONSIN
Milwaukee ●
Madison ★

IOWA
Des ★ Moines

NEBRASKA
Omaha ●
Lincoln ★

Cheyenne ★

Denver ★

COLORADO

Lake Superior

MICHIGAN
Lansing ★

L. Michigan

L. Huron

Chicago ●

ILLINOIS
Springfield ★

Detroit ●
Cleveland ●
L. Erie

INDIANA
Indianapolis ★

OHIO
Columbus ★
Cincinnati ●

Pittsburgh ●

PENNSYLVANIA
Harrisburg ★

Lake Ontario
Rochester ●
Buffalo ●

Montpelier ★
VT.
★ Concord
N.H.

MAINE
★ Augusta

NEW YORK
Albany ★

MASS.
★ Boston
★ Providence
RHODE ISLAND

Hartford ★
CONN.

Trenton ★
NEW JERSEY
New York ●

Baltimore ●
★ Philadelphia
Dover ★
DELAWARE

ATLANTIC OCEAN

Topeka ★
KANSAS
Jefferson City ★
Wichita ●

Kansas City ●
St. Louis ●

MISSOURI

KENTUCKY
Frankfort ★

WEST VIRGINIA
Charleston ★

MARYLAND
⊛ Annapolis
Washington, D.C.
Richmond ★

VIRGINIA

Santa Fe ★
Albuquerque ●
NEW MEXICO

Oklahoma City ★
Tulsa ●

OKLAHOMA

Nashville ★
TENNESSEE
Memphis ●

ARKANSAS
Little Rock ★

Raleigh ★
NORTH CAROLINA
Charlotte ●

Columbia ★
SOUTH CAROLINA

New York City skyscrapers rise over boats moving along the Hudson River.

El Paso ●

TEXAS
Austin ★
Houston ●
San Antonio ●

Fort Worth ● ● Dallas

Rio Grande

LOUISIANA
Jackson ★
MISSISSIPPI

Baton Rouge ★
New Orleans ●

Atlanta ★
Birmingham ●
ALABAMA
Montgomery ★

GEORGIA
Savannah ●

Jacksonville ●

Tallahassee ★
FLORIDA
Orlando ●
Tampa ●
Miami ●

MEXICO

Gulf of Mexico

Map Key
⊛ National capital
★ State capital
● City
•••• Country boundary
---- State boundary

N

| 0 | 400 miles |
| 0 | 400 kilometers |

◄ A scarecrow guards the fall harvest. Illinois grows more pumpkins than any other state.

THE NATIONAL CAPITAL
The District of Columbia

 LAND & WATER The National Mall, the Potomac River, and the Anacostia River are important land and water features of the District of Columbia.

 **STATEHOOD** The District of Columbia, better known as Washington, D.C., was founded in 1790, but it is not a state.

 PEOPLE & PLACES The District of Columbia's population is 702,455. The city is the seat of the U.S. government.

? **FUN FACT** The flag of the District of Columbia, with three red stars and two red stripes, is based on the shield in George Washington's family coat of arms.

The Smithsonian Institution, the world's largest museum, is actually made up of 19 museums and the National Zoo. Established in 1846, it is sometimes called the nation's attic because of its large collections.

Abraham Lincoln, who was president during the Civil War and a strong opponent of slavery, is remembered in a memorial that houses this seated statue at the west end of the National Mall.

Washington, D.C. Flag

American Beauty Rose
Official Flower

Wood Thrush
Official Bird

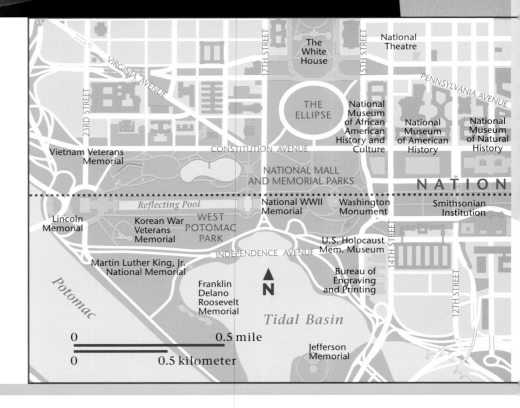

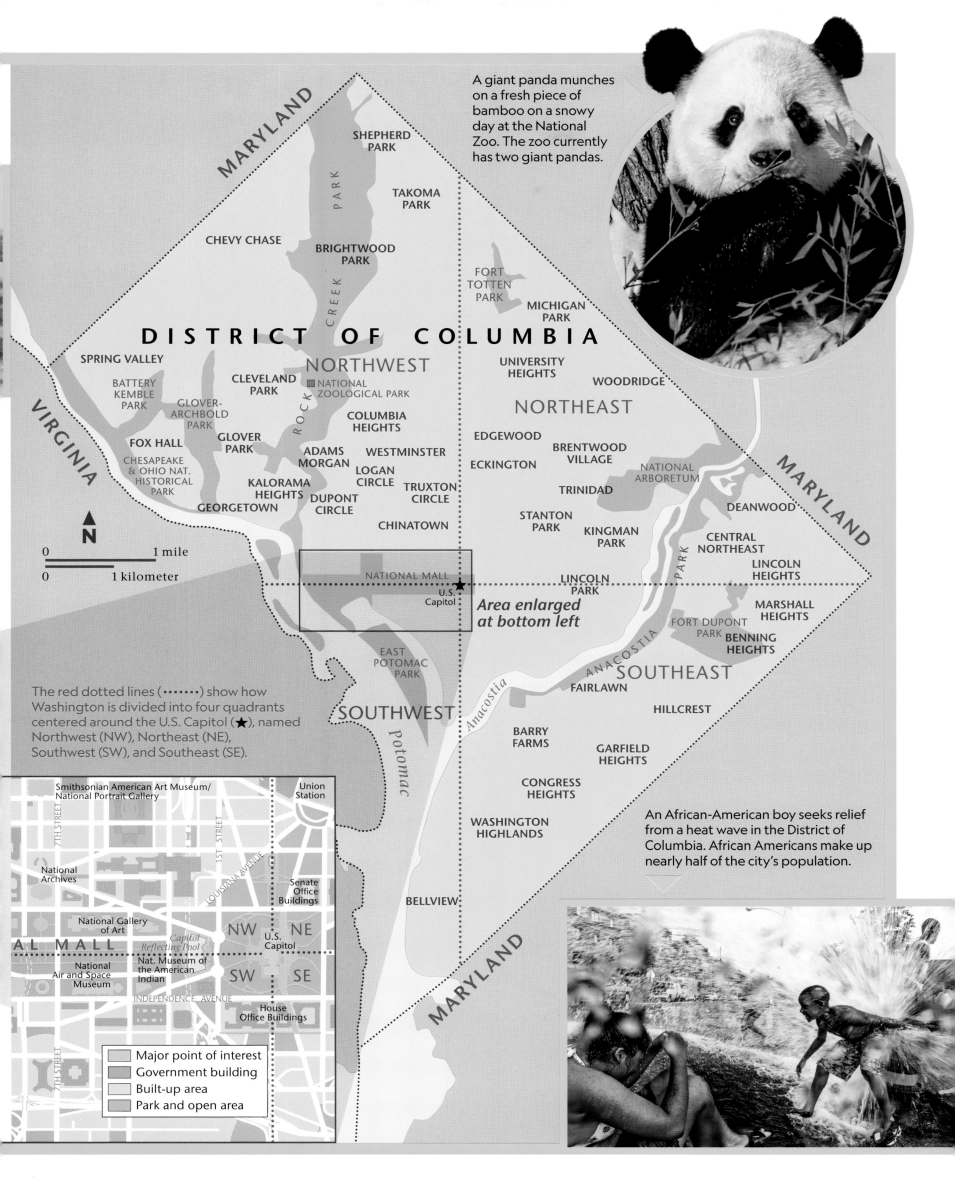

A giant panda munches on a fresh piece of bamboo on a snowy day at the National Zoo. The zoo currently has two giant pandas.

MARYLAND

SHEPHERD PARK

TAKOMA PARK

CHEVY CHASE

BRIGHTWOOD PARK

PARK

CREEK

FORT TOTTEN PARK

MICHIGAN PARK

DISTRICT OF COLUMBIA

NORTHWEST

UNIVERSITY HEIGHTS

WOODRIDGE

VIRGINIA

SPRING VALLEY

CLEVELAND PARK

NATIONAL ZOOLOGICAL PARK

BATTERY KEMBLE PARK

GLOVER-ARCHBOLD PARK

ROCK

COLUMBIA HEIGHTS

NORTHEAST

EDGEWOOD

BRENTWOOD VILLAGE

FOX HALL

GLOVER PARK

ECKINGTON

NATIONAL ARBORETUM

CHESAPEAKE & OHIO NAT. HISTORICAL PARK

ADAMS MORGAN

WESTMINSTER

TRINIDAD

DEANWOOD

KALORAMA HEIGHTS

LOGAN CIRCLE

TRUXTON CIRCLE

STANTON PARK

KINGMAN PARK

CENTRAL NORTHEAST

LINCOLN HEIGHTS

GEORGETOWN

DUPONT CIRCLE

CHINATOWN

PARK

N
0   1 mile
0   1 kilometer

NATIONAL MALL

U.S. Capitol

Area enlarged at bottom left

LINCOLN PARK

MARSHALL HEIGHTS

FORT DUPONT PARK

BENNING HEIGHTS

ANACOSTIA

EAST POTOMAC PARK

Anacostia

FAIRLAWN

SOUTHEAST

HILLCREST

The red dotted lines (••••••) show how Washington is divided into four quadrants centered around the U.S. Capitol (★), named Northwest (NW), Northeast (NE), Southwest (SW), and Southeast (SE).

SOUTHWEST

Potomac

BARRY FARMS

GARFIELD HEIGHTS

CONGRESS HEIGHTS

WASHINGTON HIGHLANDS

An African-American boy seeks relief from a heat wave in the District of Columbia. African Americans make up nearly half of the city's population.

BELLVIEW

MARYLAND

Smithsonian American Art Museum/ National Portrait Gallery

Union Station

National Archives

7TH STREET

1ST STREET

LOUISIANA AVENUE

Senate Office Buildings

National Gallery of Art

Capitol Reflecting Pool

NW

NE

AL MALL

U.S. Capitol

National Air and Space Museum

Nat. Museum of the American Indian

SW

SE

INDEPENDENCE AVENUE

House Office Buildings

7TH STREET

Major point of interest
Government building
Built-up area
Park and open area

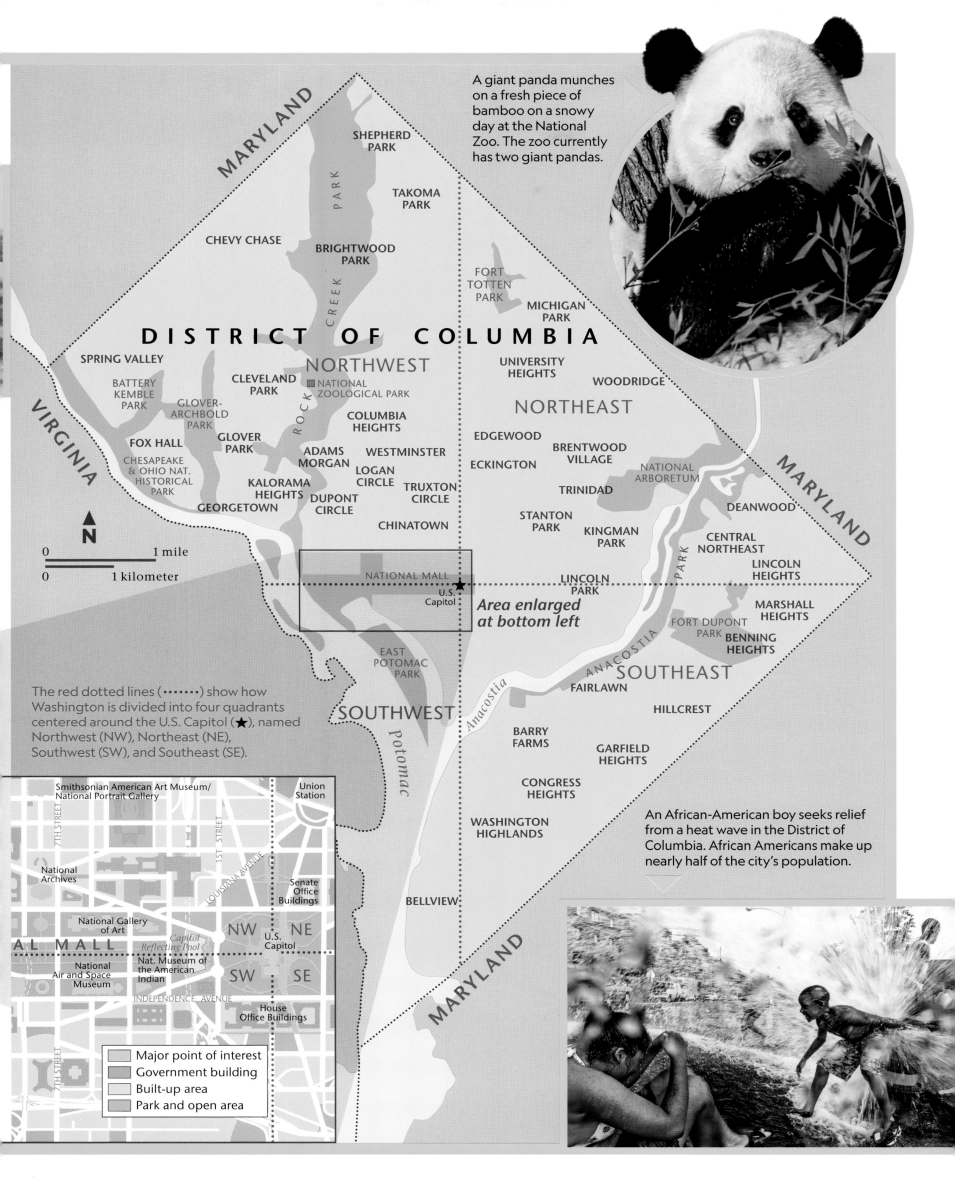

THE NORTHEAST

The earliest inhabitants of the river valleys and woodlands of the Northeast were Native American. Settlers and traders arrived from Europe and established colonies that eventually became states. Today people come from countries around the world to live here, bringing with them customs, languages, and beliefs that make the Northeast a region of great diversity. The region includes the country's financial center, New York City, and its political capital, Washington, D.C.

Black bears live throughout much of the United States, including the forests of the Northeast. Their diet includes roots, berries, and human garbage.

Water plunges as much as 110 feet (34 m) over the American Falls on the Niagara River near New York's northwestern border with the country of Canada.

CONNECTICUT

LAND & WATER Mount Frissell, the Connecticut River, and Long Island Sound are important land and water features of Connecticut.

STATEHOOD Connecticut became the 5th state in 1788.

PEOPLE & PLACES Connecticut's population is 3,572,665. Hartford is the state capital. The largest city is Bridgeport.

FUN FACT The sperm whale, Connecticut's state animal, is known for its massive head. Its brain is larger than that of any other creature known to have lived on Earth.

Lacrosse is a popular sport in schools and colleges in Connecticut and across the United States. It was derived from a game played by many Eastern Woodland Native Americans.

Connecticut State Flag

Mountain Laurel
State Flower

Robin
State Bird

The *Charles W. Morgan*, launched in 1841 and now docked in Mystic Seaport, is the only remaining wooden whaling ship in the world.

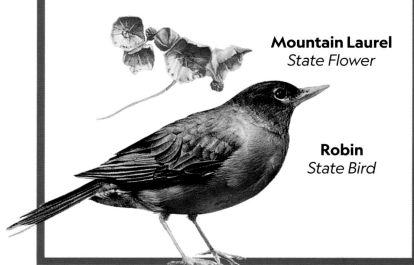

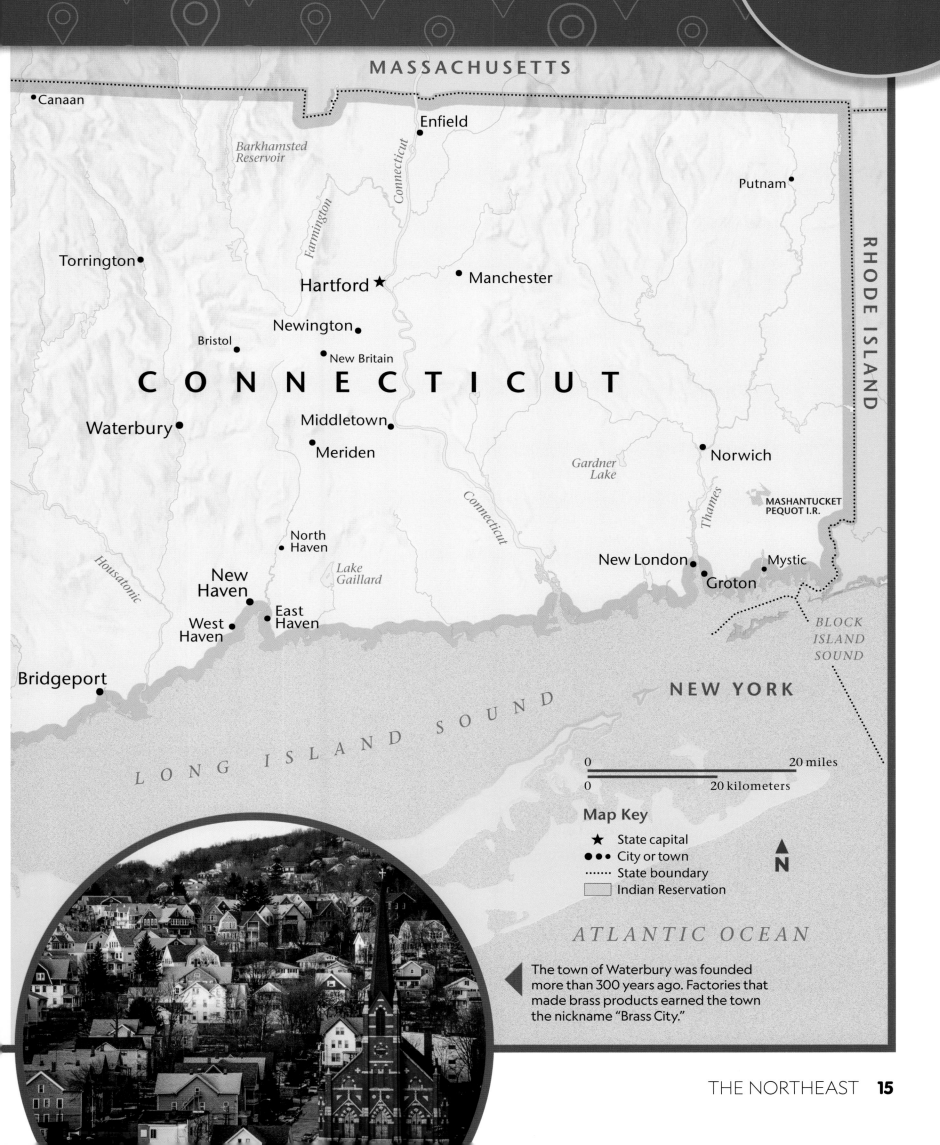

MASSACHUSETTS

RHODE ISLAND

Canaan

Enfield

Barkhamsted Reservoir

Connecticut

Putnam

Farmington

Torrington

Manchester

Hartford ★

Newington

Bristol

New Britain

CONNECTICUT

Waterbury

Middletown

Meriden

Gardner Lake

Norwich

Connecticut

MASHANTUCKET PEQUOT I.R.

Housatonic

North Haven

Lake Gaillard

Thames

New Haven

New London

Mystic

West Haven

East Haven

Groton

BLOCK ISLAND SOUND

Bridgeport

NEW YORK

LONG ISLAND SOUND

0   20 miles

0   20 kilometers

Map Key

★ State capital

●●● City or town

······ State boundary

▢ Indian Reservation

N

ATLANTIC OCEAN

The town of Waterbury was founded more than 300 years ago. Factories that made brass products earned the town the nickname "Brass City."

DELAWARE

DELAWARE

LAND & WATER
The Barrier Islands, Cypress Swamp, and Delaware Bay are important land and water features of Delaware.

The Delmarva Peninsula is a major area for raising chickens, with more than 1,500 poultry farms. The Delmarva poultry trade association is in Georgetown.

STATEHOOD Delaware became the 1st state in 1787.

PEOPLE & PLACES The population of Delaware is 967,171. Dover is the state capital. The largest city is Wilmington.

FUN FACT Each year contestants bring pumpkins and launching machines to the Punkin Chunkin World Championship in Bridgeville to see who can toss their big orange squash the farthest.

Delaware State Flag

Brightly colored umbrellas dot Cape Henlopen Beach. Sun, sand, and surf attract thousands of vacationers each year to Delaware's shore.

Patriotic boys wave American flags at a Delaware motorsports track near Delmar. Racing fans have come to the tracks since they opened in 1963.

Peach Blossom
State Flower

Blue Hen Chicken
State Bird

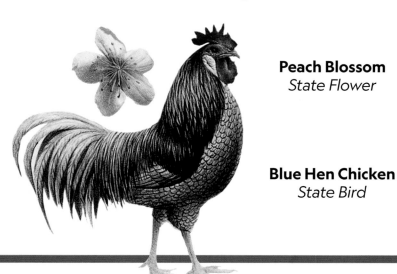

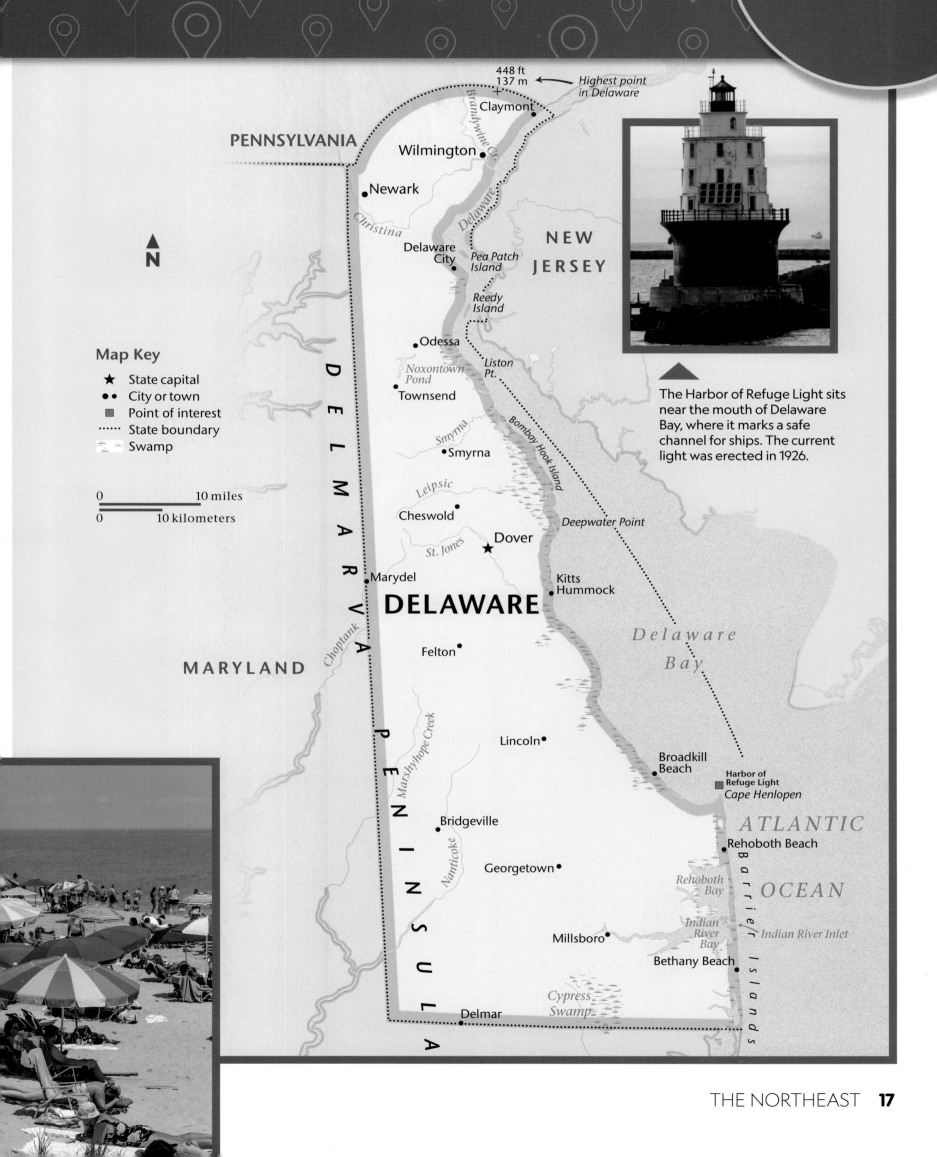

PENNSYLVANIA

448 ft
137 m ← Highest point in Delaware

Claymont

Wilmington

Newark

NEW JERSEY

Delaware City

Pea Patch Island

Reedy Island

Odessa

Noxontown Pond

Liston Pt.

Townsend

Smyrna

Smyrna

Bombay Hook Island

Leipsic

Cheswold

Deepwater Point

Dover

St. Jones

Marydel

Kitts Hummock

DELAWARE

Delaware Bay

MARYLAND

Felton

Lincoln

Broadkill Beach

Harbor of Refuge Light
Cape Henlopen

Bridgeville

ATLANTIC

Rehoboth Beach

Georgetown

Rehoboth Bay

OCEAN

Indian River Bay

Millsboro

Indian River Inlet

Bethany Beach

Delmar

Cypress Swamp

Christina

Choptank

Marshyhope Creek

Nanticoke

Map Key

★ State capital
•• City or town
■ Point of interest
⋯ State boundary
≈ Swamp

0 ——— 10 miles
0 ——— 10 kilometers

The Harbor of Refuge Light sits near the mouth of Delaware Bay, where it marks a safe channel for ships. The current light was erected in 1926.

MAINE

MAINE

LAND & WATER The Appalachian Mountains, Mount Katahdin, and the Gulf of Maine are important land and water features of Maine.

STATEHOOD Maine became the 23rd state in 1820.

PEOPLE & PLACES Maine's population is 1,338,404. Augusta is the state capital. The largest city is Portland.

FUN FACT During the last ice age, glaciers carved hundreds of bays and inlets along Maine's shoreline and created some 2,000 islands off the coast.

There are 65 lighthouses along Maine's rocky coastline, warning ships of danger. The oldest lighthouse, Portland Head Light, is located at Cape Elizabeth.

Each year Rockland hosts the Maine Lobster Festival. This celebration of the state's popular seafood delicacy attracts visitors from far and near.

Maine State Flag

Moose are North America's largest deer, averaging six feet (2 m) tall at the shoulders. This female stands knee-deep in grass near Rangeley Lake.

White Pine Cone and Tassel
State Flower

Black-Capped Chickadee
State Bird

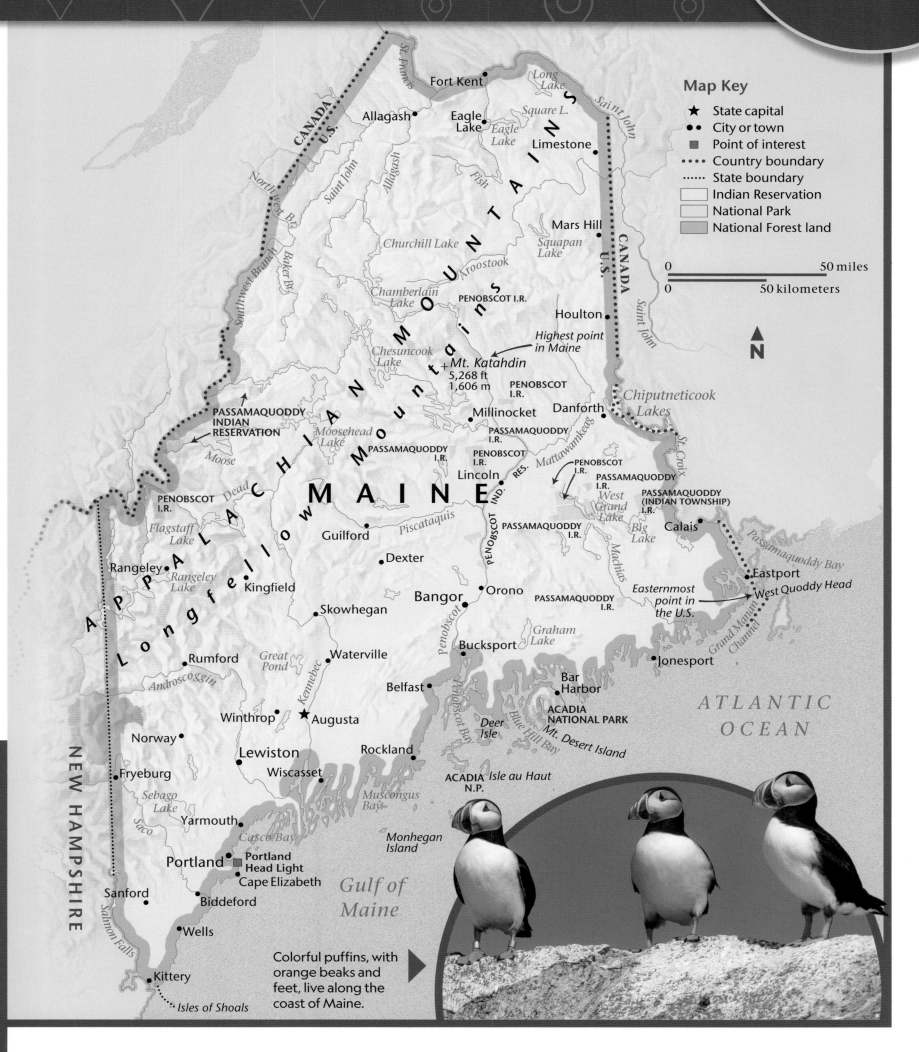

Map Key

★ State capital
•• City or town
■ Point of interest
⋯ Country boundary
⋯ State boundary
☐ Indian Reservation
☐ National Park
☐ National Forest land

0 ———————— 50 miles
0 ———————— 50 kilometers

N

CANADA
U.S.

St. Francis

Fort Kent
Long Lake
Square L.
Saint John

Allagash
Eagle Lake
Eagle Lake
Limestone

Northwest Br.

Saint John

Allagash

Fish

Mars Hill

CANADA
U.S.

Churchill Lake
Squapan Lake

Southwest Branch

Baker Br.

Chamberlain Lake

Aroostook

PENOBSCOT I.R.

Houlton

Saint John

Chesuncook Lake

Highest point in Maine

+Mt. Katahdin
5,268 ft
1,606 m

Danforth

Chiputneticook Lakes

PASSAMAQUODDY
INDIAN
RESERVATION

Moosehead Lake

PASSAMAQUODDY I.R.

Millinocket

PENOBSCOT I.R.

PENOBSCOT
I.R.

PENOBSCOT
I.R.

St. Croix

Moose

PASSAMAQUODDY
I.R.

Mattawamkeag

PENOBSCOT
I.R.

PASSAMAQUODDY
I.R.

PASSAMAQUODDY
(INDIAN TOWNSHIP)
I.R.

PENOBSCOT
I.R.

Dead

M A I N E

Lincoln

PENOBSCOT IND. RES.

West Grand Lake

Flagstaff Lake

Longfellow Mountains

Piscataquis

PASSAMAQUODDY
I.R.

Calais

Big Lake

Passamaquoddy Bay

Rangeley

Guilford

Machias

Rangeley Lake

A P P A L A C H I A N

Kingfield

Dexter

Eastport
West Quoddy Head

Easternmost point in the U.S.

Grand Manan Channel

Rumford

Skowhegan

Bangor

Orono

PASSAMAQUODDY
I.R.

Androscoggin

Great Pond

Waterville

Penobscot

Graham Lake

Bucksport

Jonesport

Belfast

Bar Harbor

A T L A N T I C
O C E A N

Norway

Winthrop

★ Augusta

Kennebec

Deer Isle

Blue Hill Bay

Mt. Desert Island

ACADIA
NATIONAL PARK

Fryeburg

Lewiston

Rockland

Penobscot Bay

Muscongus Bay

ACADIA
N.P.

Isle au Haut

Sebago Lake

Wiscasset

Saco

Yarmouth

Casco Bay

Monhegan Island

Portland ■ Portland Head Light

Cape Elizabeth

Gulf of Maine

Sanford

Biddeford

Wells

Salmon Falls

Kittery

Isles of Shoals

NEW HAMPSHIRE

Colorful puffins, with orange beaks and feet, live along the coast of Maine.

MARYLAND

MARYLAND

LAND & WATER The Appalachian Mountains, Potomac River, and Chesapeake Bay are major land and water features of Maryland.

STATEHOOD Maryland became the 7th state in 1788.

PEOPLE & PLACES Maryland's population is 6,042,718. Annapolis is the state capital. The largest city is Baltimore.

FUN FACT The name of Baltimore's professional football team—the Ravens—was inspired by a poem written by the famous American author Edgar Allan Poe, who lived in Baltimore in the mid-1800s.

Sailing is a popular pastime on Maryland's Chesapeake Bay. In the background, the Bay Bridge stretches 4.3 miles (6.9 km) across the waters of the bay.

Since the early 1700s, Baltimore, near the upper Chesapeake Bay, has been a major seaport and a focus of trade, industry, and immigration.

Maryland State Flag

Black-Eyed Susan
State Flower

Northern (Baltimore) Oriole
State Bird

Youghiogheny

Deep Creek Lake

•Cumberland

Highest point in Maryland

+*Backbone Mt.*
3,360 ft
1,024 m

Allegheny Mountains

WEST VIRGINIA

APP

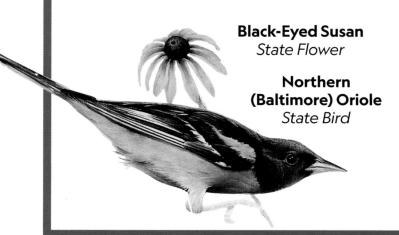

PENNSYLVANIA

Potomac

• Hagerstown

Monocacy

Frederick •

Reisterstown •

Towson •

• Parkville

Baltimore

• Dundalk

• Columbia

Gaithersburg •

M A R Y L A N D

Patuxent

Rockville •

Potomac

Silver
Spring

VIRGINIA

Bethesda •

• Bowie

Annapolis ★

• D.C.

Suitland •

Susquehanna

Elkton •

Aberdeen •

Edgewood •

Sassafras

Chester

D E L M A R V A   P E N I N S U L A

Kent
Island

Severn

Eastern
Bay

Chesapeake Bay

Easton •

DELAWARE

Choptank

The blue crab, found
in the waters of
Chesapeake Bay, is
the state crustacean
of Maryland.

N

Map Key

★ State capital

••• City or town

···· State boundary

0 ———————— 40 miles

0 ———————— 40 kilometers

St. Charles •

Cambridge •

Lexington Park •

Patuxent

Potomac

Bloodsworth
Island

*Fishing
Bay*

Nanticoke

• Salisbury

Ocean
City •

Tangier Sound

Pocomoke

Point
Lookout

Smith
Island

Chincoteague Bay

Assateague
Island

Pocomoke
Sound

VIRGINIA

*ATLANTIC
OCEAN*

Wild ponies have lived on
Assateague Island since
the 1600s. Today more than
300 ponies live on this
Atlantic barrier island.

MASSACHUSETTS

The Green Monster, Fenway Park's famous left field wall, is 37 feet (11.3 m) high. The park is home to major league baseball's Boston Red Sox.

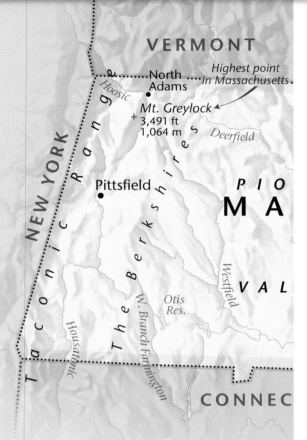

VERMONT

Highest point in Massachusetts.

North Adams

Hoosic

Mt. Greylock
+ 3,491 ft
1,064 m

Deerfield

NEW YORK

Taconic Range

Pittsfield

The Berkshires

P I O

M A

Westfield

Otis Res.

W. Branch Farmington

Housatonic

V A L

CONNEC

LAND & WATER The Berkshires, Cape Cod, and Nantucket Sound are important land and water features of Massachusetts.

STATEHOOD Massachusetts became the 6th state in 1788.

PEOPLE & PLACES The population of Massachusetts is 6,902,149. Boston is the state capital and the largest city.

FUN FACT In 1891 James Naismith wrote the original rule book for the game of basketball. Today the Basketball Hall of Fame is located in Springfield in his honor.

Cranberries are a major agricultural crop in Massachusetts, which produces 24 percent of the cranberries grown in the United States. An annual cranberry harvest festival is held in Wareham.

Massachusetts State Flag

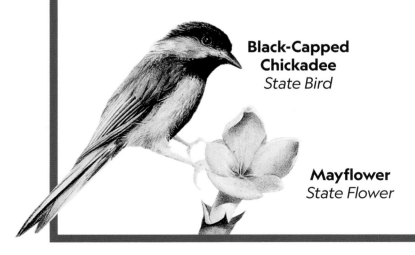
Black-Capped Chickadee
State Bird

Mayflower
State Flower

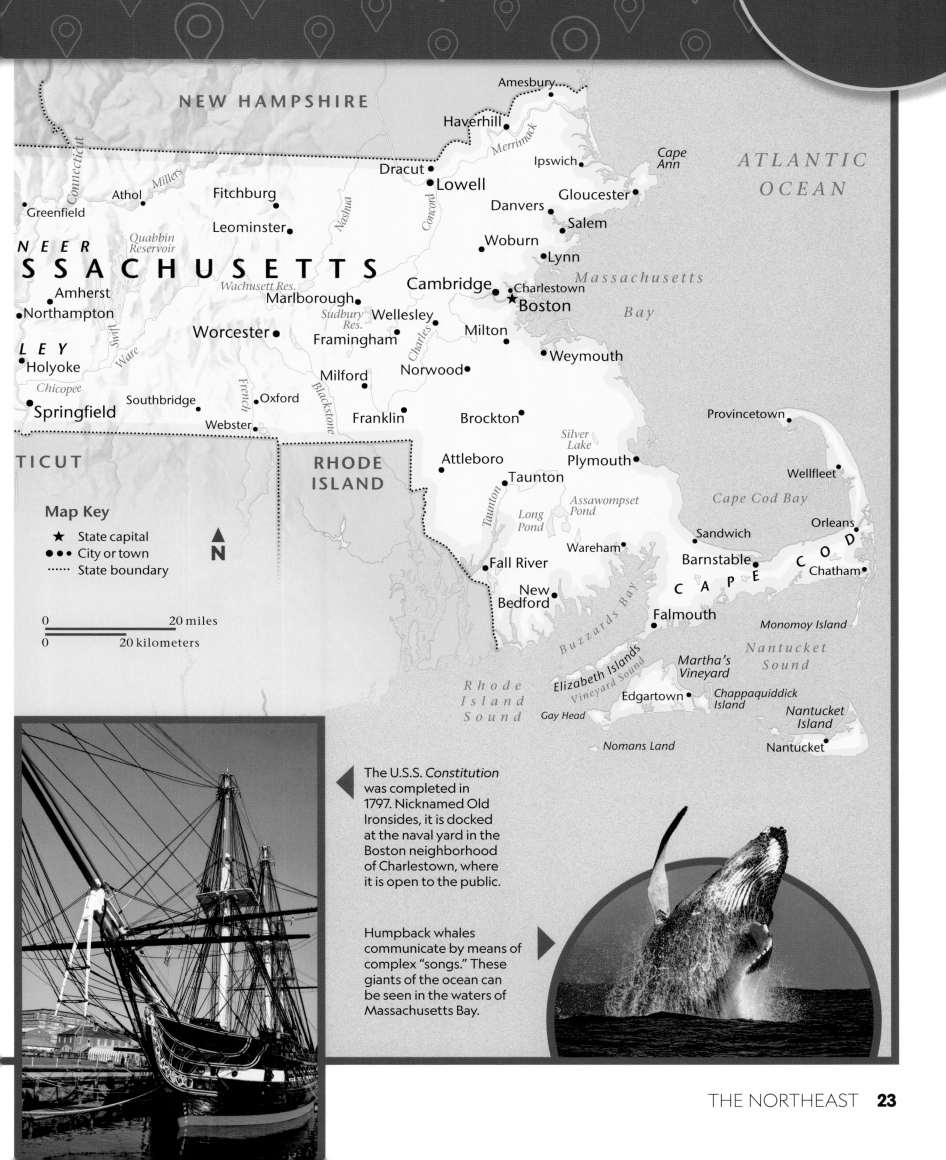

NEW HAMPSHIRE

ATLANTIC OCEAN

Amesbury
Haverhill
Dracut
Lowell
Ipswich
Cape Ann
Gloucester
Danvers
Salem
Fitchburg
Athol
Greenfield
Leominster
Woburn
Lynn
Quabbin Reservoir
Wachusett Res.
NEER
SSACHUSETTS
Massachusetts Bay
Amherst
Marlborough
Cambridge
Charlestown
Northampton
Wellesley
Boston
LEY
Worcester
Framingham
Milton
Holyoke
Sudbury Res.
Chicopee
Milford
Norwood
Weymouth
Southbridge
Oxford
Springfield
Webster
Franklin
Brockton

TICUT

RHODE ISLAND

Attleboro
Plymouth
Provincetown
Taunton
Silver Lake
Wellfleet
Cape Cod Bay

Map Key
★ State capital
••• City or town
..... State boundary

Assawompset Pond
Long Pond
Sandwich
Orleans
Wareham
Barnstable
Chatham
Fall River
CAPE COD
New Bedford
Falmouth
Monomoy Island

0 — 20 miles
0 — 20 kilometers

Buzzards Bay
Nantucket Sound
Rhode Island Sound
Elizabeth Islands
Vineyard Sound
Martha's Vineyard
Edgartown
Chappaquiddick Island
Nantucket Island
Gay Head
Nomans Land
Nantucket

The U.S.S. *Constitution* was completed in 1797. Nicknamed Old Ironsides, it is docked at the naval yard in the Boston neighborhood of Charlestown, where it is open to the public.

Humpback whales communicate by means of complex "songs." These giants of the ocean can be seen in the waters of Massachusetts Bay.

NEW HAMPSHIRE

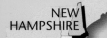

LAND & WATER The White Mountains, Mount Washington, and the Merrimack River are important land and water features of New Hampshire.

STATEHOOD New Hampshire became the 9th state in 1788.

PEOPLE & PLACES New Hampshire's population is 1,356,458. Concord is the state capital. The largest city is Manchester.

FUN FACT The first potato grown in the United States was planted in 1719 in Londonderry on the Common Field, now known simply as the Commons.

A golden dome topped by a war eagle rises above New Hampshire's State House in Concord. The pale granite building was completed in 1819.

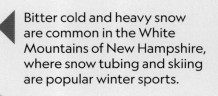

Bitter cold and heavy snow are common in the White Mountains of New Hampshire, where snow tubing and skiing are popular winter sports.

Mount Washington rises above trees rich with autumn colors. Soon winter will arrive, bringing the mountain some of the world's most extreme weather.

New Hampshire State Flag

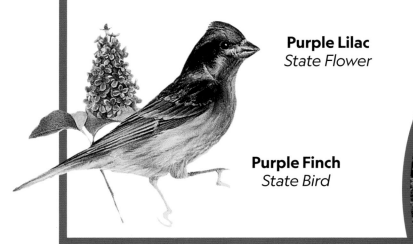

Purple Lilac
State Flower

Purple Finch
State Bird

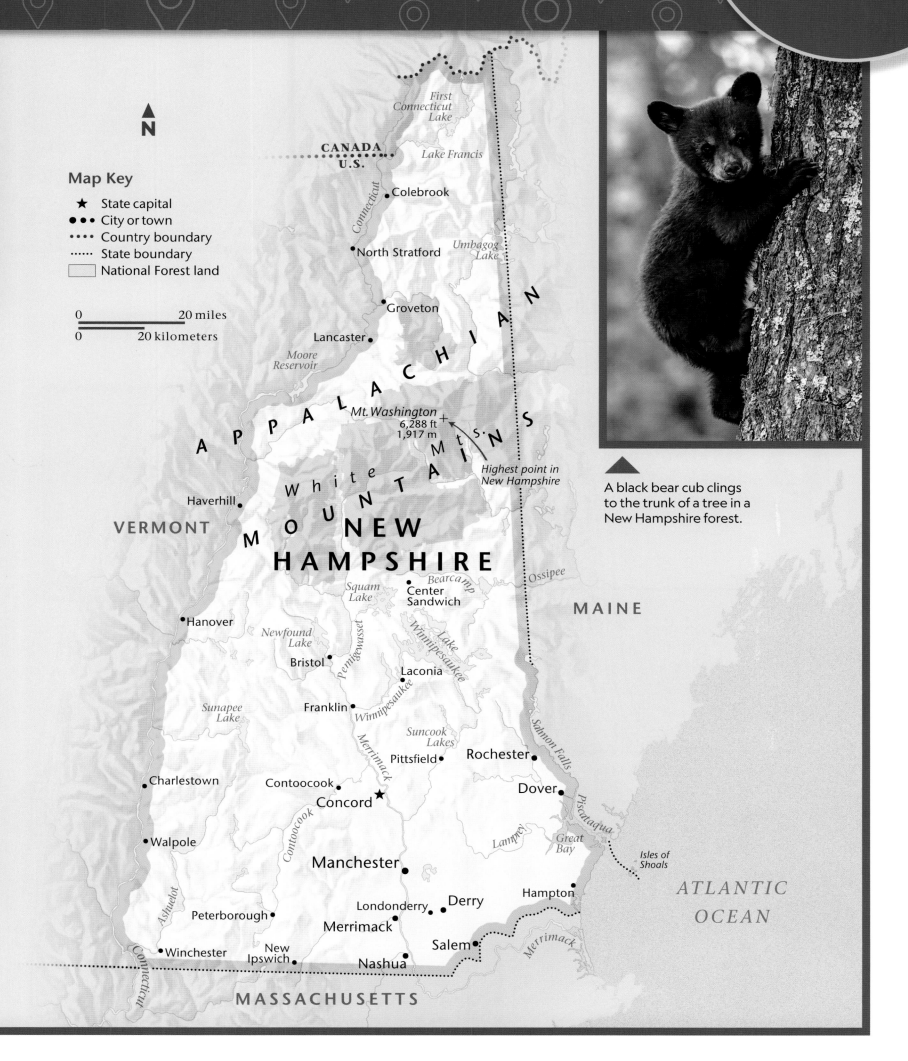

Map Key

★ State capital
●●● City or town
•••• Country boundary
••••• State boundary
☐ National Forest land

0 _____ 20 miles
0 _____ 20 kilometers

First Connecticut Lake

CANADA U.S.

Lake Francis

Colebrook

Connecticut

North Stratford

Umbagog Lake

Groveton

Lancaster

Moore Reservoir

APPALACHIAN

Mt. Washington
6,288 ft
1,917 m

White MOUNTAINS

Mts.

Highest point in New Hampshire

Haverhill

VERMONT

NEW HAMPSHIRE

Ossipee

MAINE

Squam Lake

Bearcamp

Center Sandwich

Hanover

Newfound Lake

Pemigewasset

Lake Winnipesaukee

Bristol

Laconia

Sunapee Lake

Franklin

Winnipesaukee

Suncook Lakes

Salmon Falls

Charlestown

Contoocook

Pittsfield

Rochester

Merrimack

Concord ★

Dover

Piscataqua

Walpole

Contoocook

Lamprey

Great Bay

Isles of Shoals

Manchester

Ashuelot

Peterborough

Londonderry

Derry

Hampton

ATLANTIC OCEAN

Merrimack

Winchester

New Ipswich

Merrimack

Salem

Nashua

MASSACHUSETTS

▲ A black bear cub clings to the trunk of a tree in a New Hampshire forest.

NEW JERSEY

LAND & WATER
The Kittatinny Mountains, Cape May, and the Delaware River are important land and water features of New Jersey.

STATEHOOD New Jersey became the 3rd state in 1787.

PEOPLE & PLACES New Jersey's population is 8,908,520. Trenton is the state capital. The largest city is Newark.

FUN FACT The first dinosaur skeleton found in North America was excavated at Haddonfield in 1858. It was named *Hadrosaurus* in honor of its discovery site.

Sandy beaches on the Atlantic coast of New Jersey attract vacationers from near and far. Roller coasters are just one of the exciting rides in amusement parks along the shore.

New Jersey State Flag

Sunlight reflects off the skylines of Jersey City (foreground) and New York City (across the river). The second largest city in the state, Jersey City is home to many large corporations.

Street names, such as Kentucky Avenue and Tennessee Avenue, in the board game Monopoly are taken from actual street names in Atlantic City.

American Goldfinch
State Bird

Violet
State Flower

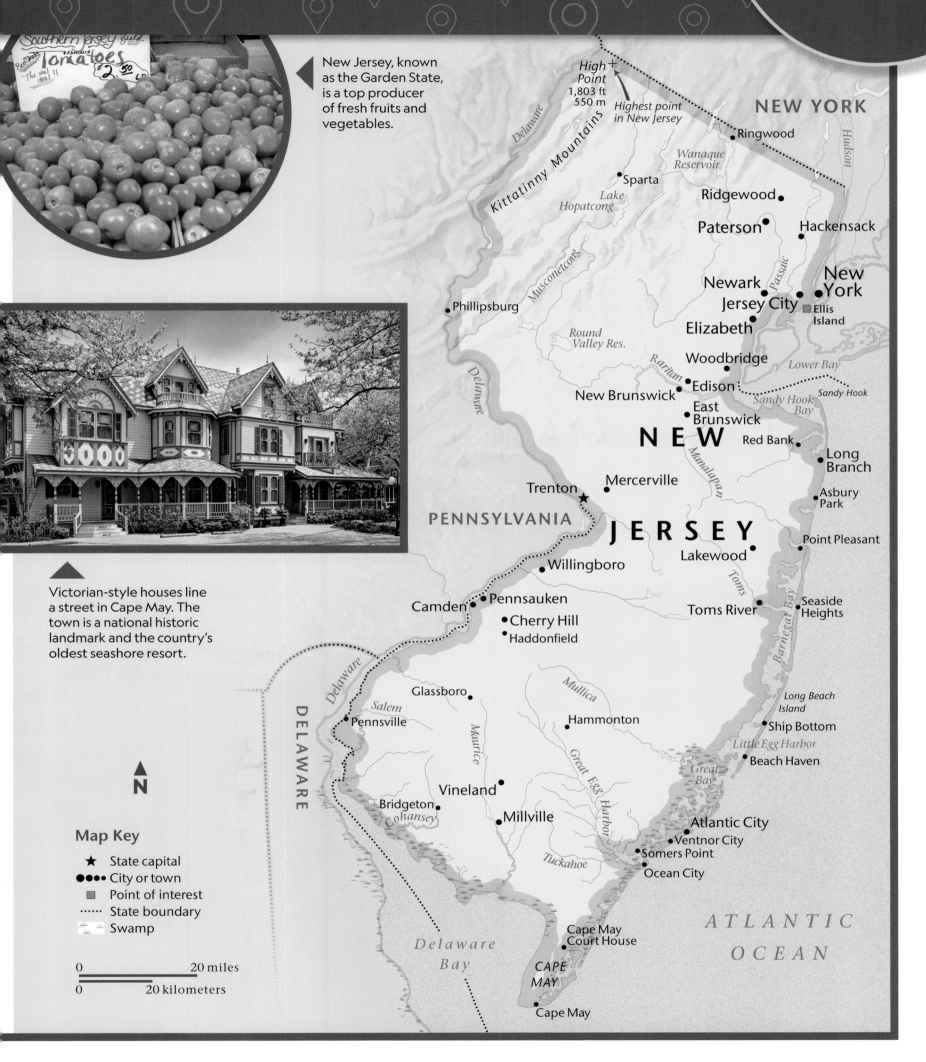

New Jersey, known as the Garden State, is a top producer of fresh fruits and vegetables.

Victorian-style houses line a street in Cape May. The town is a national historic landmark and the country's oldest seashore resort.

NEW YORK

High Point
1,803 ft
550 m
Highest point in New Jersey

Delaware

Kittatinny Mountains

Wanaque Reservoir

Ringwood

Sparta

Lake Hopatcong

Ridgewood

Paterson

Hackensack

Musconetcong

Passaic

Phillipsburg

Newark

New York

Jersey City

Ellis Island

Round Valley Res.

Elizabeth

Woodbridge

Lower Bay

Raritan

Edison

Sandy Hook

New Brunswick

Sandy Hook Bay

East Brunswick

N E W

Red Bank

Manalapan

Long Branch

Delaware

Mercerville

Asbury Park

Trenton

J E R S E Y

Point Pleasant

PENNSYLVANIA

Lakewood

Toms

Willingboro

Seaside Heights

Camden

Pennsauken

Toms River

Cherry Hill

Barnegat Bay

Haddonfield

Delaware

Long Beach Island

Glassboro

Mullica

Ship Bottom

Salem

Hammonton

Little Egg Harbor

Pennsville

Beach Haven

Maurice

Great Egg Harbor

Great Bay

DELAWARE

Vineland

Bridgeton

Cohansey

Millville

Atlantic City

Ventnor City

Tuckahoe

Somers Point

Ocean City

Cape May Court House

A T L A N T I C

O C E A N

Delaware Bay

CAPE MAY

Cape May

Map Key

★ State capital
●●● City or town
▪ Point of interest
····· State boundary
Swamp

0 ——— 20 miles
0 ——— 20 kilometers

N

NEW YORK

LAND & WATER
The Adirondack Mountains, the Finger Lakes, and the Hudson River are important land and water features of New York.

STATEHOOD
New York became the 11th state in 1788.

PEOPLE & PLACES
New York's population is 19,542,209. Albany is the state capital. The largest city is New York City.

FUN FACT
The Erie Canal, built in the 1820s, connected Buffalo to the Hudson River at Albany, allowing ships to travel from the Atlantic Ocean to the Great Lakes. The canal contributed to the growth of New York City as a major trade center.

New York State Flag

Eastern Bluebird
State Bird

Rose
State Flower

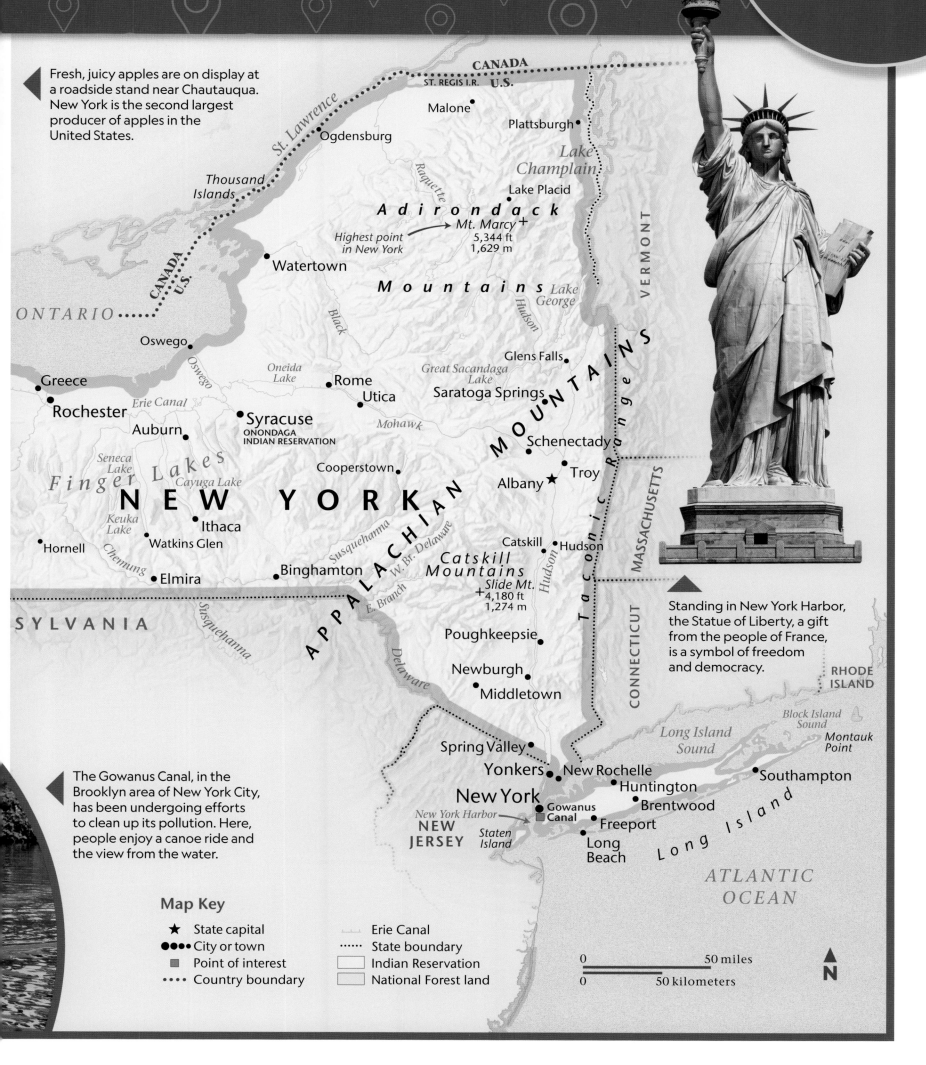

Fresh, juicy apples are on display at a roadside stand near Chautauqua. New York is the second largest producer of apples in the United States.

CANADA

ST. REGIS I.R. U.S.

Malone

Plattsburgh

St. Lawrence

Ogdensburg

Lake Champlain

Thousand Islands

Lake Placid

Raquette

A d i r o n d a c k

Mt. Marcy +

Highest point in New York

5,344 ft 1,629 m

CANADA U.S.

Watertown

M o u n t a i n s *Lake George*

VERMONT

ONTARIO

Black

Hudson

Oswego

Glens Falls

Oswego

Great Sacandaga Lake

Greece

Oneida Lake

Rome

Saratoga Springs

A P P A L A C H I A N   M O U N T A I N S

Rochester

Erie Canal

Utica

Mohawk

Auburn

Syracuse

ONONDAGA INDIAN RESERVATION

Taconic Ranges

Seneca Lake

F i n g e r   L a k e s

Cooperstown

Schenectady

MASSACHUSETTS

Cayuga Lake

N E W   Y O R K

Albany ★ Troy

Keuka Lake

Ithaca

Hornell

Watkins Glen

Susquehanna

W. Br. Delaware

Catskill

Hudson

Chemung

Binghamton

C a t s k i l l   M o u n t a i n s

Hudson

Standing in New York Harbor, the Statue of Liberty, a gift from the people of France, is a symbol of freedom and democracy.

Elmira

Slide Mt. + 4,180 ft 1,274 m

CONNECTICUT

RHODE ISLAND

SYLVANIA

E. Branch

Susquehanna

Delaware

Poughkeepsie

Block Island Sound

Newburgh

Long Island Sound

Montauk Point

The Gowanus Canal, in the Brooklyn area of New York City, has been undergoing efforts to clean up its pollution. Here, people enjoy a canoe ride and the view from the water.

Middletown

Spring Valley

Yonkers

New Rochelle

Southampton

Huntington

New York

Brentwood

New York Harbor

Gowanus Canal

Freeport

NEW JERSEY

Staten Island

Long Beach

L o n g   I s l a n d

ATLANTIC OCEAN

Map Key

★ State capital

●●●● City or town

■ Point of interest

···· Country boundary

| Erie Canal

···· State boundary

☐ Indian Reservation

☐ National Forest land

0   50 miles

0   50 kilometers

N

PENNSYLVANIA

PENNSYLVANIA

LAND & WATER The Allegheny Mountains, the Pocono Mountains, and the Susquehanna River are important land and water features of Pennsylvania.

STATEHOOD Pennsylvania became the 2nd state in 1787.

PEOPLE & PLACES Pennsylvania's population is 12,807,060. Harrisburg is the state capital. The largest city is Philadelphia.

FUN FACT The town of Hershey is known as the Chocolate Capital of the World. The Hershey Company exports its chocolate candies to some 70 countries around the world.

Pennsylvania State Flag

Mountain Laurel
State Flower

Ruffed Grouse
State Bird

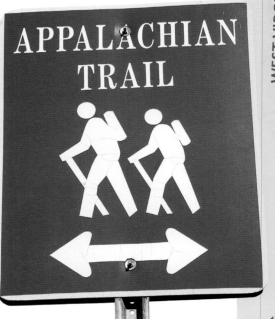

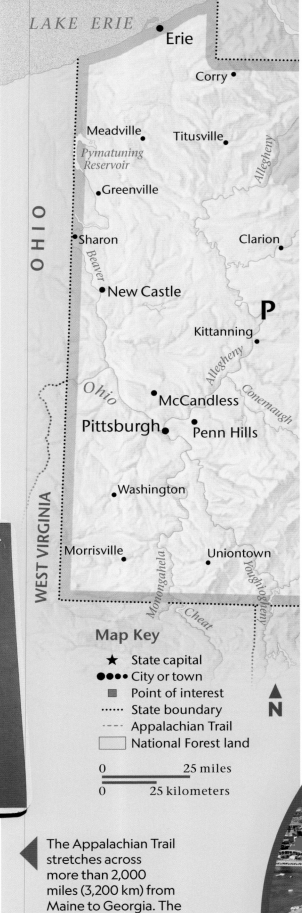

LAKE ERIE

Erie

Corry

Meadville · Titusville

Pymatuning
Reservoir

Greenville

OHIO

Sharon · Clarion

Beaver

New Castle

P

Kittanning

Ohio · McCandless

Pittsburgh · Penn Hills

Conemaugh

Washington

WEST VIRGINIA

Morrisville · Uniontown

Monongahela · Cheat · Youghiogheny

Map Key

★ State capital
●●●● City or town
■ Point of interest
...... State boundary
---- Appalachian Trail
▭ National Forest land

0 — 25 miles
0 — 25 kilometers

The Appalachian Trail stretches across more than 2,000 miles (3,200 km) from Maine to Georgia. The trail passes through 14 states, including Pennsylvania.

NEW YORK

Chemung

Susquehanna

Allegheny Reservoir

Bradford

Allegheny

Sayre

Tioga

Mansfield

Coudersport

Towanda

Wellsboro

Pine Creek

Pine Creek Gorge

Carbondale

St. Marys

Clarion

Scranton

Lake Wallenpaupack

West Branch Susquehanna

Williamsport

Wilkes-Barre

Delaware

Lock Haven

Clearfield

Bloomsburg

Susquehanna

Pocono Mts.

Stroudsburg

P E N N S Y L V A N I A

Mountains

Punxsutawney

Sunbury

Lehigh

Easton

NEW JERSEY

State College

Pottsville

Bethlehem

Indiana

Allentown

Altoona

A P P A L A C H I A N

Juniata

Blue

Mountain

Reading

Schuylkill

Raystown Lake

Tuscarora Mountain

Johnstown

Doylestown

Harrisburg

Hershey

Norristown

Levittown

Highest point in Pennsylvania

Carlisle

Three Mile Island

Elizabethtown

Upper Darby

Philadelphia

Bedford

Lancaster

Chester

Mt. Davis 3,213 ft 979 m

Chambersburg

York

Susquehanna

DELAWARE

Gettysburg

A P P.

Waynesboro

MARYLAND

Allegheny

W. VA.

MOUNTAINS

Pittsburgh was established in 1758 where the Monongahela and Allegheny Rivers meet to form the Ohio River. Today it is a center of finance, education, medicine, and robotics.

The Liberty Bell, cast in 1753 by Pennsylvania craftsmen, hangs in Philadelphia. Because of a crack, it is no longer rung.

RHODE ISLAND

RHODE ISLAND

LAND & WATER Block Island and Narragansett Bay, with its many islands, are important land and water features of Rhode Island.

STATEHOOD Rhode Island became the 13th state in 1790.

PEOPLE & PLACES Rhode Island's population is 1,057,315. Providence is the state capital and the largest city.

FUN FACT Rhode Island is the smallest U.S. state in size. It measures just 48 miles (77 km) from north to south and 37 miles (60 km) from east to west.

Sailing is a popular sport in Rhode Island. This boat is in full sail on a late summer day on Narragansett Bay.

The North Lighthouse on the northern tip of Block Island still warns ships of dangerous waters. The building, constructed in 1867, does not have a typical lighthouse design.

Rhode Island has cold, snowy winters. Skaters enjoy ice-skating on City Center public rink in front of the historic city hall in Providence.

HOPE

Rhode Island State Flag

Violet
State Flower

Rhode Island Red
State Bird

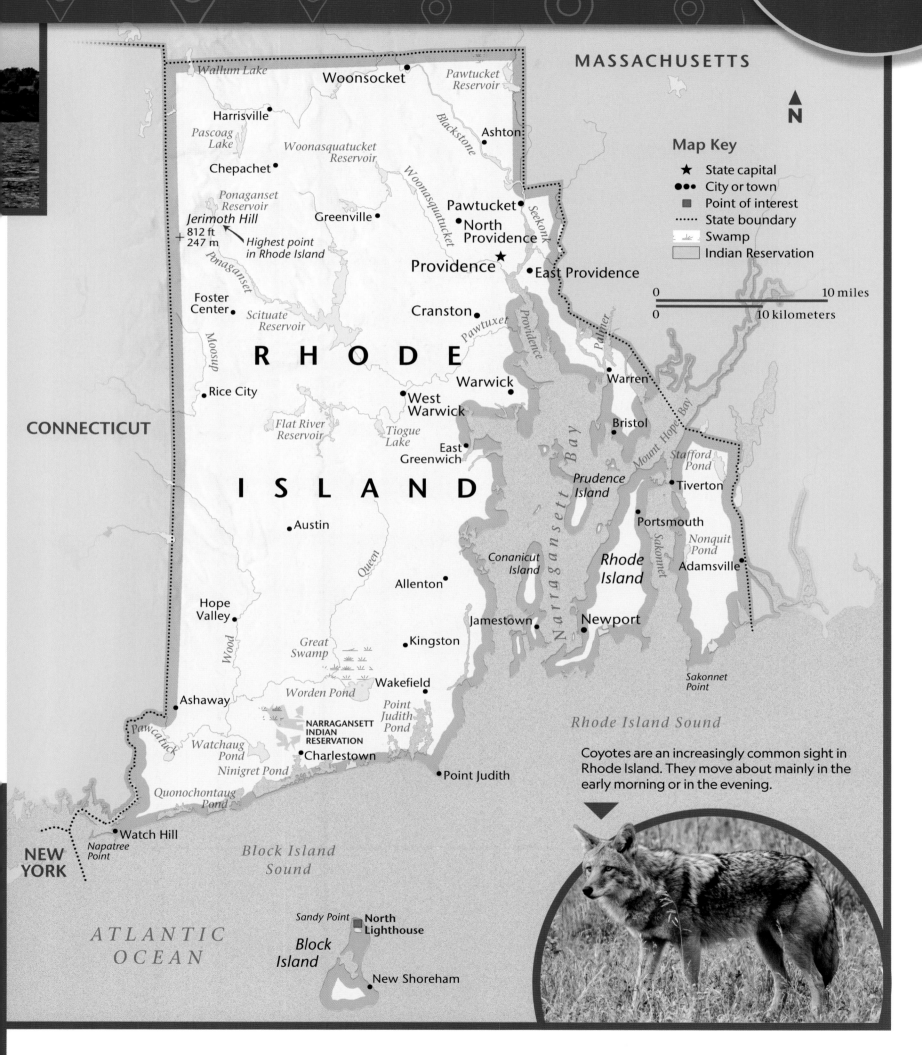

MASSACHUSETTS

CONNECTICUT

Map Key
★ State capital
●●● City or town
■ Point of interest
···· State boundary
Swamp
Indian Reservation

0   10 miles
0   10 kilometers

Wallum Lake
Woonsocket
Pawtucket Reservoir
Harrisville
Pascoag Lake
Ashton
Woonasquatucket Reservoir
Chepachet
Ponaganset Reservoir
Greenville
Jerimoth Hill
812 ft
247 m
Highest point in Rhode Island
Pawtucket
North Providence
Providence ★
East Providence
Foster Center
Scituate Reservoir
Cranston
Pawtuxet
Warren
R H O D E
Warwick
Bristol
Rice City
West Warwick
Flat River Reservoir
Tiogue Lake
East Greenwich
Prudence Island
Stafford Pond
Tiverton
I S L A N D
Austin
Conanicut Island
Rhode Island
Portsmouth
Nonquit Pond
Adamsville
Allenton
Hope Valley
Queen
Jamestown
Newport
Kingston
Great Swamp
Wakefield
Worden Pond
Point Judith Pond
Sakonnet Point
Ashaway
Pawcatuck
NARRAGANSETT INDIAN RESERVATION
Watchaug Pond
Charlestown
Ninigret Pond
Point Judith
Rhode Island Sound
Quonochontaug Pond
NEW YORK
Watch Hill
Napatree Point
Block Island Sound

Narragansett Bay
Mount Hope Bay
Sakonnet
Seekonk
Blackstone
Woonasquatucket
Providence
Palmer
Moosup
Wood

Coyotes are an increasingly common sight in Rhode Island. They move about mainly in the early morning or in the evening.

Sandy Point
North Lighthouse
Block Island
New Shoreham
ATLANTIC OCEAN

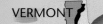

VERMONT

LAND & WATER The Green Mountains, Lake Champlain, and the Connecticut River are important land and water features of Vermont.

STATEHOOD Vermont became the 14th state in 1791.

PEOPLE & PLACES Vermont's population is 626,299. Montpelier is the state capital. The largest city is Burlington.

FUN FACT From the end of the Revolutionary War until 1791, Vermont was an independent republic with its own government and money. It even thought about uniting with Canada.

Vermont ice cream is famous worldwide. The headquarters of Ben & Jerry's in Burlington is the number one tourist attraction in the state.

People collect the sap of maple trees, which is boiled to make maple sugar and syrup. Maple production is celebrated each year at a festival in Tunbridge.

Vermont State Flag

Red Clover
State Flower

Hermit Thrush
State Bird

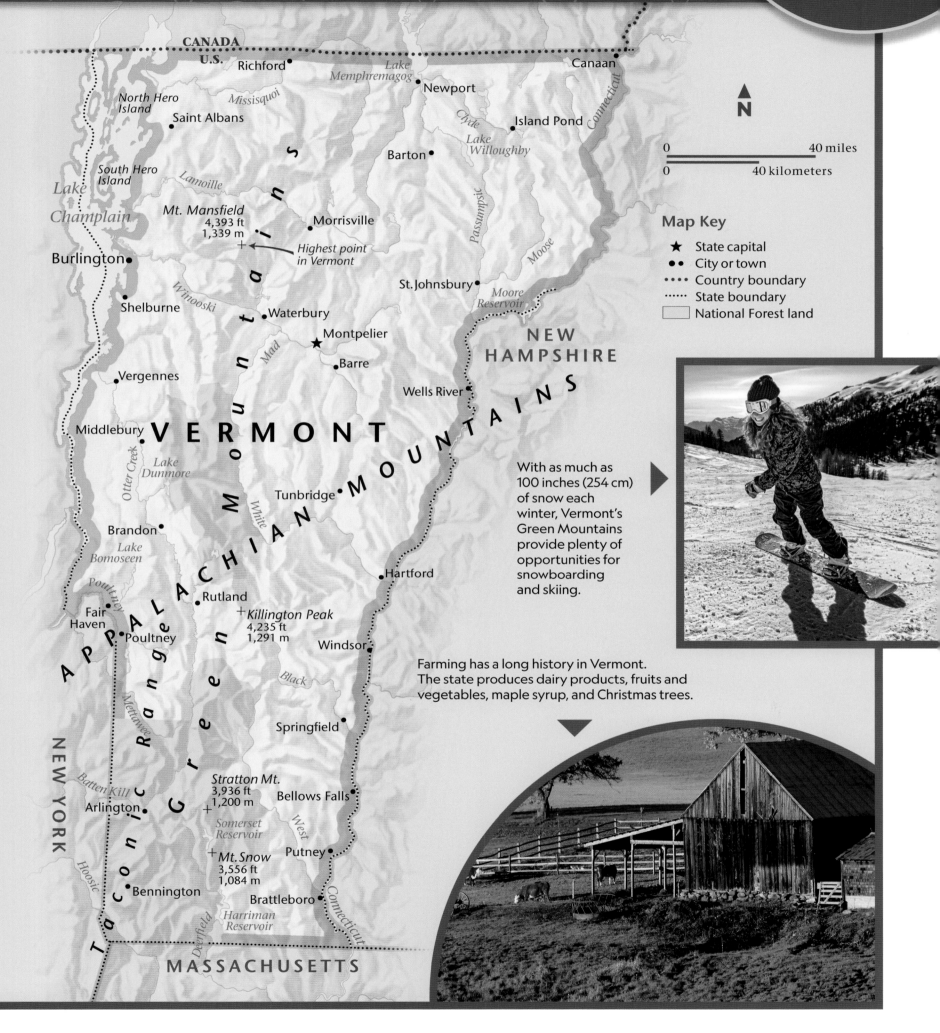

CANADA
U.S.

Richford

Lake Memphremagog

Newport

Canaan

Missisquoi

North Hero Island

Saint Albans

Clyde

Island Pond

Lake Willoughby

Barton

Connecticut

N

0   40 miles
0   40 kilometers

South Hero Island

Lamoille

Lake Champlain

Mt. Mansfield
4,393 ft
1,339 m

Morrisville

Highest point in Vermont

Passumpsic

Moose

Map Key
★   State capital
••   City or town
••••   Country boundary
····   State boundary
☐   National Forest land

Burlington

Winooski

Shelburne

Waterbury

Montpelier

Barre

St. Johnsbury

Moore Reservoir

NEW HAMPSHIRE

Vergennes

Mad

Wells River

Middlebury

VERMONT

Otter Creek

Lake Dunmore

Tunbridge

GREEN MOUNTAINS

APPALACHIAN MOUNTAINS

White

With as much as 100 inches (254 cm) of snow each winter, Vermont's Green Mountains provide plenty of opportunities for snowboarding and skiing.

Brandon

Lake Bomoseen

Poultney

Hartford

Fair Haven

Rutland

Poultney

Killington Peak
4,235 ft
1,291 m

Windsor

Black

Farming has a long history in Vermont. The state produces dairy products, fruits and vegetables, maple syrup, and Christmas trees.

Mettawee

NEW YORK

Springfield

Batten Kill

Stratton Mt.
3,936 ft
1,200 m

Bellows Falls

Arlington

Somerset Reservoir

West

Putney

Hoosic

Mt. Snow
3,556 ft
1,084 m

Bennington

Brattleboro

Connecticut

Deerfield

Harriman Reservoir

MASSACHUSETTS

THE SOUTHEAST

The Southeast is a region of varied landscapes. In the interior are old, worn-down mountains. Along the coasts there are wetlands and barrier islands. Cutting through these features are rivers that flow to the sea, linking the interior to distant places. The region's economic roots are in agriculture, especially cotton and tobacco, which were grown on large farms called plantations. Today the region is part of the Sunbelt, with rapidly growing cities and emerging high-tech industries.

Great egrets are a common sight in wetland areas of the coastal South. These young egrets in Florida stand in their treetop nest.

Live oak trees, some hundreds of years old, form a natural arch across a country road in Georgia. These trees, draped in Spanish moss, are common in the coastal Southeast.

ALABAMA

LAND & WATER The Appalachian Mountains, the Cumberland Plateau, and Mobile Bay are important land and water features of Alabama.

STATEHOOD Alabama became the 22nd state in 1819.

PEOPLE & PLACES Alabama's population is 4,887,871. Montgomery is the state capital. The largest city is Birmingham.

FUN FACT In Magnolia Springs, on Mobile Bay, mail is delivered by boat. The town has the country's only year-round, all-water mail route used by the U.S. Postal Service.

Southern Alabama has a short coastline fronting the Gulf of Mexico. The beach resort of Gulf Shores is a popular tourist destination.

A welder repairs a boat in Bayou La Batre on Alabama's Gulf Coast. The town is a center for shipbuilding and seafood processing.

This old railroad bridge, built in 1839, was a toll bridge across the Tennessee River. Today it is a pedestrian bridge.

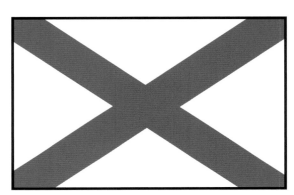

Alabama State Flag

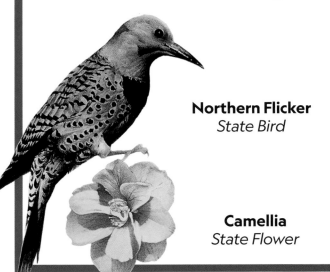

Northern Flicker
State Bird

Camellia
State Flower

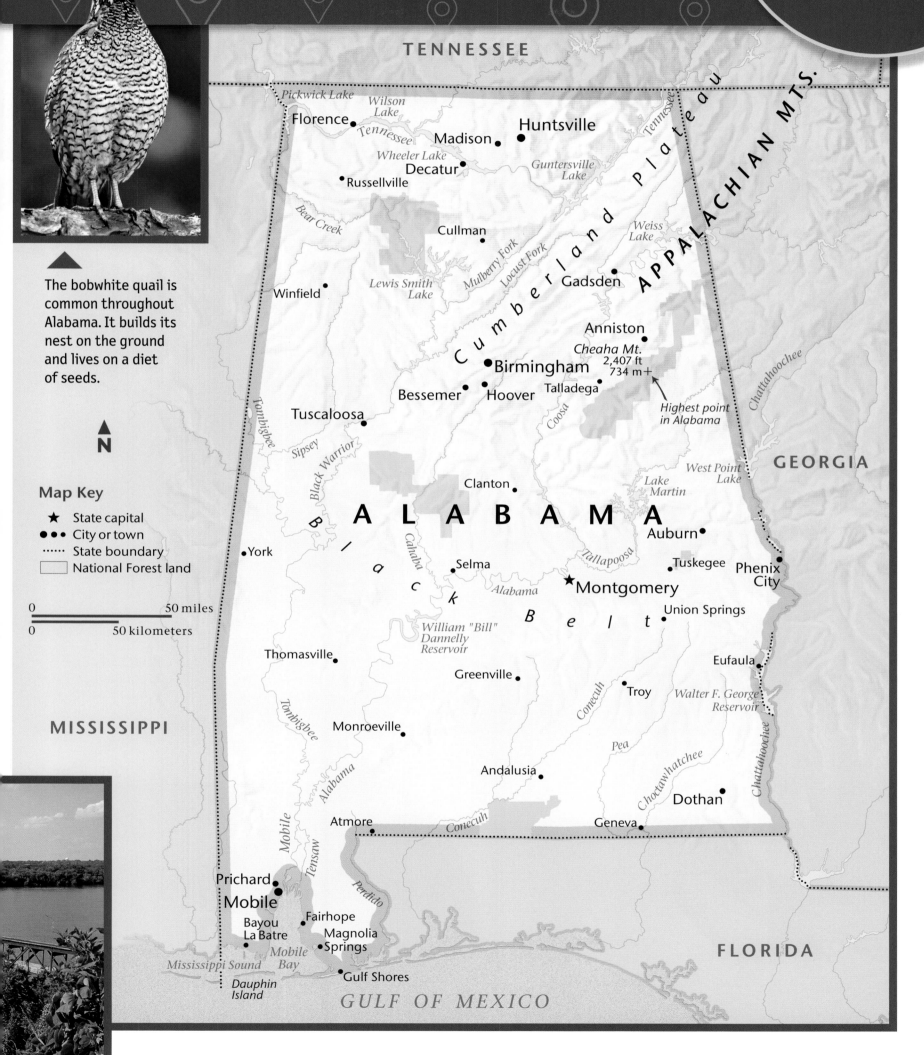

The bobwhite quail is common throughout Alabama. It builds its nest on the ground and lives on a diet of seeds.

N

Map Key

★ State capital

●●● City or town

······ State boundary

☐ National Forest land

| 0 | 50 miles |
| 0 | 50 kilometers |

TENNESSEE

Pickwick Lake

Wilson Lake

Florence

Tennessee

Madison

Huntsville

Wheeler Lake

Decatur

Russellville

Guntersville Lake

Bear Creek

Cullman

APPALACHIAN MTS.

Cumberland Plateau

Mulberry Fork

Locust Fork

Weiss Lake

Winfield

Lewis Smith Lake

Gadsden

Anniston

Cheaha Mt.
2,407 ft
734 m +

Birmingham

Highest point in Alabama

Bessemer

Hoover

Talladega

Tuscaloosa

Coosa

Sipsey

Black Warrior

Tombigbee

GEORGIA

West Point Lake

Lake Martin

Chattahoochee

ALABAMA

Clanton

Black
l
a
c
k

Cahaba

Selma

Auburn

Tallapoosa

Tuskegee

Phenix City

York

★ Montgomery

Union Springs

William "Bill" Dannelly Reservoir

Alabama

Eufaula

Thomasville

Greenville

Conecuh

Troy

Walter F. George Reservoir

Monroeville

Tombigbee

Alabama

Andalusia

Pea

Choctawhatchee

Dothan

MISSISSIPPI

Atmore

Conecuh

Geneva

Chattahoochee

Mobile

Tensaw

Prichard

Mobile

Bayou La Batre

Fairhope

Magnolia Springs

Perdido

FLORIDA

Mississippi Sound

Mobile Bay

Dauphin Island

Gulf Shores

GULF OF MEXICO

ARKANSAS

 LAND & WATER The Ouachita Mountains, the Ozark Plateau, and the Mississippi River are important land and water features of Arkansas.

STATEHOOD Arkansas became the 25th state in 1836.

PEOPLE & PLACES Arkansas has a population of 3,013,825. Little Rock is the state capital and the largest city.

FUN FACT In 1924 Crater of Diamonds State Park near Murfreesboro yielded the largest natural diamond ever found in the United States. The stone, called "Uncle Sam," weighed more than 40 carats.

Arkansas State Flag

Apple Blossom
State Flower

Mockingbird
State Bird

A farmer in eastern Arkansas checks the progress of his rice crop. The state is the leading U.S. producer of rice.

Located in the River Market District of Little Rock, the Museum of Discovery offers children interactive experiences in science, technology, engineering, and math.

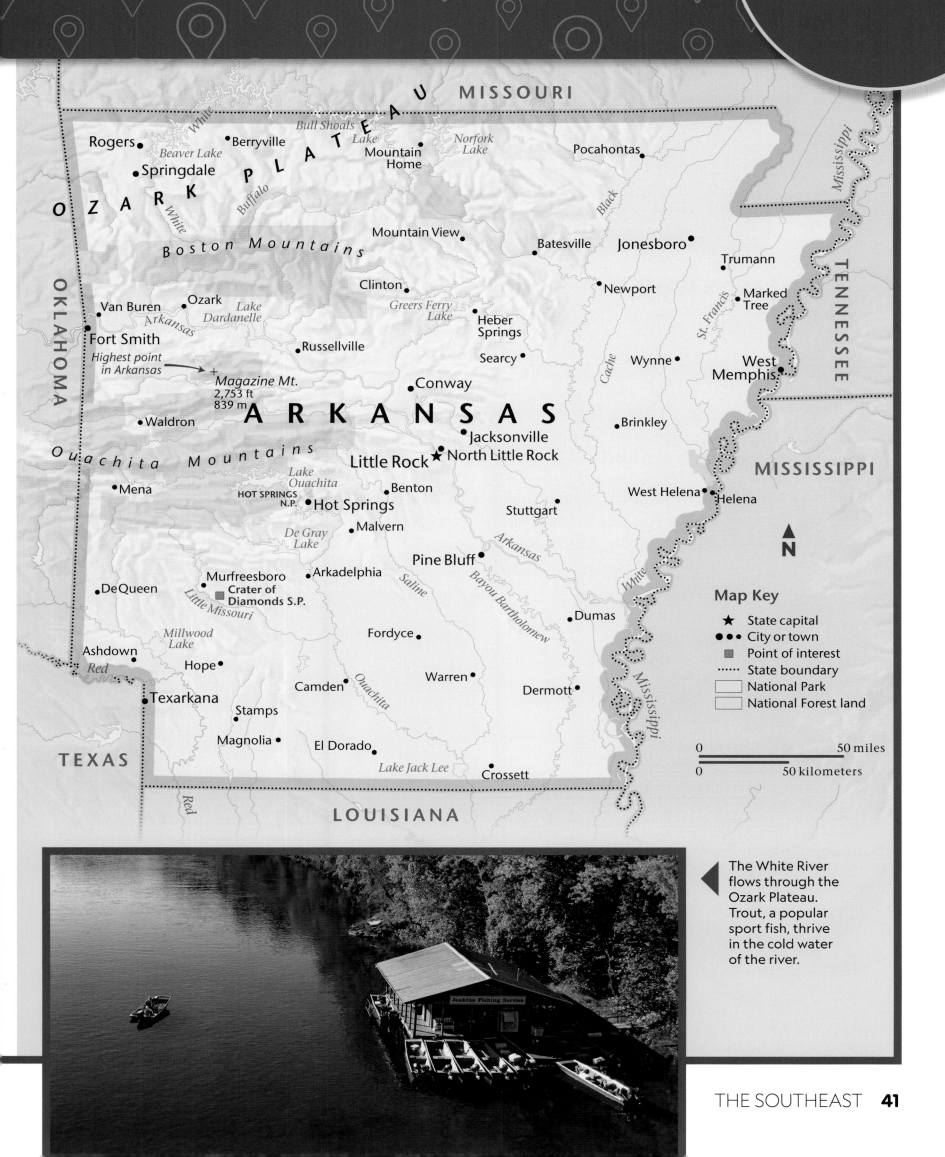

MISSOURI

OZARK PLATEAU

White
Bull Shoals Lake
Norfork Lake

Rogers
Berryville
Beaver Lake
Mountain Home
Pocahontas

Springdale

Buffalo

White

Boston Mountains

Mountain View

Batesville
Jonesboro
Trumann

Clinton
Newport
Marked Tree

Van Buren
Ozark
Lake Dardanelle
Greers Ferry Lake
Heber Springs

Arkansas

Fort Smith
Russellville
Searcy
Wynne
West Memphis

Highest point in Arkansas →
+ Magazine Mt.
2,753 ft
839 m

Conway

ARKANSAS

Waldron

Jacksonville
Little Rock ★ North Little Rock

Brinkley

Ouachita Mountains

Lake Ouachita

Mena
HOT SPRINGS N.P.
Benton
Stuttgart
West Helena
Helena

MISSISSIPPI

Hot Springs
De Gray Lake
Malvern

Arkansas

Murfreesboro
Crater of Diamonds S.P.
Arkadelphia
Pine Bluff
Saline

DeQueen
Little Missouri
Bayou Bartholomew
Dumas

Millwood Lake
Fordyce

Ashdown
Red
Hope
Warren
Dermott

Camden
Ouachita
White

Texarkana
Mississippi

Stamps

Magnolia
El Dorado

TEXAS

Lake Jack Lee
Crossett

Red

LOUISIANA

Black
Cache
St. Francis

TENNESSEE

N

Map Key
★ State capital
●●● City or town
■ Point of interest
⋯⋯ State boundary
☐ National Park
☐ National Forest land

0   50 miles
0   50 kilometers

The White River flows through the Ozark Plateau. Trout, a popular sport fish, thrive in the cold water of the river.

Jenkins Fishing Service

FLORIDA

FLORIDA

A L A B A

Pendido

Britton Hill
345 ft
105 m

Highest point in Florida

• Pensacola

• Fort Walton Beach

The manatee is the state marine mammal of Florida. It averages 10 feet (3 m) in length and can weigh 1,000 pounds (450 kg).

LAND & WATER The Florida Keys, the Everglades, and Lake Okeechobee are important land and water features of Florida.

STATEHOOD Florida became the 27th state in 1845.

PEOPLE & PLACES Florida's population is 21,299,325. Tallahassee is the state capital. The largest city is Jacksonville.

FUN FACT Everglades National Park is home to rare and endangered species such as the American crocodile, the Florida panther, and the West Indian manatee.

NASA's powerful Space Launch System, shown in this artwork, is based at the Kennedy Space Center. It will support human exploration beyond Earth's orbit.

Florida State Flag

Orange Blossom
State Flower

Mockingbird
State Bird

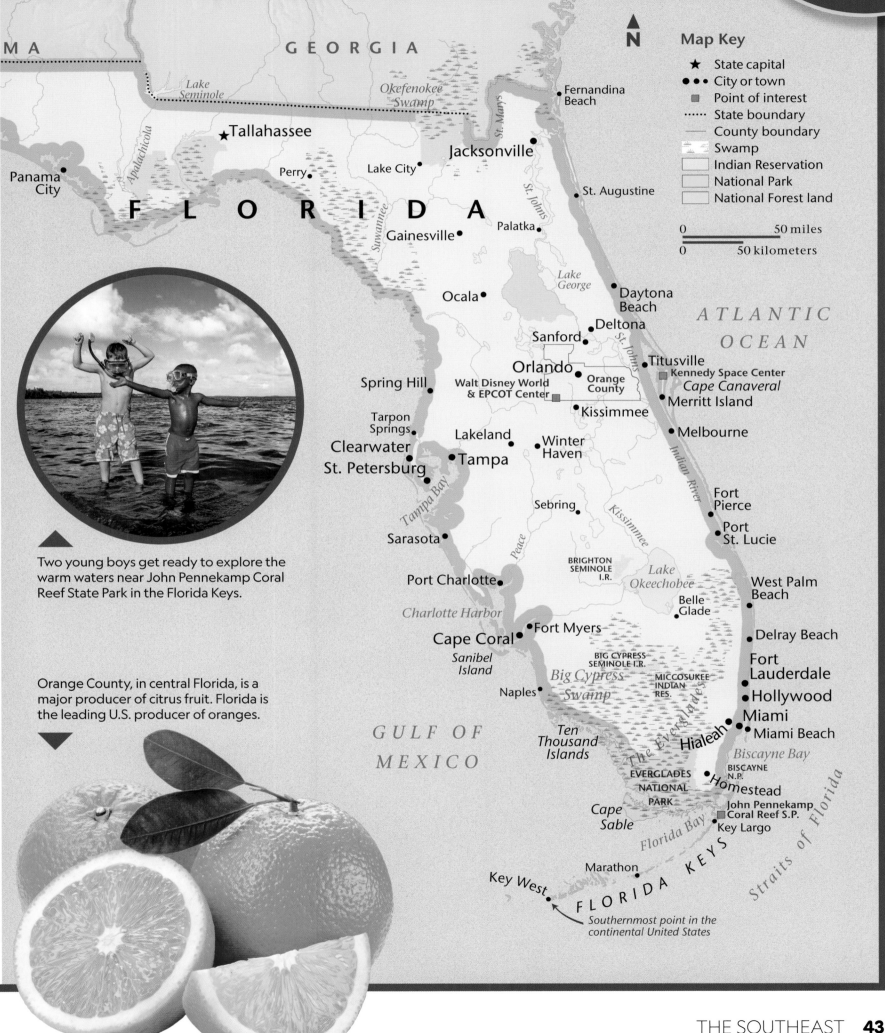

GEORGIA

MA

Lake Seminole

Okefenokee Swamp

★ Tallahassee

Panama City

Perry

Lake City

Apalachicola

F L O R I D A

Jacksonville

St. Augustine

Gainesville

Palatka

St. Johns

Suwannee

St. Marys

Fernandina Beach

Map Key

★ State capital
●●● City or town
■ Point of interest
‥‥ State boundary
— County boundary
🌿 Swamp
☐ Indian Reservation
☐ National Park
☐ National Forest land

0   50 miles
0   50 kilometers

Ocala

Lake George

Daytona Beach

Deltona

Sanford

Orlando

Walt Disney World & EPCOT Center

Orange County

Kissimmee

St. Johns

Titusville

Kennedy Space Center

Cape Canaveral

Merritt Island

ATLANTIC OCEAN

Spring Hill

Tarpon Springs

Lakeland

Winter Haven

Melbourne

Clearwater

Tampa

St. Petersburg

Tampa Bay

Sebring

Indian River

Fort Pierce

Port St. Lucie

Sarasota

Peace

Kissimmee

BRIGHTON SEMINOLE I.R.

Lake Okeechobee

West Palm Beach

Port Charlotte

Belle Glade

Delray Beach

Charlotte Harbor

Fort Myers

Cape Coral

BIG CYPRESS SEMINOLE I.R.

Fort Lauderdale

Sanibel Island

MICCOSUKEE INDIAN RES.

Hollywood

Big Cypress Swamp

Naples

Miami

The Everglades

Hialeah

Miami Beach

GULF OF MEXICO

Ten Thousand Islands

Biscayne Bay

BISCAYNE N.P.

EVERGLADES NATIONAL PARK

Homestead

John Pennekamp Coral Reef S.P.

Cape Sable

Key Largo

Florida Bay

Straits of Florida

Marathon

FLORIDA KEYS

Key West

← Southernmost point in the continental United States

Two young boys get ready to explore the warm waters near John Pennekamp Coral Reef State Park in the Florida Keys.

Orange County, in central Florida, is a major producer of citrus fruit. Florida is the leading U.S. producer of oranges.

GEORGIA

LAND & WATER The Sea Islands, the Okefenokee Swamp, and the Savannah River are important land and water features of Georgia.

STATEHOOD Georgia became the 4th state in 1788.

PEOPLE & PLACES Georgia's population is 10,519,475. Atlanta is the state capital and the largest city.

FUN FACT The Georgia Aquarium in Atlanta is the largest aquarium in the world. It features more than 100,000 animals living in more than eight million gallons (30.3 million L) of water.

Built for the 1996 Olympic Games, Centennial Olympic Park in Atlanta is the site of festivals and community events that attract an estimated three million visitors each year.

Nearly half the peanut crop in the United States is grown in Georgia. Sylvester claims to be the peanut capital of the world.

Georgia State Flag

Alligators, which can live more than 50 years, are found in marshes, rivers, and swamps, including the Okefenokee National Wildlife Refuge.

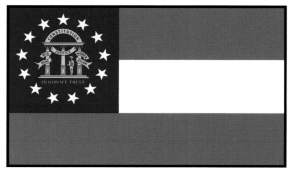

Cherokee Rose
State Flower

Brown Thrasher
State Bird

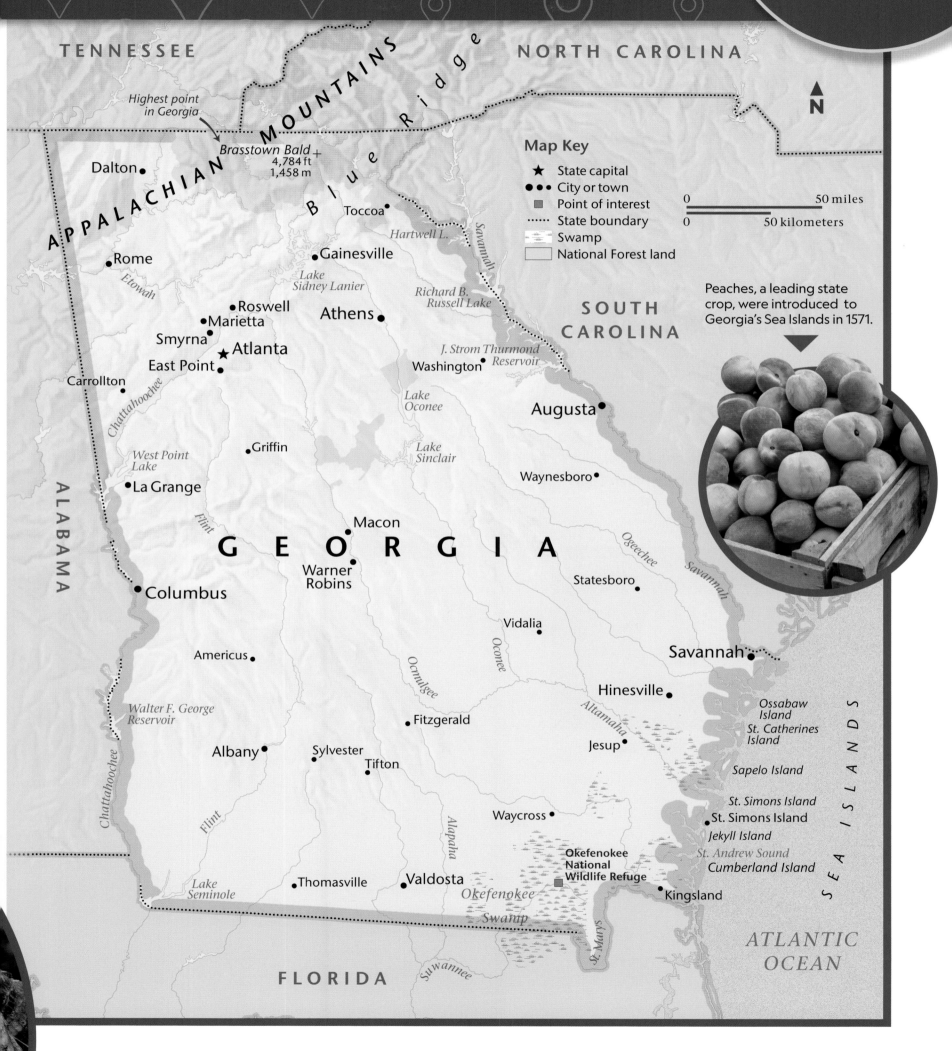

TENNESSEE

NORTH CAROLINA

N

APPALACHIAN MOUNTAINS

Blue Ridge

Highest point in Georgia

Brasstown Bald +
4,784 ft
1,458 m

Dalton

Rome

Etowah

Toccoa

Hartwell L.

Gainesville

Savannah

Lake
Sidney Lanier

*Richard B.
Russell Lake*

SOUTH
CAROLINA

Roswell

Marietta

Athens

Smyrna

Atlanta

*J. Strom Thurmond
Reservoir*

East Point

Washington

Carrollton

Chattahoochee

*Lake
Oconee*

Augusta

Griffin

*West Point
Lake*

*Lake
Sinclair*

Waynesboro

La Grange

Macon

GEORGIA

Flint

Warner
Robins

Ogeechee

Statesboro

Columbus

ALABAMA

Vidalia

Oconee

Savannah

Americus

Ocmulgee

Hinesville

Altamaha

Ossabaw
Island

St. Catherines
Island

*Walter F. George
Reservoir*

Fitzgerald

Jesup

Sapelo Island

Albany

Sylvester

Tifton

St. Simons Island

St. Simons Island

Jekyll Island

Alapaha

Waycross

St. Andrew Sound

Okefenokee
National
Wildlife Refuge

Cumberland Island

Flint

*Lake
Seminole*

Thomasville

Valdosta

*Okefenokee
Swamp*

Kingsland

St. Marys

SEA ISLANDS

Chattahoochee

Suwannee

FLORIDA

ATLANTIC
OCEAN

Map Key

★ State capital
●●● City or town
■ Point of interest
···· State boundary
〜 Swamp
▭ National Forest land

0 ——————— 50 miles
0 ——————— 50 kilometers

Peaches, a leading state crop, were introduced to Georgia's Sea Islands in 1571.
▼

KENTUCKY

KENTUCKY

Shaker Village in Pleasant Hill preserves the culture and history of the Shaker social movement.

LAND & WATER Mammoth Cave, Lake Cumberland, and the Ohio River are important land and water features of Kentucky.

STATEHOOD Kentucky became the 15th state in 1792.

PEOPLE & PLACES Kentucky's population is 4,468,402. Frankfort is the state capital. The largest city is Louisville/Jefferson County.

FUN FACT The song "Happy Birthday to You," one of the most popular songs in the English language, was written in 1893 by two sisters living in Louisville.

Abraham Lincoln, the 16th U.S. president, was born near Hodgenville. His profile appears on the penny.

ILLINOIS

Marion

MISSOURI

Paducah
Calvert City
Kentucky Lake

Mayfield

Fulton   Murray

Ohio

Cumberland

Tradewater

Lake Barkley

Wabash

Mississippi

Tennessee

Kentucky State Flag

The setting sun turns the sky red over Cave Run Lake. The lake's natural beauty makes it a popular vacation spot.

Goldenrod
State Flower

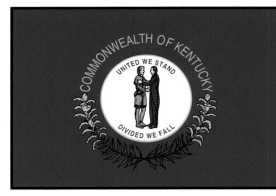

Cardinal
State Bird

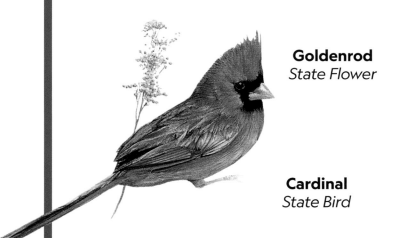

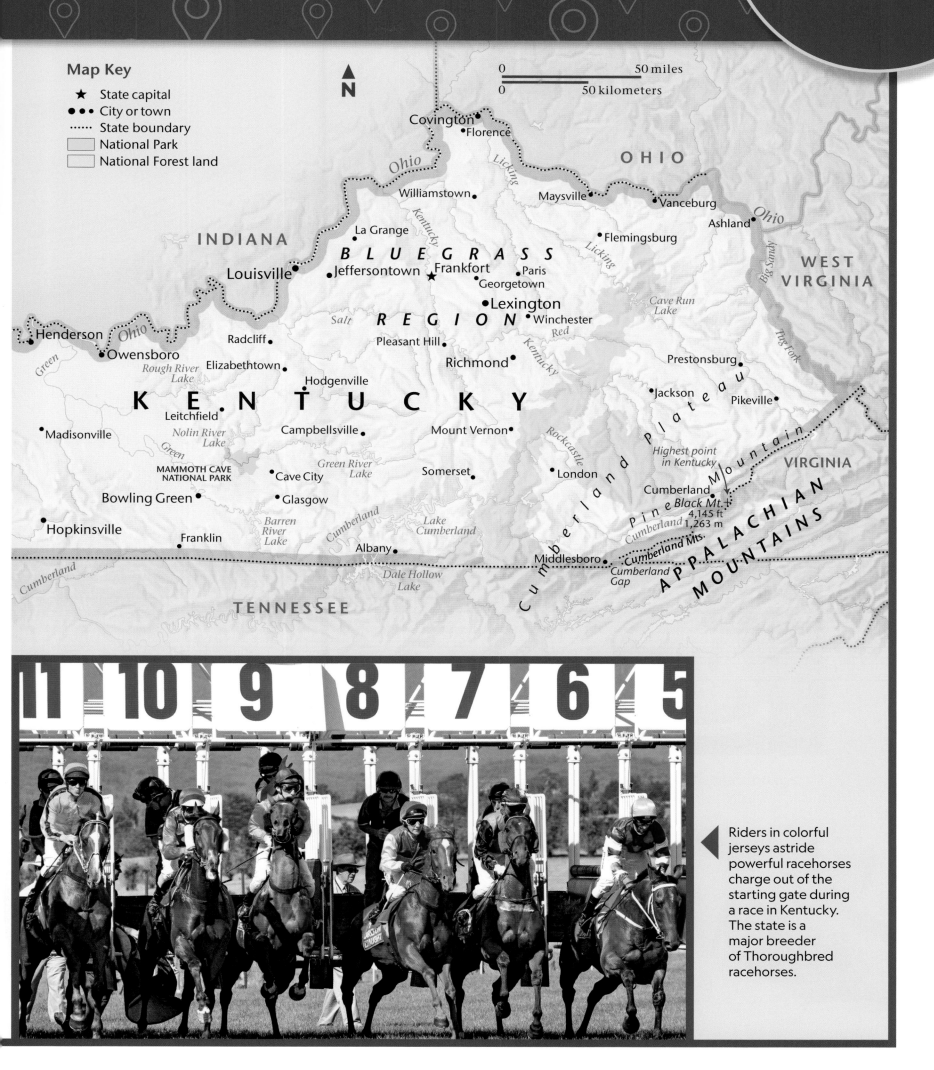

Map Key
★ State capital
●●● City or town
•••• State boundary
National Park
National Forest land

N

0   50 miles
0   50 kilometers

OHIO

INDIANA

Covington
Florence

Williamstown

Maysville

Vanceburg

Ashland

Flemingsburg

WEST
VIRGINIA

La Grange

Ohio

Licking

Licking

Kentucky

Big Sandy

Tug Fork

Ohio

BLUEGRASS

Louisville

Jeffersontown

Frankfort

Paris

Georgetown

Cave Run
Lake

Henderson

Ohio

REGION

Salt

Lexington

Winchester

Red

Green

Owensboro

Rough River
Lake

Radcliff

Pleasant Hill

Kentucky

Prestonsburg

Elizabethtown

Richmond

Jackson

Pikeville

KENTUCKY

Hodgenville

Leitchfield

Madisonville

Nolin River
Lake

Campbellsville

Mount Vernon

Cumberland Plateau

Highest point
in Kentucky

VIRGINIA

Green

MAMMOTH CAVE
NATIONAL PARK

Cave City

Green River
Lake

Somerset

Rockcastle

London

Cumberland

Pine Mountain

Black Mt.
4,145 ft
1,263 m

APPALACHIAN

Bowling Green

Glasgow

Cumberland

Barren
River
Lake

Lake
Cumberland

Cumberland Mts.

MOUNTAINS

Hopkinsville

Franklin

Albany

Middlesboro

Cumberland
Gap

Cumberland

Dale Hollow
Lake

TENNESSEE

11 10 9 8 7 6 5

◀ Riders in colorful jerseys astride powerful racehorses charge out of the starting gate during a race in Kentucky. The state is a major breeder of Thoroughbred racehorses.

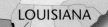

LOUISIANA

LAND & WATER Driskill Mountain, Lake Pontchartrain, and the Mississippi River are important land and water features of Louisiana.

STATEHOOD Louisiana became the 18th state in 1812.

PEOPLE & PLACES Louisiana's population is 4,659,978. Baton Rouge is the state capital. The largest city is New Orleans.

FUN FACT The Louisiana state capitol building in Baton Rouge is the tallest of all the state capitols. It is a limestone skyscraper that stands 450 feet (137 m) tall and has 34 stories!

The steamboat *Natchez*, an authentic paddle-wheel boat, churns up water as it provides tourists with a view of New Orleans from the Mississippi River.

Louisiana is the leading U.S. producer of shrimp. Most of it is harvested from the Barataria-Terrebonne National Estuary of the Mississippi River.

Springhill
Caddo Lake
Caddo Black Bayou Preserve
Bossier City
Shreveport
Lake Bistineau
Mansfield
Red
Toledo Bend Reservoir
Natchitoches
Many
Leesville
TEXAS
De Ridder
Sabine
Lake Charles
Calcasieu Lake
Sabine Lake

Louisiana State Flag

UNION JUSTICE CONFIDENCE

Magnolia
State Flower

Brown Pelican
State Bird

Musicians practice on a park bench in New Orleans. The city is the birthplace of jazz, a music form that originated in African-American communities.

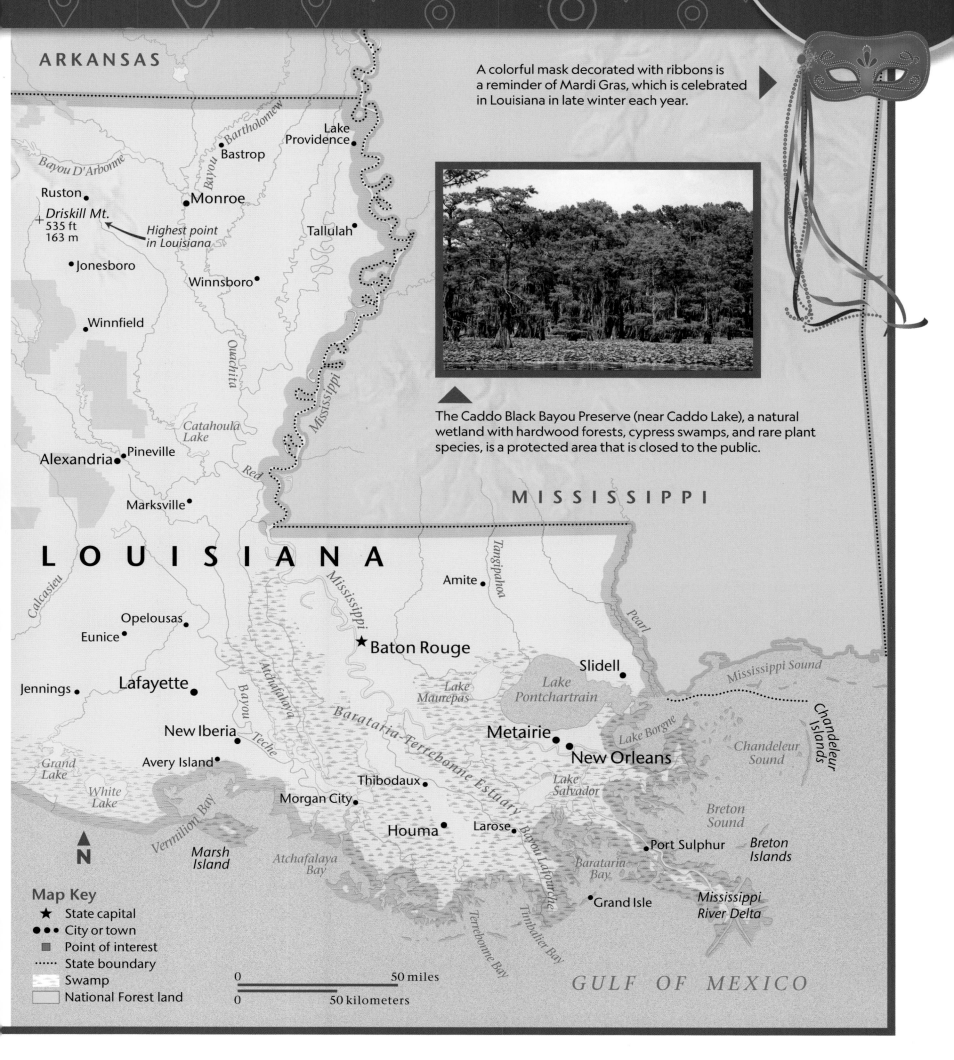

ARKANSAS

Bayou D'Arbonne

Lake Providence

Bastrop

Bayou Bartholomew

Ruston

Monroe

+ *Driskill Mt.*
535 ft
163 m

Highest point in Louisiana

Tallulah

Jonesboro

Winnsboro

Winnfield

Ouachita

Catahoula Lake

Alexandria • Pineville

Red

Marksville

L O U I S I A N A

Mississippi

MISSISSIPPI

Amite

Tangipahoa

Opelousas

Eunice

Baton Rouge ★

Atchafalaya

Bayou Teche

Lafayette

Jennings

Baratataria-Terrebonne Estuary

Slidell

Lake Maurepas

Lake Pontchartrain

Mississippi Sound

Metairie

New Orleans

Lake Borgne

Chandeleur Sound

Chandeleur Islands

New Iberia

Avery Island

Grand Lake

White Lake

Thibodaux

Morgan City

Lake Salvador

Breton Sound

Breton Islands

Vermilion Bay

Houma

Larose

Bayou Lafourche

Port Sulphur

Calcasieu

Marsh Island

Atchafalaya Bay

Baratataria Bay

Grand Isle

Mississippi River Delta

N

Terrebonne Bay

Timbalier Bay

GULF OF MEXICO

Map Key
★ State capital
••• City or town
■ Point of interest
••• State boundary
〰 Swamp
▢ National Forest land

0 ——————— 50 miles
0 ——————— 50 kilometers

A colorful mask decorated with ribbons is a reminder of Mardi Gras, which is celebrated in Louisiana in late winter each year. ▶

The Caddo Black Bayou Preserve (near Caddo Lake), a natural wetland with hardwood forests, cypress swamps, and rare plant species, is a protected area that is closed to the public.

Mississippi is the leading producer of catfish in the United States. A part of the Mississippi River Valley known as the Delta is the main producing area.

LAND & WATER The Mississippi Petrified Forest, the Tennessee-Tombigbee Waterway, and the Mississippi River are important land and water features of Mississippi.

STATEHOOD Mississippi became the 20th state in 1817.

PEOPLE & PLACES The population of Mississippi is 2,986,530. Jackson is the state capital and the largest city.

FUN FACT Jim Henson, creator of Kermit the Frog, Miss Piggy, Big Bird, and other famous Muppets, was born in Greenville.

Two bridges cross the Mississippi River between Vicksburg, Mississippi, and Delta, Louisiana. Cars and trucks use one bridge (left). The other is for trains.

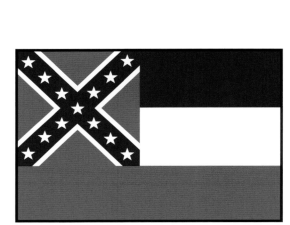

Mississippi State Flag

A sandy beach near Biloxi, on the state's Gulf of Mexico coast, is ready for sunseeking tourists.

Mockingbird
State Bird

Magnolia
State Flower

▲ More than 800 cotton farms produce over 1.4 million bales (about 500 pounds/227 kg per bale) of cotton each year in Mississippi.

N

Map Key

★ State capital
•• City or town
■ Point of interest
⋯ State boundary
▢ Indian Reservation
▢ National Forest land

0 ——————— 50 miles
0 ——————— 50 kilometers

ARKANSAS

TENNESSEE

Southaven

Corinth

Pickwick Lake

Woodall Mt.
806 ft
246 m

Senatobia

Booneville

Sardis Lake

New Albany

Tennessee-Tombigbee Waterway

Little Tallahatchie

Highest point in Mississippi

Colewater

Oxford

Tupelo

Yocona

Clarksdale

Water Valley

Houston

Aberdeen

Yalobusha

Shelby

Tallahatchie

Tombigbee

Ruleville

West Point

D E L T A

Winona

Columbus

Indianola

Greenville

Yazoo

Kosciusko

Louisville

MISSISSIPPI

Big Black

Yazoo City

Carthage

Philadelphia
MISSISSIPPI CHOCTAW INDIAN RESERVATION

Mississippi Petrified Forest

Ross Barnett Reservoir

Pearl

Ridgeland

Meridian

Vicksburg

Forest

Jackson

Brandon

Newton

Deer Creek

Mississippi

Yazoo

LOUISIANA

Crystal Springs

ALABAMA

Quitman

Hazlehurst

Magee

Leaf

Chickasawhay

Natchez

Collins

Waynesboro

Brookhaven

Ellisville

Pearl

Homochitto

McComb

Columbia

Hattiesburg

Centreville

Leaf

Lucedale

Wiggins

Black Creek

Pascagoula

Mississippi

Gulfport

Biloxi

Pascagoula

Bay St. Louis

Mississippi Sound

GULF OF MEXICO

NORTH CAROLINA

 LAND & WATER Mount Mitchell, Lake Norman, and the Cape Fear River are important land and water features of North Carolina.

 STATEHOOD North Carolina became the 12th state in 1789.

 PEOPLE & PLACES North Carolina's population is 10,383,620. Raleigh is the state capital. The largest city is Charlotte.

? **FUN FACT** The University of North Carolina, the first public university in the United States, opened its doors in 1795 with two professors and 41 students.

North Carolina State Flag

Cardinal
State Bird

Flowering Dogwood
State Flower

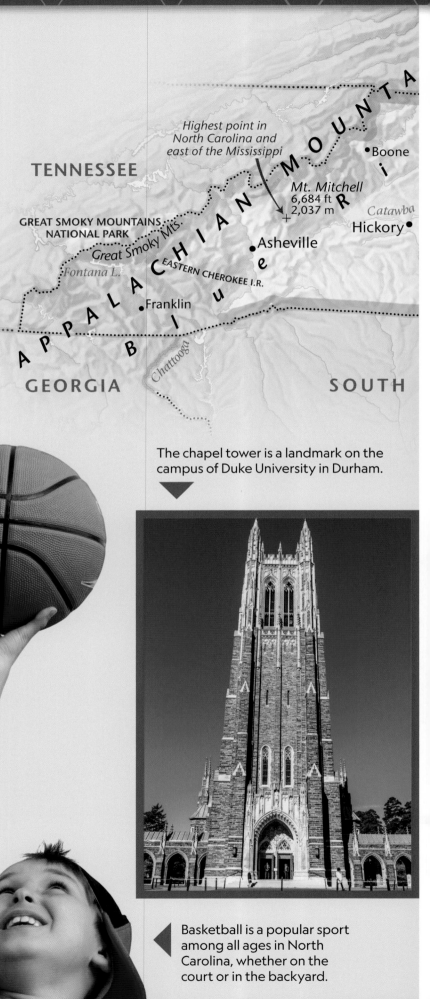

TENNESSEE

GREAT SMOKY MOUNTAINS NATIONAL PARK

Great Smoky Mts.

Fontana L.

EASTERN CHEROKEE I.R.

•Franklin

Chattooga

GEORGIA

Highest point in North Carolina and east of the Mississippi

APPALACHIAN MOUNTAINS

•Boone

Mt. Mitchell
6,684 ft
2,037 m

Catawba

Hickory•

•Asheville

Blue Ridge

SOUTH

The chapel tower is a landmark on the campus of Duke University in Durham.

Basketball is a popular sport among all ages in North Carolina, whether on the court or in the backyard.

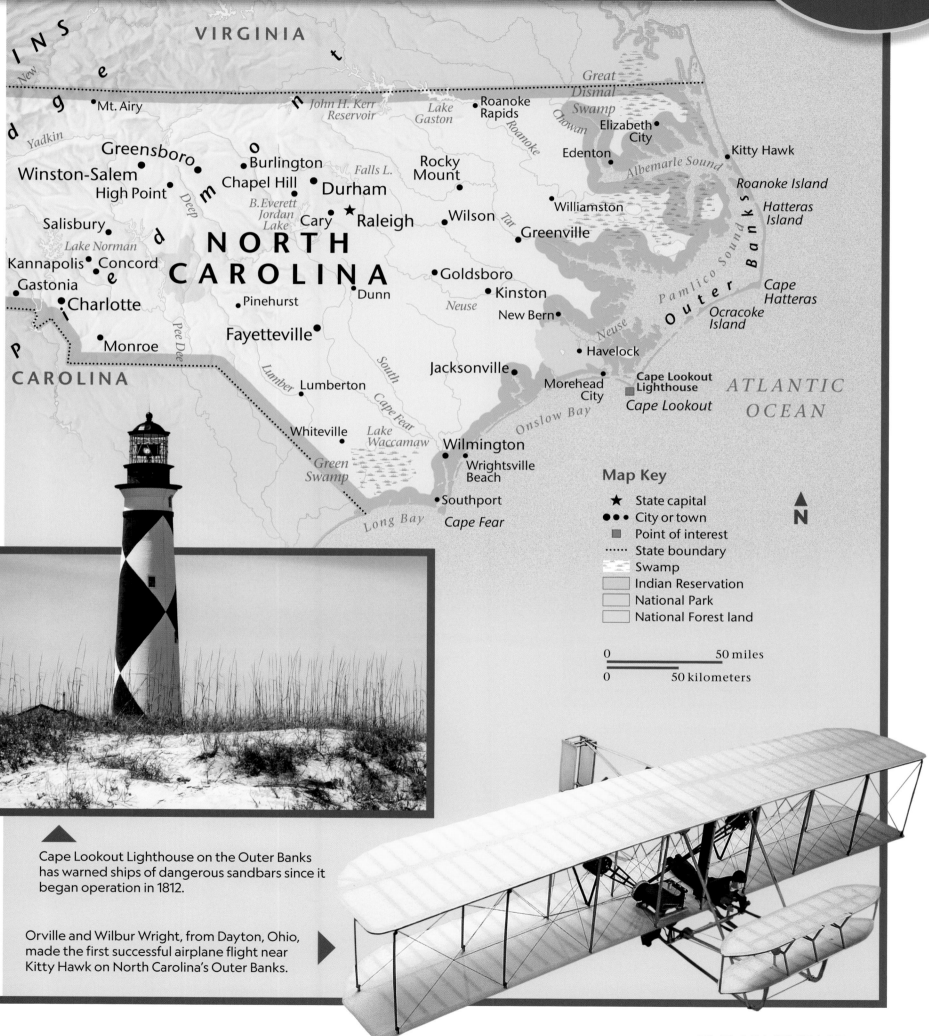

VIRGINIA

Great Dismal Swamp

New

INS
e
d
g
e

•Mt. Airy

Yadkin

Greensboro
•Burlington
John H. Kerr Reservoir
Lake Gaston
Roanoke Rapids
Chowan
Elizabeth City
Kitty Hawk
Edenton
Albemarle Sound
Roanoke Island

Winston-Salem
Chapel Hill
•**Durham**
Falls L.
Rocky Mount
Williamston
Hatteras Island

High Point
Deep
B. Everett Jordan Lake
Cary
★ Raleigh
•Wilson
Tar
Greenville

Salisbury
m
o
n
t

Lake Norman
d

Kannapolis
•Concord
NORTH CAROLINA
Goldsboro
Kinston
Neuse
New Bern

Gastonia
e
Dunn
Pamlico Sound
Outer Banks
Cape Hatteras
Ocracoke Island

•**Charlotte**
Pinehurst
South
Neuse
Havelock

•Monroe
P
i
Fayetteville
Lumber
Cape Fear
Jacksonville
Morehead City
Cape Lookout Lighthouse
Cape Lookout
ATLANTIC OCEAN

CAROLINA
Pee Dee
Lumberton
Onslow Bay

Whiteville
Lake Waccamaw
Wilmington
Wrightsville Beach

Green Swamp
Southport
Cape Fear
Long Bay

Roanoke

Map Key

★ State capital
••• City or town
■ Point of interest
······ State boundary
Swamp
Indian Reservation
National Park
National Forest land

N

0 ——————— 50 miles
0 ——————— 50 kilometers

Cape Lookout Lighthouse on the Outer Banks has warned ships of dangerous sandbars since it began operation in 1812.

Orville and Wilbur Wright, from Dayton, Ohio, made the first successful airplane flight near Kitty Hawk on North Carolina's Outer Banks.

SOUTH CAROLINA

LAND & WATER Sumter National Forest, Lake Marion, and the Great Pee Dee River are important land and water features of South Carolina.

STATEHOOD South Carolina became the 8th state in 1788.

PEOPLE & PLACES South Carolina's population is 5,084,127. Columbia is the state capital. The largest city is Charleston.

FUN FACT Sweetgrass baskets have been made in the coastal lowland region for more than 300 years. They were originally used in the planting and processing of rice.

South Carolina State Flag

Highest point in South Carolina

Sassafras Mt.
3,560 ft
1,085 m

Map Key
★ State capital
•• City or town
····· State boundary
Swamp
National Park
National Forest land

| 0 | | 50 miles |
| 0 | | 50 kilometers |

SUMTER NATIONAL FOREST

Greer
Greenville
Easley
Simpsonville
Clemson
Hartwell Lake
Anderson
Lake Keowee
Lake Greenwood
Richard B. Russell Lake
SUMTER NATIONAL FOREST
J. Strom Thurmond Reservoir

Blue Ridge
Chattooga
Tugaloo
Savannah

GEORGIA

Large container ships carrying valuable manufactured goods link South Carolina to the global economy. Charleston is the state's largest port.

Yellow Jessamine
State Flower

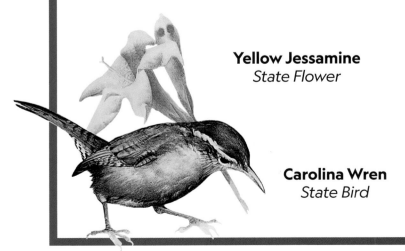

Carolina Wren
State Bird

NORTH CAROLINA

Gaffney
Spartanburg
York
Rock Hill
Union
Lancaster
Cheraw
SUMTER NATIONAL FOREST
Winnsboro
Dillon
Darlington
Florence
Newberry
Loris
Lake Murray
Saluda
Irmo
S O U T H
West Columbia
Columbia
Sumter
Lake City
CONGAREE NATIONAL PARK
C A R O L I N A
Myrtle Beach
Aiken
S. Fork Edisto
N. Fork Edisto
Orangeburg
Lake Marion
Georgetown
Williston
Lake Moultrie
North Island
Bamberg
Moncks Corner
Savannah
Allendale
Summerville
Cape Island
Walterboro
North Charleston
Mount Pleasant
Charleston
Edisto Island
Beaufort
St. Helena Sound
St. Helena Island
Parris Island
Port Royal Sound
Hilton Head Island
Hilton Head Island
Daufuskie Island

Wylie Lake
Broad
Catawba
Wateree Lake
Wateree
Great Pee Dee
Little Pee Dee
Congaree
Black
Great Pee Dee
Waccamaw
Long Bay
Santee
Edisto
Cooper

Piedmont

Coastal Plain

Lowcountry

Sea Islands

ATLANTIC OCEAN

Hard-packed sands on a Hilton Head Island beach are perfect for a family bicycle outing.

Loggerhead turtles, which are an endangered species, lay their eggs in nests that they dig in the sand in the coastal area known as the Lowcountry.

TENNESSEE

TENNESSEE

LAND & WATER The Cumberland Plateau, Reelfoot Lake, and the Tennessee River are important land and water features of Tennessee.

STATEHOOD Tennessee became the 16th state in 1796.

PEOPLE & PLACES Tennessee's population is 6,770,010. Nashville/Davidson County is the state capital and the largest city.

FUN FACT In 1811–1812 three major earthquakes, known as the New Madrid earthquakes, changed the landscape in parts of Tennessee and neighboring Missouri. The ground in northwest Tennessee sank, creating Reelfoot Lake.

Tennessee State Flag

Iris
State Flower

Mockingbird
State Bird

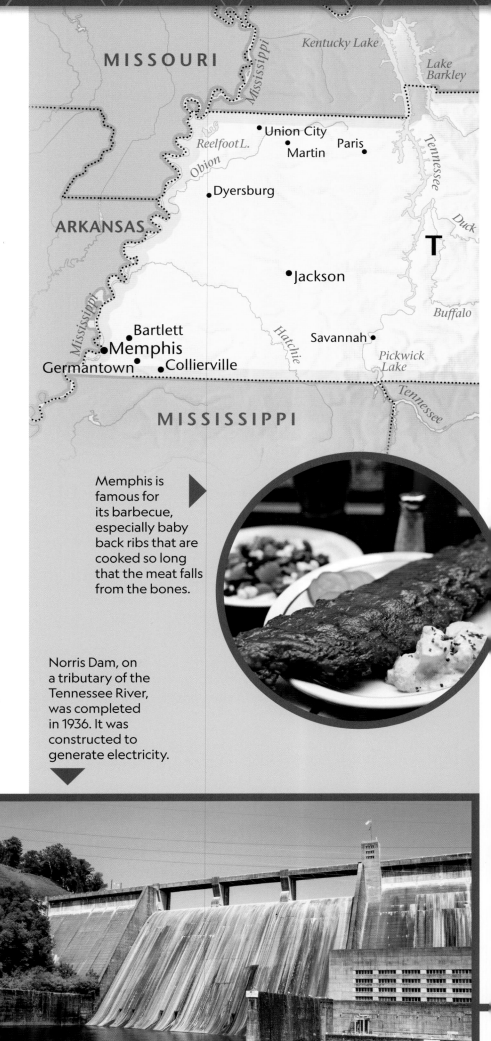

MISSOURI

Kentucky Lake

Lake Barkley

Mississippi

Reelfoot L.
Union City
Martin
Paris

Obion
Dyersburg

ARKANSAS

Tennessee

Duck

T

Jackson

Buffalo

Mississippi

Bartlett
Memphis
Germantown
Collierville

Hatchie

Savannah

Pickwick Lake

Tennessee

MISSISSIPPI

Memphis is famous for its barbecue, especially baby back ribs that are cooked so long that the meat falls from the bones.

Norris Dam, on a tributary of the Tennessee River, was completed in 1936. It was constructed to generate electricity.

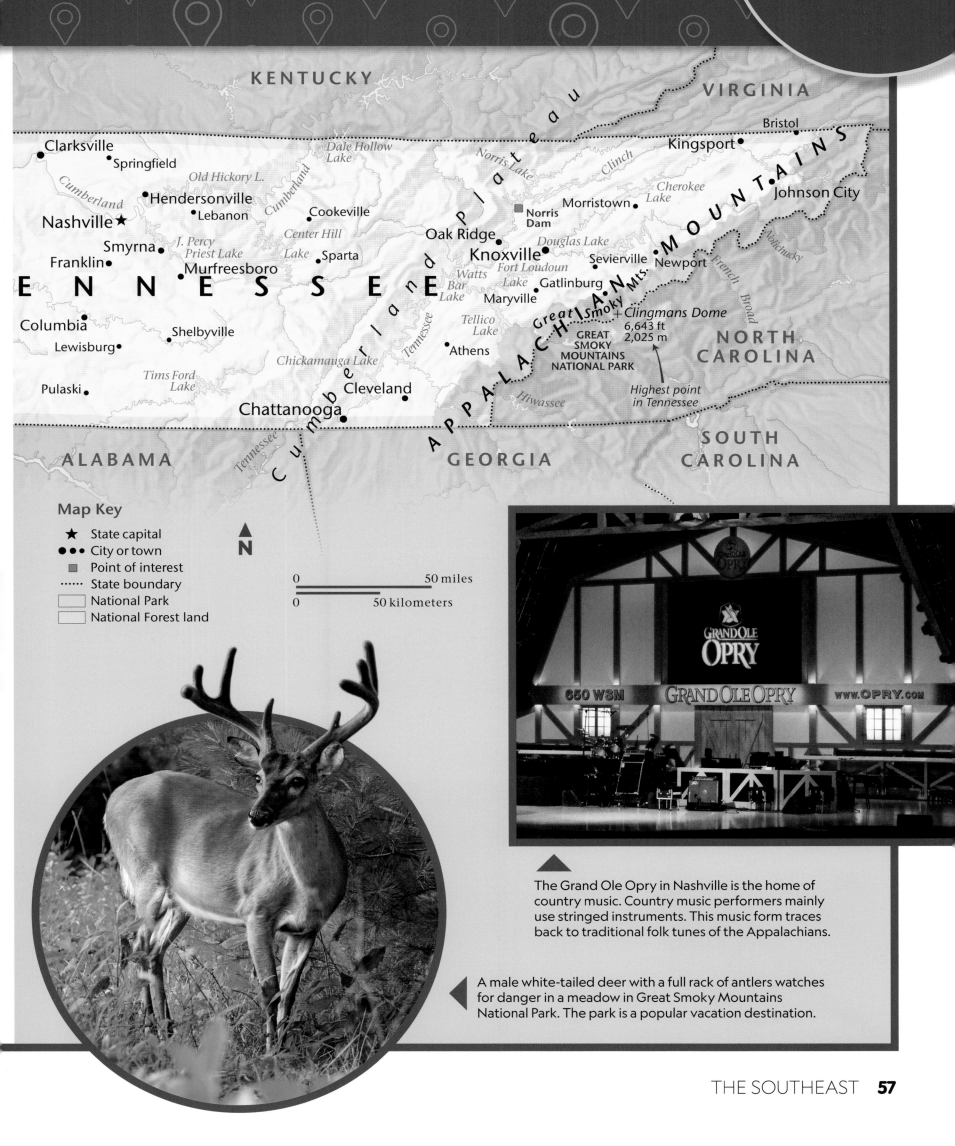

KENTUCKY

VIRGINIA

Clarksville
Springfield
Old Hickory L.
Dale Hollow Lake
Norris Lake
Clinch
Bristol
Kingsport
Hendersonville
Lebanon
Cookeville
Cumberland
Cumberland
Morristown
Cherokee Lake
Johnson City
Nashville ★
Center Hill Lake
Oak Ridge
Norris Dam
Smyrna
J. Percy Priest Lake
Sparta
Knoxville
Douglas Lake
Sevierville
Newport
French Broad
Nolichucky
Franklin
Murfreesboro
Watts Bar Lake
Fort Loudoun Lake
Gatlinburg
Columbia
Shelbyville
Tellico Lake
Maryville
+ Clingmans Dome 6,643 ft 2,025 m
NORTH CAROLINA
Lewisburg
Chickamauga Lake
Athens
GREAT SMOKY MOUNTAINS NATIONAL PARK
Highest point in Tennessee
Pulaski
Tims Ford Lake
Cleveland
Chattanooga
Hiwassee

T E N N E S S E E

Cumberland Plateau

A P P A L A C H I A N   M O U N T A I N S

Great Smoky Mts.

ALABAMA
Tennessee
GEORGIA
SOUTH CAROLINA

Map Key

★ State capital
●●● City or town
■ Point of interest
⋯⋯ State boundary
▢ National Park
▢ National Forest land

N

| 0 | 50 miles |
| 0 | 50 kilometers |

The Grand Ole Opry in Nashville is the home of country music. Country music performers mainly use stringed instruments. This music form traces back to traditional folk tunes of the Appalachians.

A male white-tailed deer with a full rack of antlers watches for danger in a meadow in Great Smoky Mountains National Park. The park is a popular vacation destination.

VIRGINIA

 LAND & WATER The Blue Ridge mountains, Shenandoah National Park, and the James River are important land and water features of Virginia.

STATEHOOD Virginia became the 10th state in 1788.

PEOPLE & PLACES Virginia's population is 8,517,685. Richmond is the state capital. The largest city is Virginia Beach.

FUN FACT Eight U.S. presidents—Washington, Jefferson, Madison, Monroe, Harrison, Tyler, Taylor, and Wilson—were born in Virginia, more than in any other state.

Virginia State Flag

Flowering Dogwood
State Flower

Cardinal
State Bird

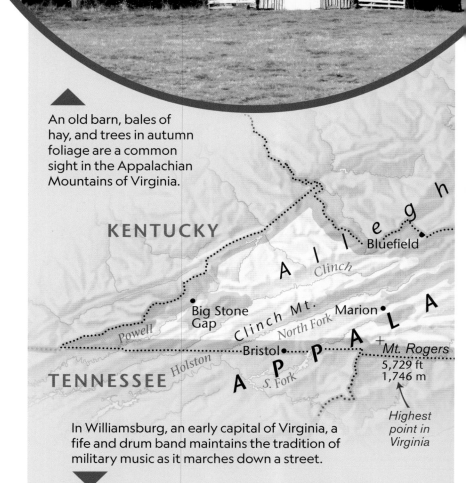

An old barn, bales of hay, and trees in autumn foliage are a common sight in the Appalachian Mountains of Virginia.

KENTUCKY

Bluefield

Allegh

Clinch

Big Stone Gap

Clinch Mt.

Marion

Powell

North Fork

Bristol

+ Mt. Rogers
5,729 ft
1,746 m

TENNESSEE

Holston

S. Fork

APPALA

Highest point in Virginia

In Williamsburg, an early capital of Virginia, a fife and drum band maintains the tradition of military music as it marches down a street.

NEW JERSEY

MARYLAND

DELAWARE

DELMARVA PENINSULA

WEST VIRGINIA

Potomac

Winchester

Leesburg

Reston

Front Royal

Shenandoah

D.C.

Arlington

Manassas

Alexandria

Luray Caverns

Luray

Woodbridge

Harrisonburg

Culpeper

Chesapeake Bay

SHENANDOAH NATIONAL PARK

Fredericksburg

Rappahannock

Potomac

Allegheny Mountains

Shenandoah Mountain

Cowpasture

MOUNTAINS

BLUE RIDGE

PIEDMONT

Lake Anna

Chincoteague

New

Lexington

James

VIRGINIA

Charlottesville

APPALACHIAN

Richmond

York

Appomattox

Williamsburg

Cape Charles

Lynchburg

Yorktown

Roanoke

Petersburg

James

Hampton

Blacksburg

Smith Mountain Lake

Newport News

Virginia Beach

Radford

Roanoke (Staunton)

Nottoway

Norfolk

New

Portsmouth

Chesapeake

John H. Kerr Reservoir

Lake Gaston

Great Dismal Swamp

Danville

Roanoke

ATLANTIC OCEAN

NORTH CAROLINA

N

A great blue heron uses its sharp eyes to watch the water in a river near Richmond for a dinner of fish or frogs.

Map Key

★ State capital
●●● City or town
■ Point of interest
⋯ State boundary
Swamp
National Park
National Forest land

0 — 50 miles
0 — 50 kilometers

Winding under the Appalachian Mountains, Luray Caverns was created as water dissolved rocks and the minerals dripped down to create formations called stalactites and stalagmites.

WEST VIRGINIA

LAND & WATER
The Allegheny Mountains, the Ohio River, and the New River are important land and water features of West Virginia.

STATEHOOD
West Virginia became the 35th state in 1863.

PEOPLE & PLACES
West Virginia's population is 1,805,832. Charleston is the state capital and the largest city.

FUN FACT
One of the oldest and largest burial mounds is located in Moundsville along the Ohio River. Built by the Adena people, the mound is more than 2,000 years old.

West Virginia State Flag

West Virginia's rivers offer some of the best white-water rafting in the eastern United States. The Gauley River is called the Beast of the East.

A coal miner's helmet recalls the history of mining in West Virginia. The state produced 12 percent of U.S. coal in 2017, second only to Wyoming.

Foliage turns red in the Dolly Sods Wilderness in the Monongahela National Forest. The area is named for an early settler family.

Rhododendron
State Flower

Cardinal
State Bird

KENTUCKY

Point Pleasant

Huntington

Ohio

Big Sandy

Guyandotte

Tug Fork

Williamson

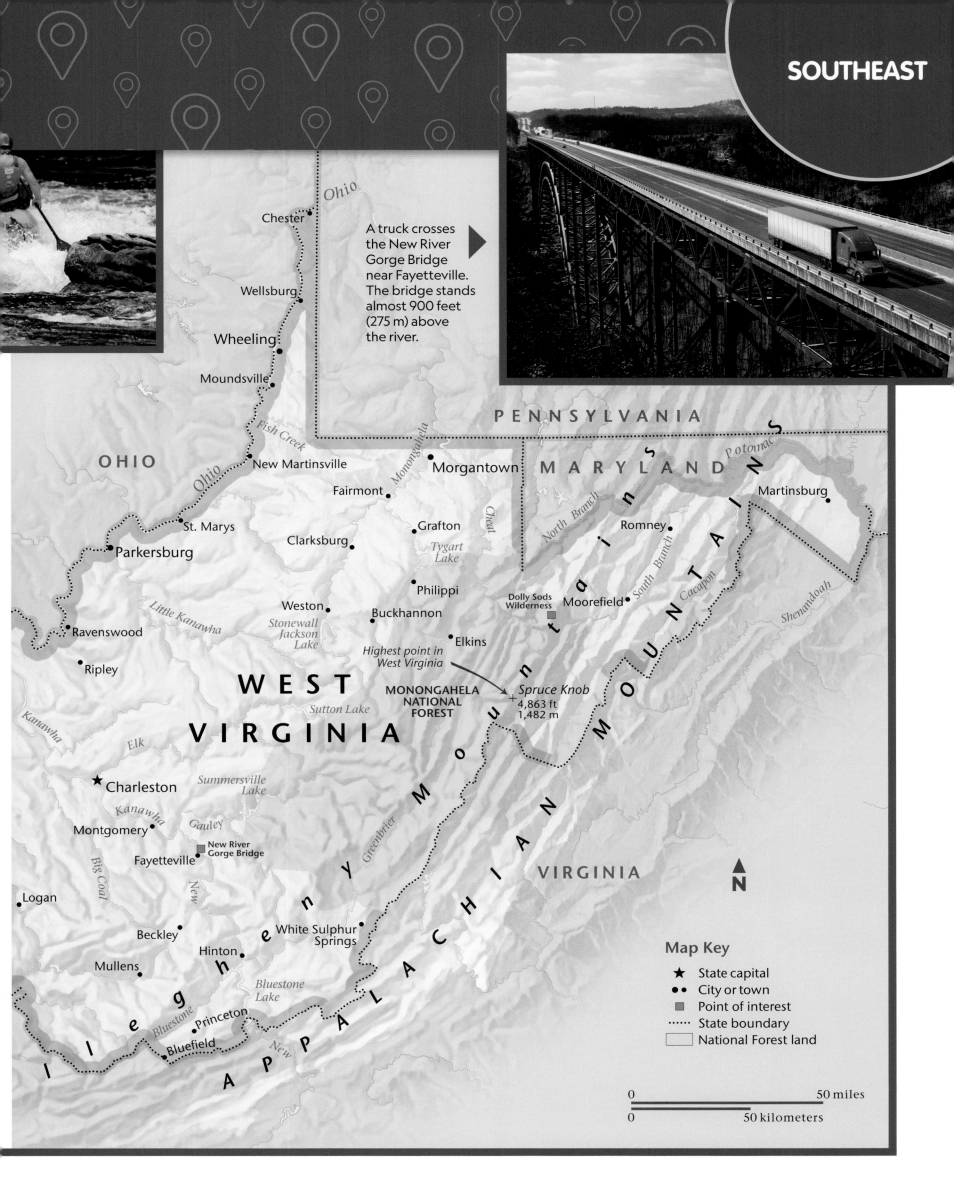

A truck crosses the New River Gorge Bridge near Fayetteville. The bridge stands almost 900 feet (275 m) above the river.

OHIO

PENNSYLVANIA

MARYLAND

Chester

Wellsburg

Wheeling

Moundsville

Ohio

Fish Creek

New Martinsville

Monongahela

Fairmont

Morgantown

Martinsburg

St. Marys

Parkersburg

Clarksburg

Grafton

Cheat

Romney

North Branch

Potomac

South Branch

Cacapon

Ravenswood

Ripley

Little Kanawha

Weston

Stonewall Jackson Lake

Philippi

Buckhannon

Dolly Sods Wilderness

Moorefield

Shenandoah

Tygart Lake

Elkins

WEST VIRGINIA

Highest point in West Virginia

MONONGAHELA NATIONAL FOREST

+ *Spruce Knob* 4,863 ft 1,482 m

Sutton Lake

Kanawha

Elk

★ Charleston

Summersville Lake

Kanawha

Gauley

Montgomery

New River Gorge Bridge

Fayetteville

Big Coal

New

Logan

Beckley

Hinton

White Sulphur Springs

Mullens

Bluestone Lake

Bluestone

Princeton

Bluefield

New

VIRGINIA

A l l e g h e n y   M o u n t a i n s

A P P A L A C H I A N   M O U N T A I N S

N

Map Key

★ State capital

● City or town

■ Point of interest

⋯ State boundary

▭ National Forest land

0 — 50 miles
0 — 50 kilometers

THE MIDWEST

The Midwest is a region of prairies, lakes, and rivers. The Mississippi River and its tributaries drain America's interior. The region supports some of the most productive agriculture in the world, including the crops corn, wheat, and soybeans. Industries such as food processing, steel, and automobile production led to the growth of cities such as Chicago, Illinois, and Detroit, Michigan, but these industries are now being replaced by technology and information-based businesses.

Dairy cows are an important part of the region's economy. The Midwest supplies much of the country's milk, cheese, and butter.

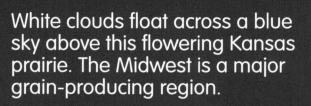

White clouds float across a blue sky above this flowering Kansas prairie. The Midwest is a major grain-producing region.

ILLINOIS

ILLINOIS

LAND & WATER
The Shawnee National Forest, the Illinois River, and Lake Michigan are important land and water features of Illinois.

STATEHOOD
Illinois became the 21st state in 1818.

PEOPLE & PLACES
Illinois has a population of 12,741,080. Springfield is the state capital. The largest city is Chicago.

FUN FACT
The Chicago River is dyed green on St. Patrick's Day to honor Chicago's large Irish population. The formula for the green dye is a closely kept secret.

Illinois State Flag

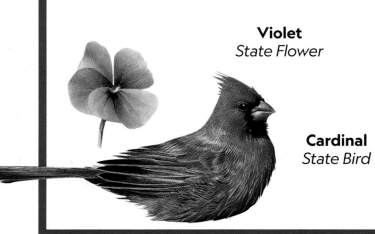

Violet
State Flower

Cardinal
State Bird

The Pilsen neighborhood on Chicago's lower west side is known for its colorful street murals. This painting celebrates women in the multicultural population of this immigrant neighborhood.

Pig races are a fun-filled highlight of the annual Illinois State Fair in Springfield.

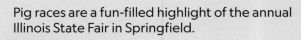

WRIGLEY FIELD
HOME OF
CHICAGO CUBS

PIRATES   TOP 9TH   CUBS
1   4

The tomb of Abraham Lincoln, the country's 16th president, attracts visitors to Oak Ridge Cemetery in Springfield.

N

Map Key

★ State capital
●●●● City or town
⋯⋯ State boundary
☐ National Forest land

| 0 | 50 miles |
| 0 | 50 kilometers |

Wrigley Field in Chicago is affected by wind conditions more than any other major league baseball park due to its location near Lake Michigan.

WISCONSIN

LAKE MICHIGAN

MICHIGAN

Highest point in Illinois

‡ Charles Mound
1,235 ft
376 m

Chicago River

Freeport
Waukegan
Rockford
Schaumburg
Elgin
Evanston
DeKalb
Cicero
Chicago
IOWA
Sterling
Dixon
Naperville
Aurora
Green
Rock Island
Moline
Joliet
Geneseo
Fox
Des Plaines
Illinois
Kewanee
Kankakee
Vermilion
Galesburg
Kankakee
Pontiac
Iroquois
Spoon
Peoria
Mackinaw
Pekin
Normal
Bloomington
Rantoul

ILLINOIS

Sangamon
Lincoln
Champaign
Danville
Salt Creek
Urbana
Embarras
Quincy
Decatur
Wabash
McKee Creek
Sangamon
Springfield ★
Mississippi
Taylorville
Lake Shelbyville
Charleston
Illinois
INDIANA
Greenup
Kaskaskia
Effingham
Vandalia
Embarras
Alton
Carlyle Lake
Lawrenceville
Granite City
Little Wabash
Missouri
East St. Louis
Belleville
Centralia
Rend Lake
Kaskaskia
MISSOURI
Kaskaskia Island
Big Muddy
Marion
Harrisburg
Carbondale
Ohio
SHAWNEE NATIONAL FOREST
Ohio
Cumberland
KENTUCKY
Cairo
Tennessee
Mississippi

INDIANA

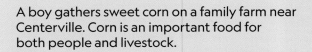

LAND & WATER
The Hoosier National Forest, Lake Michigan, and the Wabash River are important land and water features of Indiana.

STATEHOOD
Indiana became the 19th state in 1816.

PEOPLE & PLACES
Indiana's population is 6,691,878. Indianapolis is the state capital and the largest city.

FUN FACT
The intersection of U.S. Highway 40 and U.S. Highway 41, at Wabash Avenue and Seventh Street in Terre Haute, is called the Crossroads of America.

The Indianapolis Motor Speedway is the largest sports stadium in the world. It has more than 250,000 permanent seats and hosts the famous Indy 500 race.

The Hoosiers of Indiana University, in Bloomington, are part of the powerful Big Ten Conference in college football. Sports are an important tradition and a favorite pastime in Indiana.

A boy gathers sweet corn on a family farm near Centerville. Corn is an important food for both people and livestock.

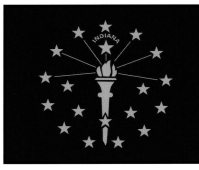

Indiana State Flag

Peony
State Flower

Cardinal
State Bird

LAKE MICHIGAN

MICHIGAN

East Chicago
Hammond
Gary
Michigan City
Elkhart
Angola
INDIANA DUNES
NATIONAL PARK
South
Bend
Mishawaka
Portage
Goshen
Merrillville
Valparaiso

Plymouth

Auburn

Warsaw

Fort Wayne

St. Joseph
Maumee

Map Key

★ State capital
●●● City or town
■ Point of interest
···· State boundary
National Park
National Forest land

Kankakee

Tippecanoe

Eel

St. Marys

Rensselaer

Huntington

Wabash

Iroquois

Wabash

Mississinewa
Lake

0   100 miles
0   100 kilometers

Kokomo
Marion

Lafayette

I N D I A N A

OHIO

Muncie
Highest point
in Indiana

White

Lebanon
Noblesville
Anderson

Carmel
Hoosier Hill
1,257 ft
383 m

Sugar Creek

ILLINOIS

Wabash

Sugar Creek

New
Castle
Richmond

Indianapolis
Motor Speedway

Lawrence
Centerville

Indianapolis ★
Beech Grove

Plainfield
Connersville

Greenwood
Big Blue

Cagles Mill
Lake

Mill Creek

Shelbyville
Brookville
Lake

White

Franklin
Whitewater

Great Miami

Terre
Haute
Eel
Martinsville
Lake
Lemon

Bloomington
Columbus

Monroe
Lake
Sand Creek

Lawrenceburg

HOOSIER
NATIONAL
FOREST

Ohio

Salt Cr.

Bedford
Muscatatuck

Vincennes
Washington
East Fork White

Blue

Patoka

HOOSIER
NATIONAL
FOREST

Ohio

Patoka
Lake

New Albany

Mount
Vernon
Evansville
Jeffersonville

K E N T U C K Y

Ohio

IOWA

LAND & WATER
Hawkeye Point and the Missouri and Mississippi Rivers are important land and water features of Iowa.

STATEHOOD
Iowa became the 29th state in 1846.

PEOPLE & PLACES
Iowa's population is 3,156,145. Des Moines is the state capital and the largest city.

FUN FACT
Iowa's nickname, the Hawkeye State, comes from Black Hawk, the Sauk warrior who fought unsuccessfully to regain tribal lands in the Black Hawk War of 1832.

Iowa State Flag

Wild Rose
State Flower

American Goldfinch
State Bird

Hogs outnumber people almost seven to one in Iowa, which produces nearly one-third of all hogs raised in the United States.

SOUTH DAKOTA

Hawkeye Point +
1,670 ft
509 m
Highest point in Iowa

• Sheldon

Big Sioux

Le Mars •

• Sioux City

Missouri

Little Sioux

• Onawa

NEBRASKA

Boyer

N

•• Council Bluffs

• Glenwood

Missouri

Map Key
★ State capital
••• City or town
■ Point of interest
⋯⋯ State boundary
☐ Indian Reservation

0 ————————— 50 miles
0 ————————— 50 kilometers

A young Meskwaki boy, dressed in colorful ceremonial clothing, prepares to participate in his tribe's annual powwow near Tama.

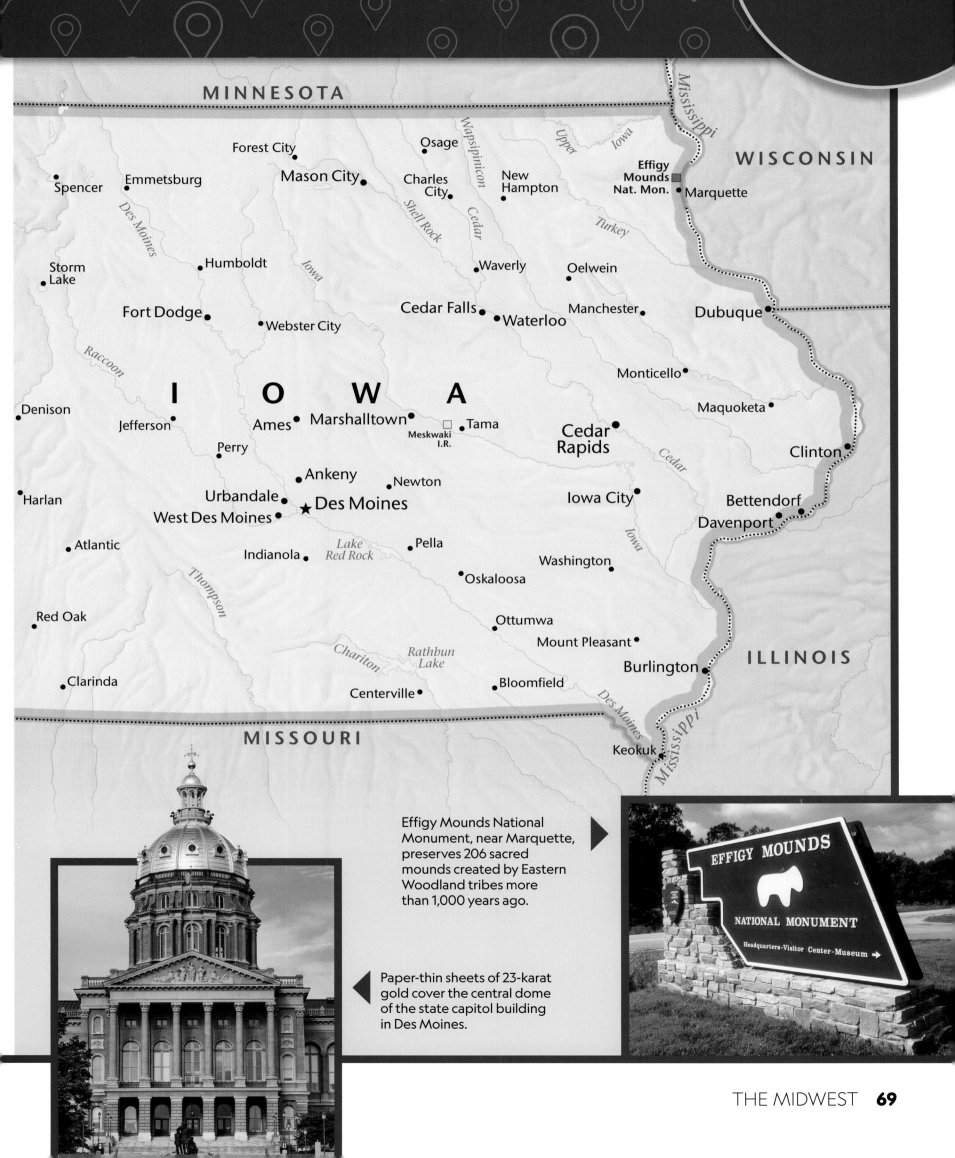

MINNESOTA

WISCONSIN

Spencer
Emmetsburg
Forest City
Osage
Charles City
New Hampton
Mason City
Wapsipinicon
Effigy Mounds Nat. Mon.
Marquette

Des Moines
Storm Lake
Humboldt
Shell Rock
Iowa
Cedar
Waverly
Oelwein
Turkey

Fort Dodge
Webster City
Cedar Falls
Waterloo
Manchester
Dubuque

Raccoon
I O W A
Monticello

Denison
Jefferson
Ames
Marshalltown
Tama
Meskwaki I.R.
Cedar Rapids
Maquoketa

Perry
Cedar
Clinton

Harlan
Urbandale
Ankeny
Newton
Iowa City
Bettendorf

West Des Moines
★ Des Moines
Davenport

Atlantic
Indianola
Lake Red Rock
Pella
Washington
Iowa

Thompson
Oskaloosa

Red Oak
Ottumwa
Mount Pleasant
I L L I N O I S

Chariton
Rathbun Lake

Clarinda
Centerville
Bloomfield
Burlington

MISSOURI
Des Moines
Keokuk
Mississippi

Effigy Mounds National Monument, near Marquette, preserves 206 sacred mounds created by Eastern Woodland tribes more than 1,000 years ago.

Paper-thin sheets of 23-karat gold cover the central dome of the state capitol building in Des Moines.

EFFIGY MOUNDS
NATIONAL MONUMENT
Headquarters-Visitor Center-Museum →

KANSAS

LAND & WATER Mount Sunflower, the Flint Hills, and the Missouri River are important land and water features of Kansas.

STATEHOOD Kansas became the 34th state in 1861.

PEOPLE & PLACES The population of Kansas is 2,911,505. Topeka is the state capital. The largest city is Wichita.

FUN FACT Pizza Hut, the world's largest pizza chain, opened its first restaurant in Wichita in 1958. Today the company has more than 16,900 restaurants in at least 105 countries.

Kansas State Flag

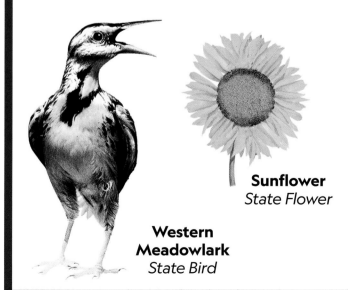

Western Meadowlark *State Bird*

Sunflower *State Flower*

A statue of the Tin Man, a character from *The Wonderful Wizard of Oz*, the popular fantasy book partly set in Kansas, sits in a garden.

Map Key

★ State capital
●●● City or town
■ Point of interest
····· State boundary
▨ Indian Reservation

0   50 miles
0   50 kilometers

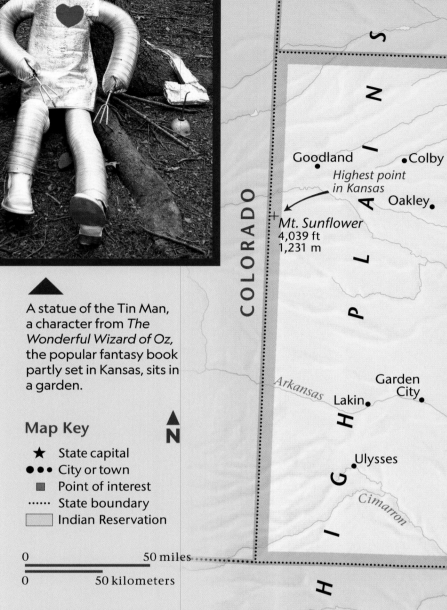

COLORADO

HIGH PLAINS

Goodland   •Colby
Highest point in Kansas
→ *Mt. Sunflower* 4,039 ft 1,231 m
Oakley•

Arkansas   Lakin•   Garden City•

•Ulysses

Cimarron

N

Monument Rocks, located south of Oakley, were once part of an ancient inland seabed. Over millions of years, erosion by wind and water has created these chalk formations.

NEBRASKA

Norton

Phillipsburg

Prairie Dog Creek

North Fork Solomon

Belleville

Concordia

Clay
Center

Seneca

SAC AND FOX
I.R.

KICKAPOO
I.R.

IOWA
I.R.

Hiawatha

Holton

Atchison

Little Blue

Big Blue

Missouri

Beloit

Plainville

South Fork Solomon

S m o k y   H i l l s

Republican

Solomon

Tuttle
Creek
Lake

POTAWATOMI
I.R.

Leavenworth

Fort
Leavenworth

WaKeeney

Monument
Rocks

Russell

Smoky Hill

Manhattan

Saline

Salina

Abilene

Junction City

Wamego

Perry
Lake

Kansas

Topeka ★

Lawrence

Kansas City

Overland Park

Olathe

Milford
Lake

Smoky Hill

Missouri

MISSOURI

K A N S A S

Ness City

Great Bend

Walnut Creek

Arkansas

Cheyenne Bottoms

Marion
Lake

Osage City

Emporia

John Redmond
Reservoir

Osawatomie

Marais des Cygnes

Buckner Creek

Hesston

Newton

Flint Hills

Verdigris

Burlington

Hutchinson

El Dorado
Lake

Dodge City

Cheney
Reservoir

El Dorado

Chanute

Fort Scott

Greensburg

Pratt

Kingman

Wichita

Neosho

Parsons

Red Hills

Medicine Lodge

Medicine
Lodge

Walnut

Elk

Elk City
Lake

Independence

Coffeyville

Cimarron

Arkansas

Arkansas
City

Arkansas

Caney

OKLAHOMA

Tornadoes, massive twisting storm systems, are a frequent occurrence in the south-central plains of the U.S. Known as Tornado Alley, this area, which includes Kansas, most commonly experiences these violent storms between April and June.

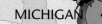

MICHIGAN

 LAND & WATER The Upper and Lower Peninsulas and Lakes Superior, Michigan, and Huron are important land and water features of Michigan.

 STATEHOOD Michigan became the 26th state in 1837.

PEOPLE & PLACES Michigan's population is 9,995,915. Lansing is the state capital. The largest city is Detroit.

FUN FACT The Detroit River is home to the only floating post office in the United States. Operating since 1874, the post office, which even has its own zip code, is located on a tugboat.

Michigan State Flag

A statue of Austin Blair, governor of Michigan during the Civil War, stands in front of the state capitol in Lansing.

Boys explore nature's wonders on the bank of a river near Niles. The town sits on the site of Fort St. Joseph, built by the French in 1691.

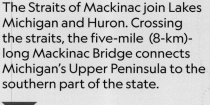

The Straits of Mackinac join Lakes Michigan and Huron. Crossing the straits, the five-mile (8-km)-long Mackinac Bridge connects Michigan's Upper Peninsula to the southern part of the state.

Apple Blossom
State Flower

Robin
State Bird

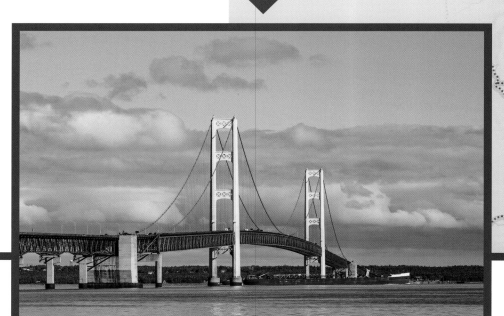

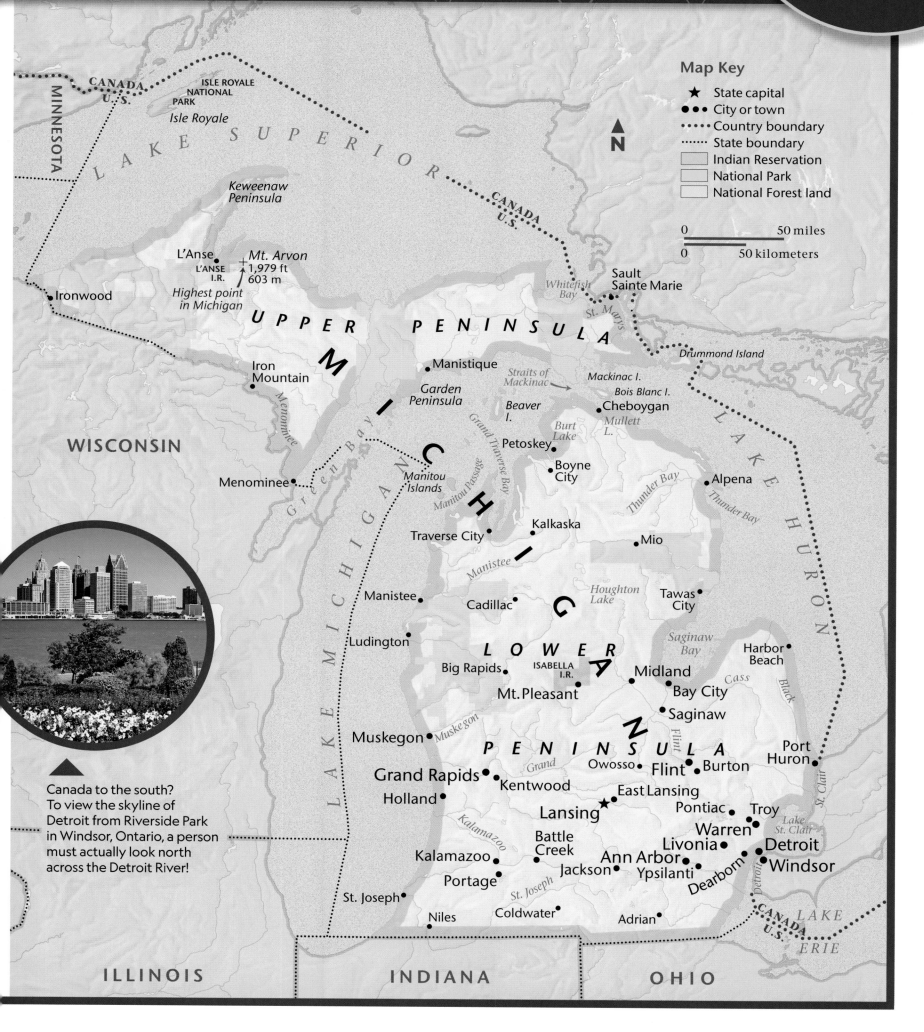

CANADA
U.S.

MINNESOTA

ISLE ROYALE
NATIONAL
PARK

Isle Royale

L A K E   S U P E R I O R

*Keweenaw
Peninsula*

CANADA
U.S.

Map Key

★ State capital
••• City or town
••••• Country boundary
••••• State boundary
☐ Indian Reservation
☐ National Park
☐ National Forest land

N

0   50 miles
0   50 kilometers

L'Anse
L'ANSE
I.R.
Mt. Arvon
1,979 ft
603 m
*Highest point
in Michigan*

Ironwood

*Whitefish
Bay*

Sault
Sainte Marie

St. Marys

U P P E R   P E N I N S U L A

Drummond Island

Iron
Mountain

Manistique

*Garden
Peninsula*

*Straits of
Mackinac*

Mackinac I.

Bois Blanc I.

*Beaver
I.*

Cheboygan

*Mullett
L.*

L A K E   H U R O N

WISCONSIN

Menominee

M I C H I G A N

*Burt
Lake*

Petoskey

Boyne
City

Alpena

Menominee

*Manitou
Islands*

Green Bay

Grand Traverse Bay

Manitou Passage

Kalkaska

Thunder Bay

Thunder Bay

Mio

Traverse City

Manistee

*Houghton
Lake*

Tawas
City

Manistee

Cadillac

L O W E R

*Saginaw
Bay*

Harbor
Beach

Ludington

Big Rapids

ISABELLA
I.R.

Midland

Cass

Black

Mt. Pleasant

Bay City

Saginaw

Muskegon

Muskegon

P E N I N S U L A

Flint

Port
Huron

Grand Rapids

Grand

Owosso

Flint

Burton

St. Clair

Kentwood

East Lansing

Holland

Lansing ★

Pontiac

Troy

Kalamazoo

Battle
Creek

Warren

*Lake
St. Clair*

Kalamazoo

Livonia

Detroit

Ann Arbor

Portage

Jackson

Ypsilanti

Dearborn

Windsor

St. Joseph

St. Joseph

Detroit

Niles

Coldwater

Adrian

CANADA
U.S.

L A K E
E R I E

ILLINOIS

INDIANA

OHIO

▲

Canada to the south?
To view the skyline of
Detroit from Riverside Park
in Windsor, Ontario, a person
must actually look north
across the Detroit River!

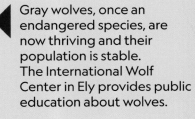

LAND & WATER Chippewa National Forest, Lake Superior, and the Mississippi River are important land and water features of Minnesota.

STATEHOOD Minnesota became the 32nd state in 1858.

PEOPLE & PLACES Minnesota's population is 5,611,179. St. Paul is the state capital. The largest city is Minneapolis.

FUN FACT Modern in-line skates were invented by two Minnesota students. Looking for a way to practice hockey in the summer, they replaced their skate blades with wheels.

Gray wolves, once an endangered species, are now thriving and their population is stable. The International Wolf Center in Ely provides public education about wolves.

Some people in Minnesota sit for hours in "ice shacks" and fish through holes cut in the ice of frozen lakes.

Minnesota State Flag

The skyline of Minneapolis rises above Lake Harriet, part of a popular recreation area called Chain of Lakes.

Showy Lady's Slipper
State Flower

Common Loon
State Bird

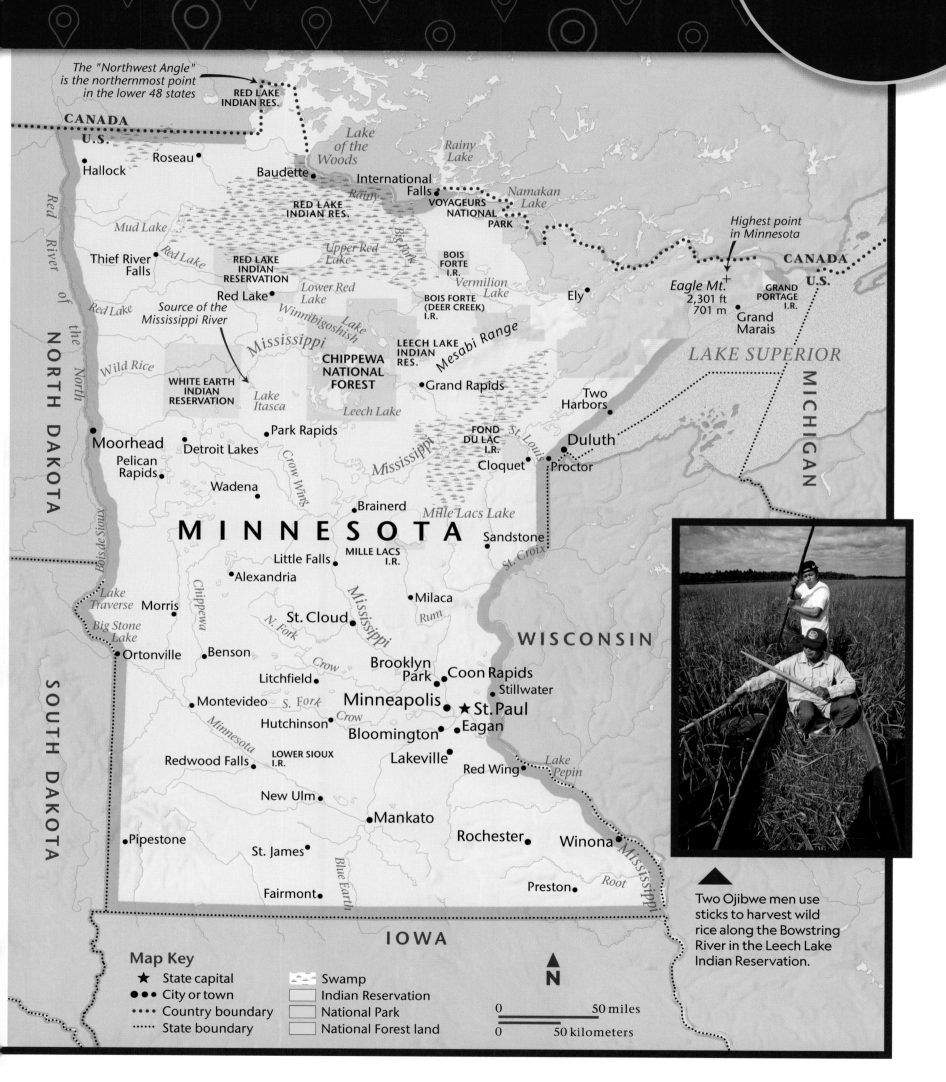

The "Northwest Angle" is the northernmost point in the lower 48 states

RED LAKE INDIAN RES.

CANADA
U.S.

Roseau

Hallock

Lake of the Woods

Baudette

Rainy Lake

International Falls

Namakan Lake

VOYAGEURS NATIONAL PARK

Red River of the North

Mud Lake

RED LAKE INDIAN RES.

Rainy

Big Fork

BOIS FORTE I.R.

Vermilion Lake

CANADA
U.S.

Highest point in Minnesota

Thief River Falls

Red Lake

Upper Red Lake

RED LAKE INDIAN RESERVATION

BOIS FORTE (DEER CREEK) I.R.

Ely

Eagle Mt. 2,301 ft 701 m

GRAND PORTAGE I.R.

Red Lake

Source of the Mississippi River

Red Lake

Lower Red Lake

Lake Winnibigoshish

Mississippi

LEECH LAKE INDIAN RES.

Mesabi Range

Grand Marais

LAKE SUPERIOR

Wild Rice

WHITE EARTH INDIAN RESERVATION

Lake Itasca

CHIPPEWA NATIONAL FOREST

Grand Rapids

Two Harbors

MICHIGAN

Leech Lake

St. Louis

Moorhead

Detroit Lakes

Park Rapids

FOND DU LAC I.R.

Duluth

Pelican Rapids

Crow Wing

Mississippi

Cloquet

Proctor

NORTH DAKOTA

Wadena

Brainerd

Mille Lacs Lake

Bois de Sioux

MINNESOTA

Sandstone

St. Croix

Little Falls

MILLE LACS I.R.

Lake Traverse

Alexandria

Morris

Milaca

Rum

WISCONSIN

Big Stone Lake

Chippewa

St. Cloud

Mississippi

Ortonville

Benson

N. Fork

Crow

Brooklyn Park

Coon Rapids

SOUTH DAKOTA

Litchfield

Stillwater

Montevideo

S. Fork

Minneapolis

★ St. Paul

Crow

Hutchinson

Bloomington

Eagan

Minnesota

Redwood Falls

LOWER SIOUX I.R.

Lakeville

Red Wing

Lake Pepin

New Ulm

Mississippi

Pipestone

Mankato

Rochester

Winona

St. James

Blue Earth

Fairmont

Preston

Root

Mississippi

IOWA

Map Key
★ State capital
●●● City or town
•••• Country boundary
•••• State boundary

Swamp
Indian Reservation
National Park
National Forest land

N

0   50 miles
0   50 kilometers

Two Ojibwe men use sticks to harvest wild rice along the Bowstring River in the Leech Lake Indian Reservation.

MISSOURI

LAND & WATER
Mark Twain National Forest and the Missouri and Mississippi Rivers are important land and water features of Missouri.

STATEHOOD
Missouri became the 24th state in 1821.

PEOPLE & PLACES
Missouri's population is 6,126,452. Jefferson City is the state capital. The largest city is Kansas City.

FUN FACT
The Pony Express, established in 1860, carried letters and newspapers from St. Joseph, Missouri, to Sacramento, California, making the journey of 1,800 miles (2,897 km) in just 10 days. It ended in 1861 with the completion of the transcontinental telegraph.

Missouri State Flag

Eastern Bluebird
State Bird

Hawthorn
State Flower

▲
The Lewis and Clark expedition, which explored the northwestern part of the Louisiana Purchase, set off from St. Charles, traveling up the Missouri River. The city celebrates the historic journey with much fanfare.

◀ Gateway Arch, completed in 1965, recognizes the role St. Louis played in the westward expansion of the United States. Trams carry one million tourists to the top of the arch each year.

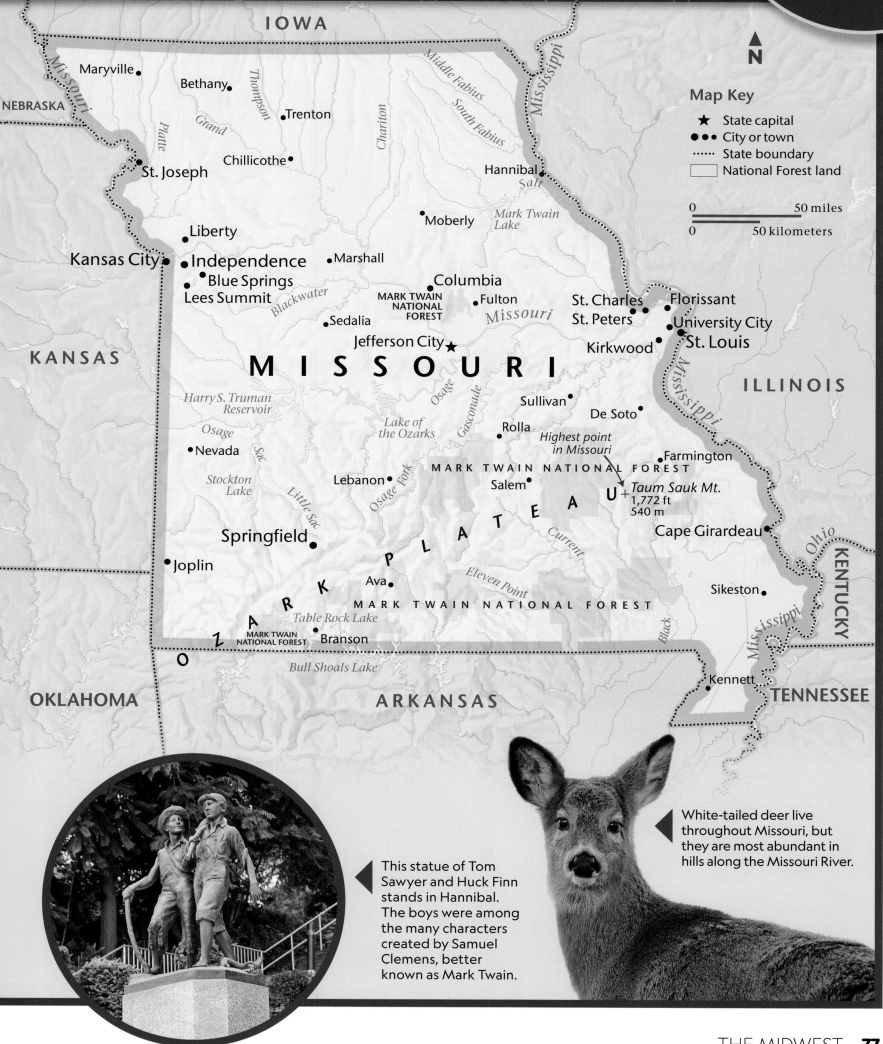

IOWA

NEBRASKA

Maryville

Bethany

Thompson

Trenton

Grand

Chariton

Middle Fabius

South Fabius

Mississippi

Chillicothe

Hannibal

Salt

St. Joseph

Platte

Missouri

Moberly

Mark Twain Lake

Liberty

Kansas City

Independence

Marshall

Columbia

Blue Springs

Lees Summit

Blackwater

MARK TWAIN NATIONAL FOREST

Fulton

Missouri

St. Charles

St. Peters

Florissant

University City

St. Louis

Sedalia

Kirkwood

KANSAS

Jefferson City ★

M I S S O U R I

Harry S. Truman Reservoir

Osage

Osage

Gasconade

Sullivan

De Soto

ILLINOIS

Mississippi

Lake of the Ozarks

Rolla

Highest point in Missouri

MARK TWAIN NATIONAL FOREST

Farmington

Nevada

Sac

Stockton Lake

Lebanon

Osage Fork

Salem

Taum Sauk Mt.
1,772 ft
540 m

Little Sac

Current

Cape Girardeau

Ohio

Springfield

O Z A R K   P L A T E A U

KENTUCKY

Joplin

Ava

Eleven Point

Sikeston

MARK TWAIN NATIONAL FOREST

Table Rock Lake

MARK TWAIN NATIONAL FOREST

Branson

Black

Bull Shoals Lake

Mississippi

Kennett

OKLAHOMA

ARKANSAS

TENNESSEE

Map Key
★ State capital
●●● City or town
···· State boundary
▢ National Forest land

0 ————— 50 miles
0 ————— 50 kilometers

N

◀ This statue of Tom Sawyer and Huck Finn stands in Hannibal. The boys were among the many characters created by Samuel Clemens, better known as Mark Twain.

◀ White-tailed deer live throughout Missouri, but they are most abundant in hills along the Missouri River.

NEBRASKA

NEBRASKA

LAND & WATER
The Sand Hills and the Platte and Missouri Rivers are important land and water features of Nebraska.

STATEHOOD
Nebraska became the 37th state in 1867.

PEOPLE & PLACES
Nebraska's population is 1,929,268. Lincoln is the state capital. The largest city is Omaha.

FUN FACT
The largest remaining area of original native prairie in the United States is in the Sand Hills region. It is an important stopover for migrating sandhill cranes.

Nebraska State Flag

Goldenrod
State Flower

Western Meadowlark
State Bird

Two black-tailed prairie dogs watch for signs of danger at the entrance to their burrow in the Fort Niobrara National Wildlife Refuge.

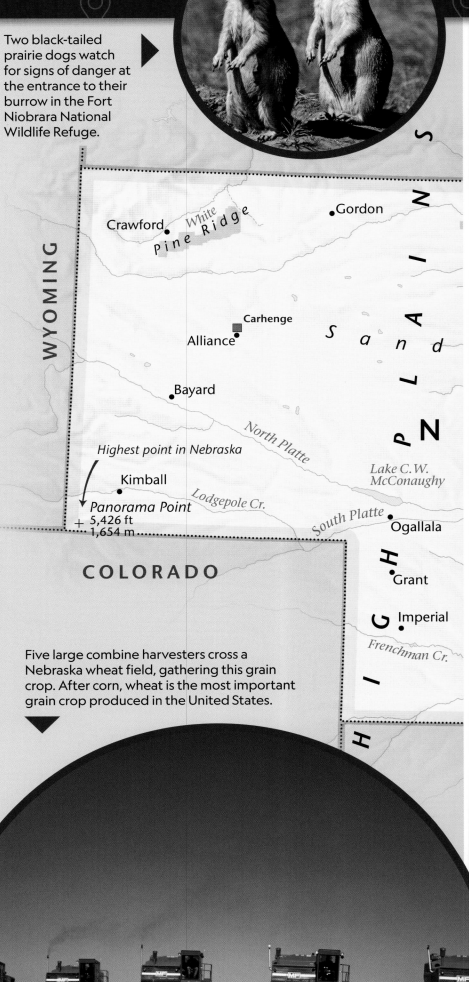

WYOMING

Crawford • White
Pine Ridge
•Gordon

Carhenge ■
Alliance•

S a n d

•Bayard

North Platte

Highest point in Nebraska

P L A I N S

Lake C.W.
McConaughy

•Kimball

Lodgepole Cr.

South Platte•
•Ogallala

Panorama Point
+ 5,426 ft
1,654 m

COLORADO

•Grant

•Imperial

Frenchman Cr.

H I G H

Five large combine harvesters cross a Nebraska wheat field, gathering this grain crop. After corn, wheat is the most important grain crop produced in the United States.

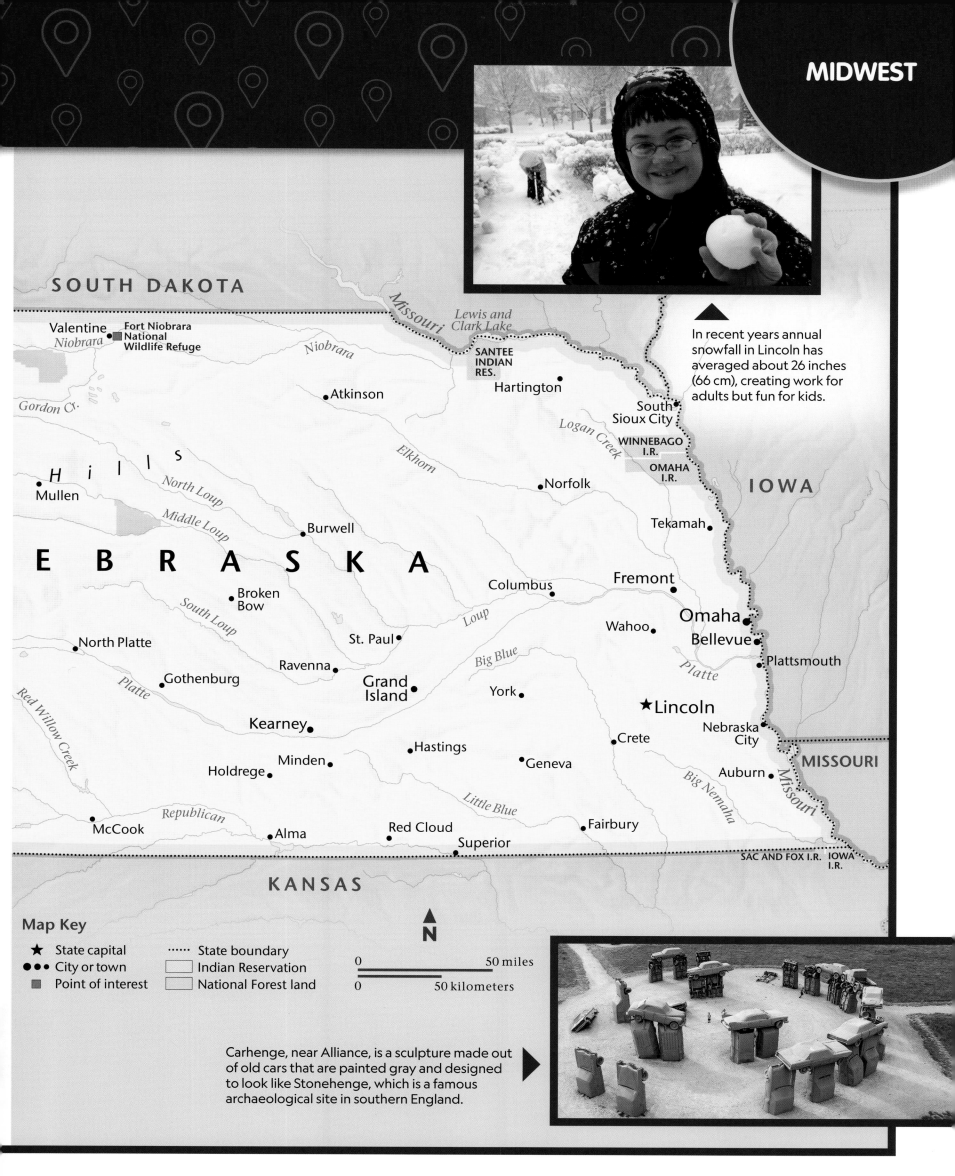

SOUTH DAKOTA

Valentine
Niobrara
Fort Niobrara
National
Wildlife Refuge
Gordon Cr.
Niobrara
Atkinson
Lewis and
Clark Lake
Missouri
SANTEE
INDIAN
RES.
Hartington
South
Sioux City
WINNEBAGO
I.R.
Logan Creek
OMAHA
I.R.
IOWA

In recent years annual
snowfall in Lincoln has
averaged about 26 inches
(66 cm), creating work for
adults but fun for kids.

H i l l s
Mullen
North Loup
Middle Loup
Elkhorn
Norfolk
Tekamah

N E B R A S K A
Broken
Bow
Burwell
South Loup
St. Paul
Columbus
Loup
Fremont
Wahoo
Omaha
Bellevue
Plattsmouth
North Platte
Gothenburg
Platte
Ravenna
Grand
Island
Big Blue
York
Lincoln
Nebraska
City
Kearney
Hastings
Geneva
Crete
MISSOURI
Holdrege
Minden
Auburn
Big Nemaha
Missouri
Red Willow Creek
Republican
McCook
Alma
Little Blue
Red Cloud
Superior
Fairbury
SAC AND FOX I.R. IOWA
I.R.

KANSAS

N

Map Key
★ State capital
•••• City or town
■ Point of interest
······ State boundary
☐ Indian Reservation
☐ National Forest land

0   50 miles
0   50 kilometers

Carhenge, near Alliance, is a sculpture made out
of old cars that are painted gray and designed
to look like Stonehenge, which is a famous
archaeological site in southern England.

NORTH DAKOTA

LAND & WATER
The Badlands, the Red River of the North, and the Missouri River are important land and water features of North Dakota.

STATEHOOD
North Dakota became the 39th state in 1889.

PEOPLE & PLACES
North Dakota's population is 760,077. Bismarck is the state capital. The largest city is Fargo.

FUN FACT
North Dakota leads the United States in honey production, with more than 33 million pounds (14 million kg) produced annually. In addition to honey, bees produce wax and help pollinate crops.

North Dakota State Flag

Wild Prairie Rose
State Flower

Western Meadowlark
State Bird

Cowboys on the fence watch the excitement of the rodeo during the Slope County Fair in Amidon.

Fossils of prehistoric life, such as this leaf, can be found in North Dakota's sedimentary rock formations.

American bison are native to the Great Plains, but now they are found mainly in parks such as Sullys Hill National Game Preserve.

CANADA
U.S.

MONTANA

Williston

Missouri

Yellowstone

Watford City

THEODORE ROOSEVELT N.P. (NORTH UNIT)

Theodore Roosevelt N.P. (Elkhorn Ranch Site)

THEODORE ROOSEVELT N.P. (SOUTH UNIT)

Medora ■ Painted Canyon

Badlands

Amidon

+*White Butte*
3,506 ft
1,069 m
Highest point in North Dakota

Little Missouri

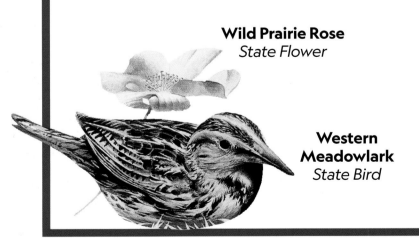

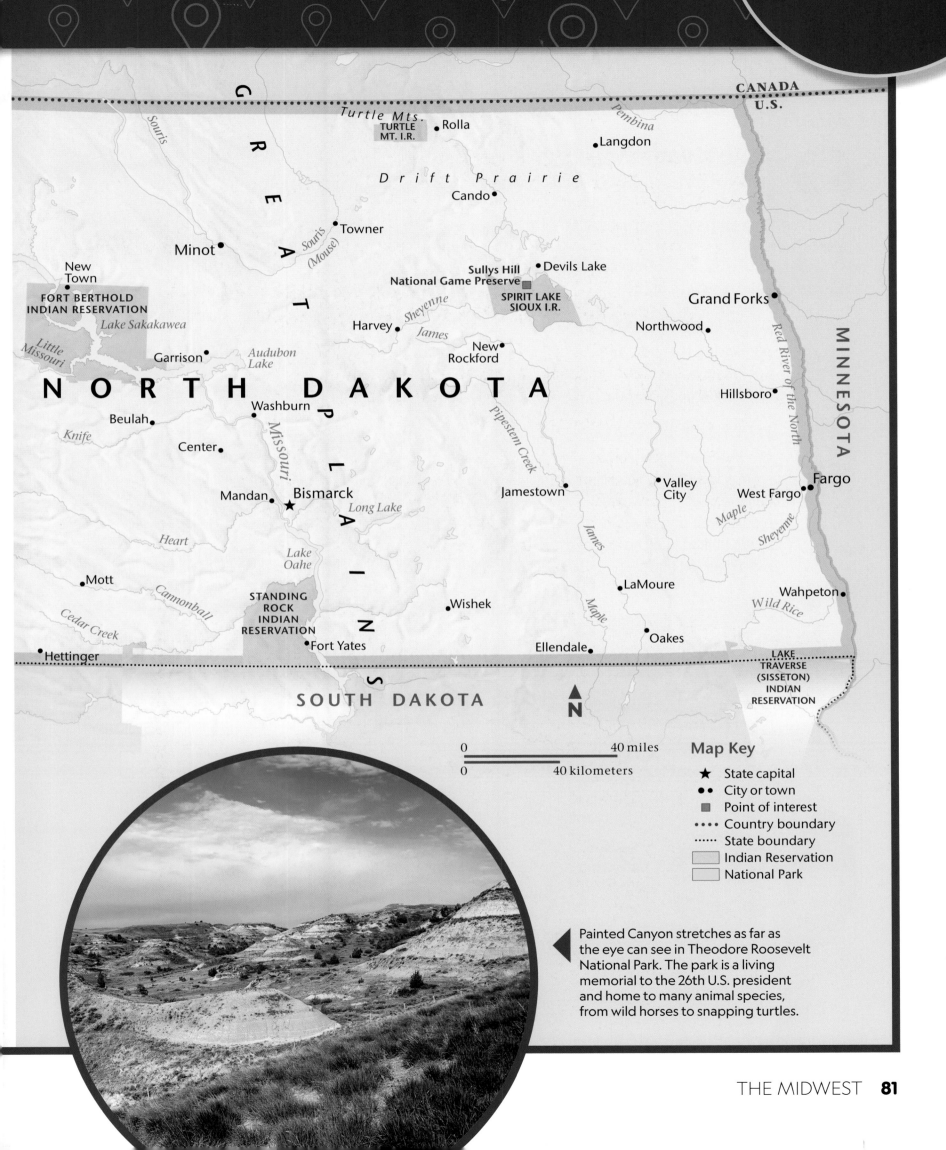

CANADA
U.S.

G R E A T

Turtle Mts.
TURTLE
MT. I.R.
• Rolla

• Langdon

D r i f t   P r a i r i e

• Cando

Souris

• Minot

Souris
(Mouse)

• Towner

New
Town

FORT BERTHOLD
INDIAN RESERVATION

Lake Sakakawea

Little
Missouri

• Garrison

Audubon
Lake

Sheyenne

• Harvey

James

Sullys Hill
National Game Preserve

• Devils Lake

SPIRIT LAKE
SIOUX I.R.

Grand Forks •

Northwood •

New
Rockford •

N O R T H   D A K O T A

Knife

• Beulah

• Washburn

Missouri

Hillsboro •

Red River of the North

M I N N E S O T A

• Center

A

P L A I N S

Pipestem Creek

Valley
City •

West Fargo •

Fargo •

Maple

• Mandan

Bismarck ★

Long Lake

Jamestown •

Heart

Lake
Oahe

James

Sheyenne

• Mott

Cannonball

STANDING
ROCK
INDIAN
RESERVATION

LaMoure •

Wahpeton •

Cedar Creek

Wild Rice

• Hettinger

• Fort Yates

• Wishek

Maple

Ellendale •

Oakes •

LAKE
TRAVERSE
(SISSETON)
INDIAN
RESERVATION

S O U T H   D A K O T A

↑N

0 _____ 40 miles
0 _____ 40 kilometers

Map Key

★ State capital
•• City or town
■ Point of interest
···· Country boundary
···· State boundary
▢ Indian Reservation
▢ National Park

◄ Painted Canyon stretches as far as
the eye can see in Theodore Roosevelt
National Park. The park is a living
memorial to the 26th U.S. president
and home to many animal species,
from wild horses to snapping turtles.

OHIO

LAND & WATER Wayne National Forest, Lake Erie, and the Ohio River are important land and water features of Ohio.

STATEHOOD Ohio became the 17th state in 1803.

PEOPLE & PLACES Ohio's population is 11,689,442. Columbus is the state capital and the largest city.

FUN FACT Ohio's nickname, the Buckeye State, comes from a local tree. The tree's name comes from Native Americans, who thought its seeds looked like the eye of a male deer, or buck.

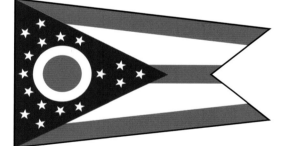

Ohio State Flag

Scarlet Carnation
State Flower

Cardinal
State Bird

▲ Fourth of July fireworks light up the nighttime sky above Columbus. The city has been the state capital since 1816.

▲ Colorful guitars mark the entrance to the Rock and Roll Hall of Fame in downtown Cleveland.

The Blue Streak is the oldest operating roller coaster at Cedar Point Amusement Park in Sandusky. This popular ride is named after a local high school sports team. ▼

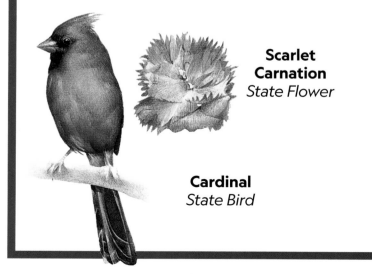

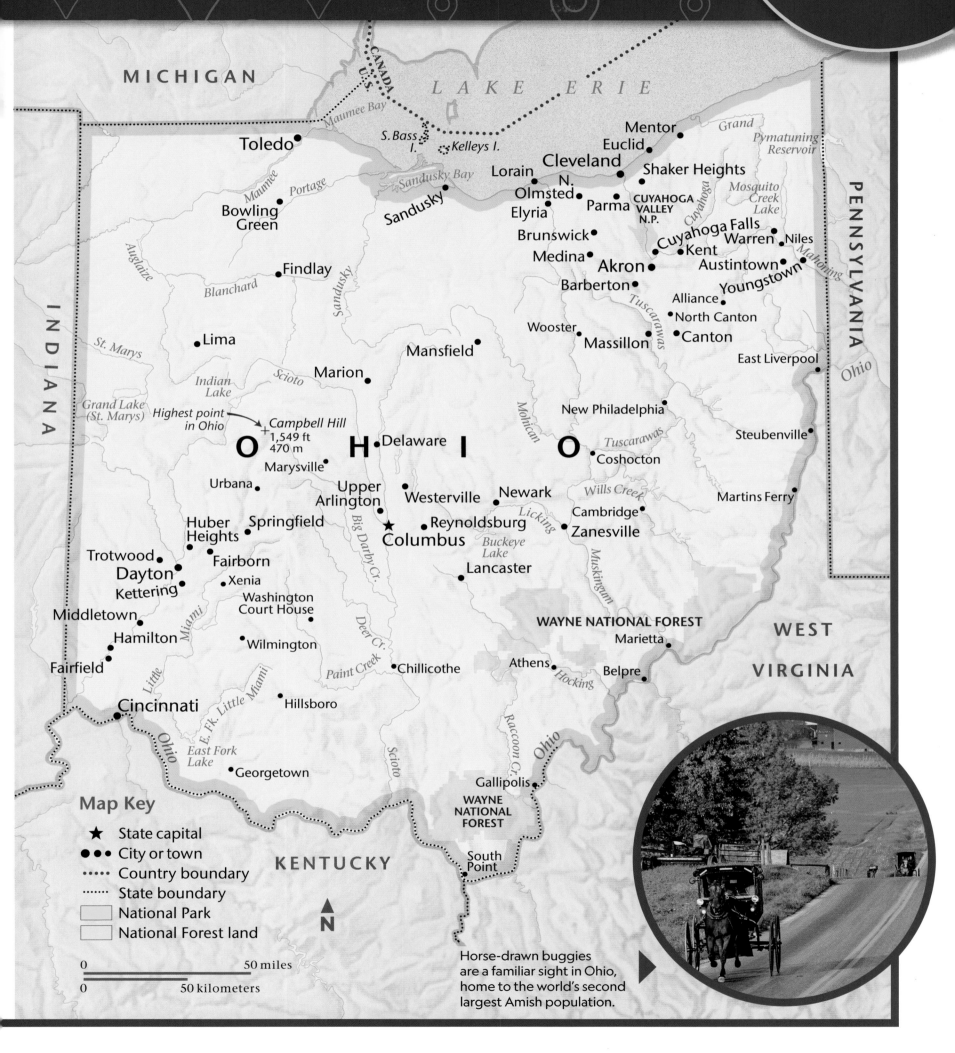

SOUTH DAKOTA

LAND & WATER The Black Hills, Badlands National Park, and the Missouri River are important land and water features of South Dakota.

STATEHOOD South Dakota became the 40th state in 1889.

PEOPLE & PLACES South Dakota's population is 882,235. Pierre is the state capital. The largest city is Sioux Falls.

FUN FACT A dinosaur nicknamed Sue was unearthed on the Cheyenne River Indian Reservation in 1990. It is the world's largest, most complete, and best preserved specimen of a *Tyrannosaurus rex*.

A mountain cottontail nibbles on some grass in Wind Cave National Park.

MONTANA

Little Missouri

North Fork

South Fork

• Buffalo

WYOMING

•Belle Fourche

• Sturgis
• Deadwood

Black Hills

Rapid City.

Black Elk Peak (Harney Peak) +
7,242 ft
2,207 m

■ Mount Rushmore N.M.

Highest point in South Dakota

WIND CAVE N.P.

Hot Springs •

•Edgemont

Cheyenne

South Dakota State Flag

Carvings on Mount Rushmore in the Black Hills honor four past U.S. presidents (from left to right): George Washington, Thomas Jefferson, Theodore Roosevelt, and Abraham Lincoln.

Pasqueflower
State Flower

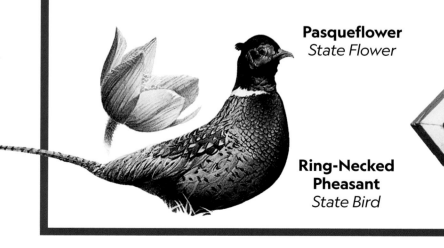

BEWARE
TYRANNOSAURUS
AHEAD

Widespread dinosaur fossils in South Dakota prompted this humorous sign.

Ring-Necked Pheasant
State Bird

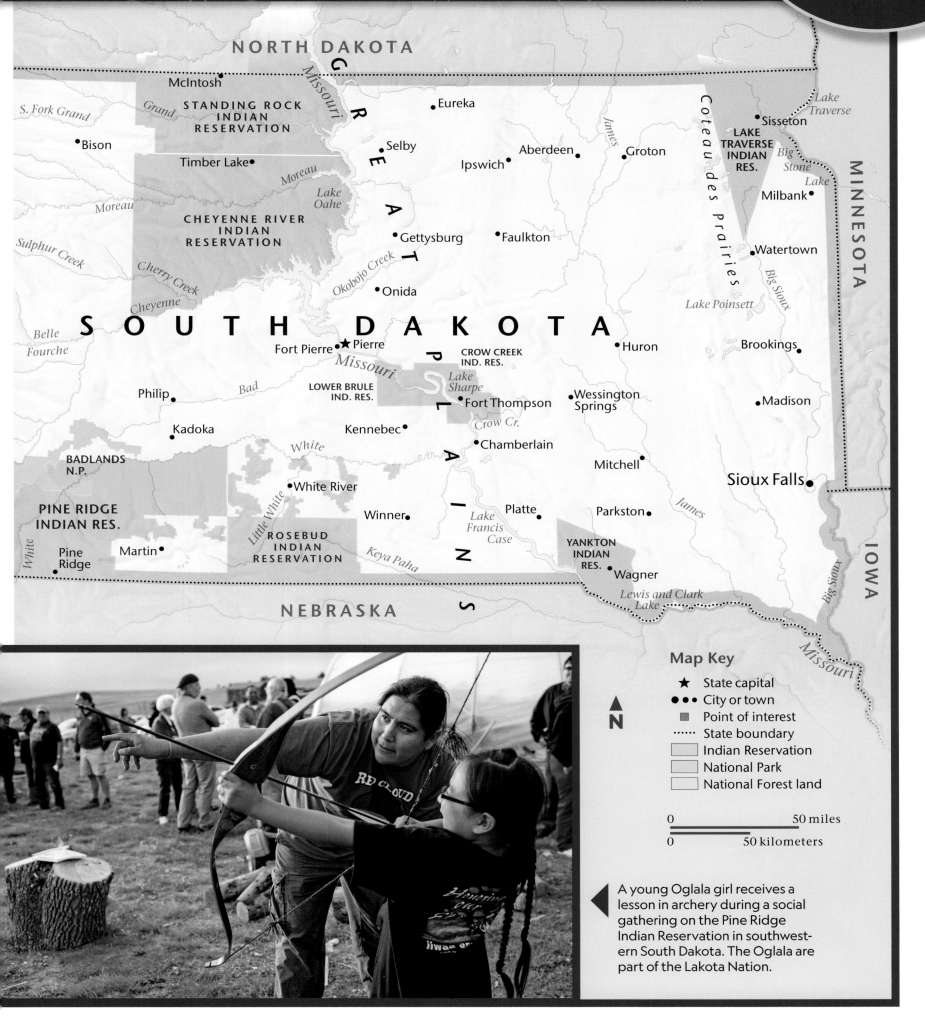

NORTH DAKOTA

McIntosh

Eureka

S. Fork Grand

Grand

STANDING ROCK
INDIAN
RESERVATION

Selby

Bison

Timber Lake

Moreau

Aberdeen

Groton

Ipswich

Coteau des Prairies

Sisseton

LAKE
TRAVERSE
INDIAN
RES.

Lake
Traverse

Big
Stone
Lake

Milbank

MINNESOTA

Sulphur Creek

Moreau

Lake
Oahe

CHEYENNE RIVER
INDIAN
RESERVATION

Gettysburg

Faulkton

Watertown

Cherry Creek

Okobojo Creek

Onida

Lake Poinsett

Big Sioux

Belle
Fourche

Cheyenne

S O U T H   D A K O T A

Fort Pierre

Pierre

Missouri

Huron

Brookings

Philip

Bad

CROW CREEK
IND. RES.

LOWER BRULE
IND. RES.

Lake
Sharpe

Fort Thompson

Wessington
Springs

Madison

Kadoka

Kennebec

White

Crow Cr.

Chamberlain

Mitchell

BADLANDS
N.P.

White River

PINE RIDGE
INDIAN RES.

Winner

Little White

ROSEBUD
INDIAN
RESERVATION

Lake
Francis
Case

Platte

Parkston

James

Sioux Falls

Pine
Ridge

Martin

Keya Paha

YANKTON
INDIAN
RES.

Wagner

Big Sioux

IOWA

NEBRASKA

Lewis and Clark
Lake

Missouri

G R E A T   P L A I N S

Map Key

★ State capital
●●● City or town
■ Point of interest
⋯⋯ State boundary
▨ Indian Reservation
▨ National Park
▨ National Forest land

N

0 ——————— 50 miles
0 ——————— 50 kilometers

◄ A young Oglala girl receives a lesson in archery during a social gathering on the Pine Ridge Indian Reservation in southwestern South Dakota. The Oglala are part of the Lakota Nation.

WISCONSIN

Bald eagles are found throughout Wisconsin. Almost 1,700 active nests were spotted in 2018.

LAND & WATER The Door Peninsula and Lakes Superior and Michigan are important land and water features of Wisconsin.

STATEHOOD
Wisconsin became the 30th state in 1848.

PEOPLE & PLACES Wisconsin's population is 5,813,568. Madison is the state capital. The largest city is Milwaukee.

FUN FACT Laura Ingalls Wilder was born in Pepin in 1867. Her famous Little House books are based on her childhood in the forests and prairies of the Midwest.

A Menominee boy works hard to control his rearing horse on the Menominee Indian Reservation near Keshena.

In a winter version of sailing, ice boats compete in a race on the frozen surface of Lake Winnebago near Oshkosh.

WISCONSIN
FORWARD
1848

Wisconsin State Flag

Robin
State Bird

Wood Violet
State Flower

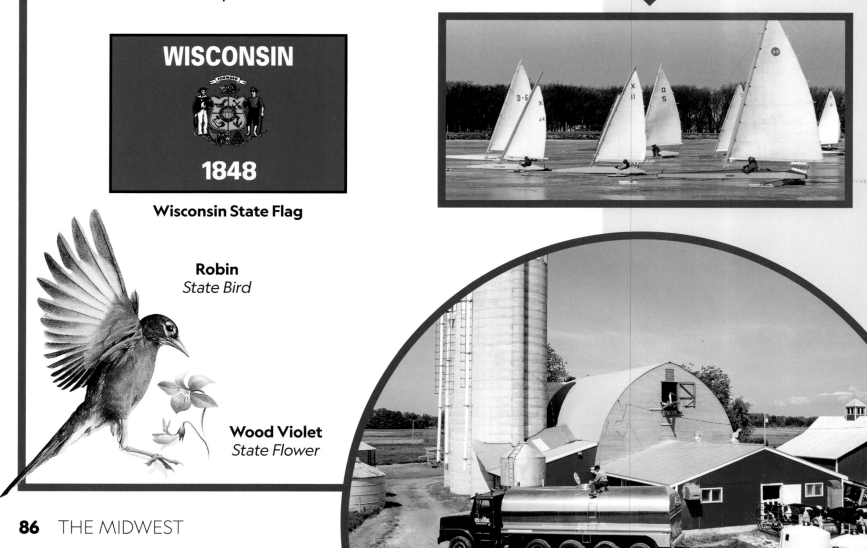

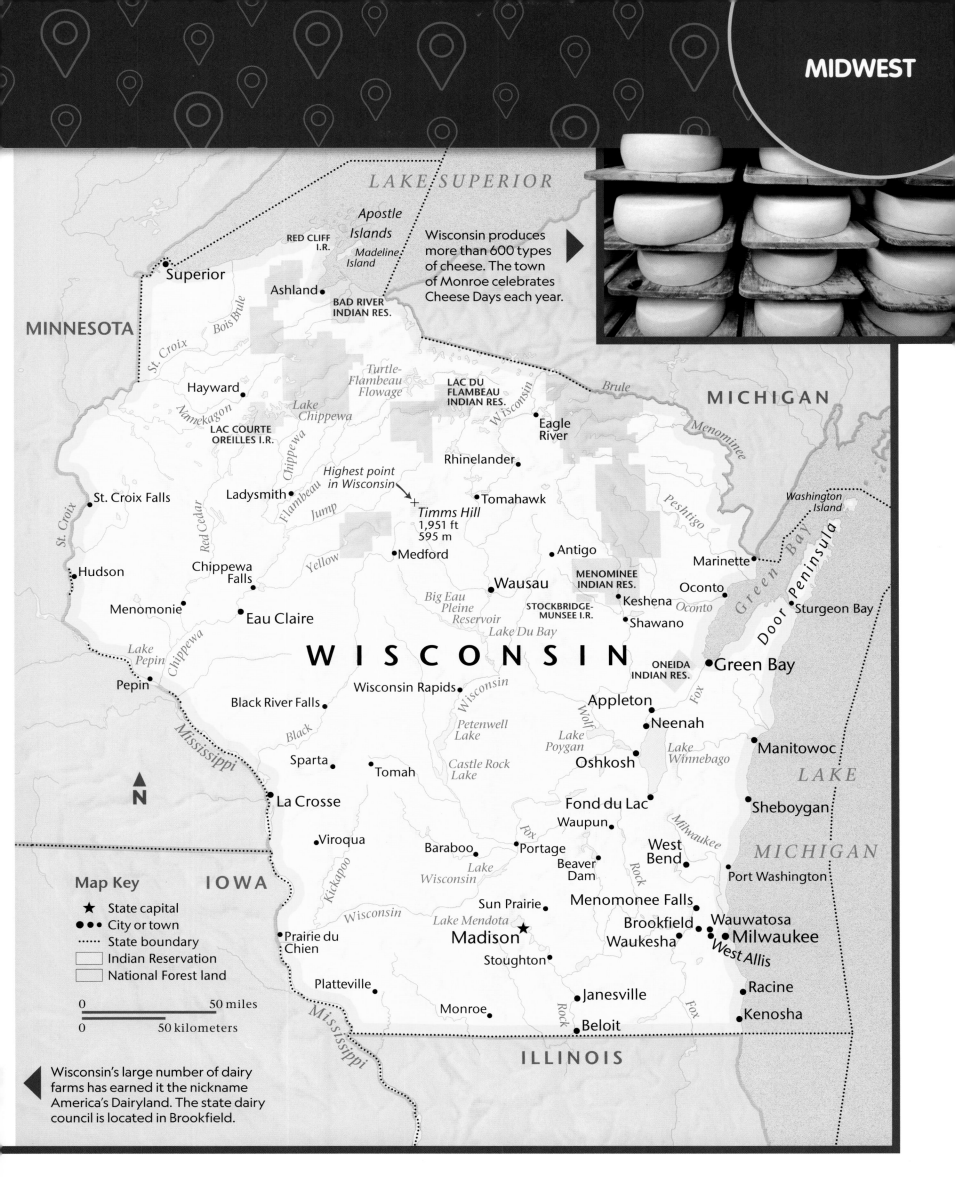

LAKE SUPERIOR

Apostle
Islands

RED CLIFF
I.R.

Madeline
Island

• Superior

Ashland •

BAD RIVER
INDIAN RES.

MINNESOTA

Wisconsin produces
more than 600 types
of cheese. The town
of Monroe celebrates
Cheese Days each year.

Bois Brule

St. Croix

Hayward •

Namekagon

LAC COURTE
OREILLES I.R.

*Lake
Chippewa*

Turtle-
Flambeau
Flowage

LAC DU
FLAMBEAU
INDIAN RES.

Wisconsin

Brule

MICHIGAN

Menominee

Eagle
River •

Rhinelander •

Peshtigo

St. Croix Falls •

Ladysmith •

Flambeau

Chippewa

Jump

Highest point
in Wisconsin

Timms Hill
1,951 ft
595 m

• Tomahawk

*Washington
Island*

Marinette •

St. Croix

Hudson •

Chippewa
Falls •

Red Cedar

Yellow

• Medford

• Antigo

MENOMINEE
INDIAN RES.

Oconto •

Sturgeon Bay •

Menomonie •

Eau Claire •

*Big Eau
Pleine
Reservoir*

• Wausau

STOCKBRIDGE-
MUNSEE I.R.

Keshena •

Oconto

Shawano •

Door Peninsula

*Lake
Pepin*

Chippewa

WISCONSIN

Lake Du Bay

ONEIDA
INDIAN RES.

• Green Bay

Green Bay

Pepin •

Wisconsin Rapids •

Wisconsin

Appleton •

Fox

Black River Falls •

Black

*Petenwell
Lake*

Neenah •

Wolf

*Lake
Poygan*

*Lake
Winnebago*

Manitowoc •

Sparta •

Tomah •

*Castle Rock
Lake*

Oshkosh •

Mississippi

La Crosse •

Fond du Lac •

Sheboygan •

Waupun •

LAKE

Viroqua •

Fox

Baraboo •

Portage •

Milwaukee

West
Bend •

MICHIGAN

Beaver
Dam •

Port Washington •

Kickapoo

*Lake
Wisconsin*

Sun Prairie •

Menomonee Falls •

Rock

Wauwatosa •

Map Key

IOWA

★ State capital
••• City or town
······ State boundary
☐ Indian Reservation
☐ National Forest land

0   50 miles
0   50 kilometers

Wisconsin

Prairie du
Chien •

Lake Mendota

Madison ★

Brookfield •

Waukesha •

Milwaukee •

West Allis •

Stoughton •

Platteville •

Janesville •

Racine •

Monroe •

Rock

Fox

Kenosha •

Beloit •

Mississippi

ILLINOIS

Wisconsin's large number of dairy
farms has earned it the nickname
America's Dairyland. The state dairy
council is located in Brookfield.

THE SOUTHWEST

The Southwest region reaches from the Gulf Coast in the east to canyonlands in the west. Native Americans, descendants of early Spanish settlers, and recent immigrants from Mexico and Central America give this region a very diverse population. Agriculture, cattle ranching, and the oil industry are major economic activities. The Southwest's rapidly growing population is putting pressure on the region's water resources.

Wild horse herds are a common sight on open prairies and parklands of the Southwest. This horse roams free in Monument Valley, Arizona.

A rainbow frames Big Bend National Park's Cerro Castellon, in Texas. This eroded mount of volcanic rock rises almost 3,300 feet (1,006 m) above the desert floor.

ARIZONA

 **LAND & WATER** The Colorado Plateau, the Grand Canyon, and the Colorado River are important land and water features of Arizona.

STATEHOOD Arizona became the 48th state in 1912.

PEOPLE & PLACES Arizona's population is 7,171,646. Phoenix is the state capital and the largest city.

FUN FACT Of the 21 Native American reservations in Arizona, the largest belongs to the Navajo Nation. Native peoples and the federal government own almost 70 percent of the state's land area.

Daring boaters get soaked as they run the rapids on the fast-flowing waters of the Colorado River in Grand Canyon National Park.

Arizona State Flag

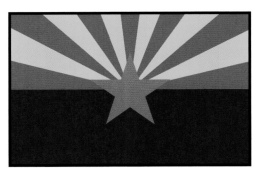

Saguaro cactus, found in the Sonoran Desert, can grow more than 30 feet (9 m) tall.

A Navajo woman works at her loom, weaving a traditional rug. Symbols in this rug reflect parts of Navajo history.

Cactus Wren
State Bird

Saguaro
State Flower

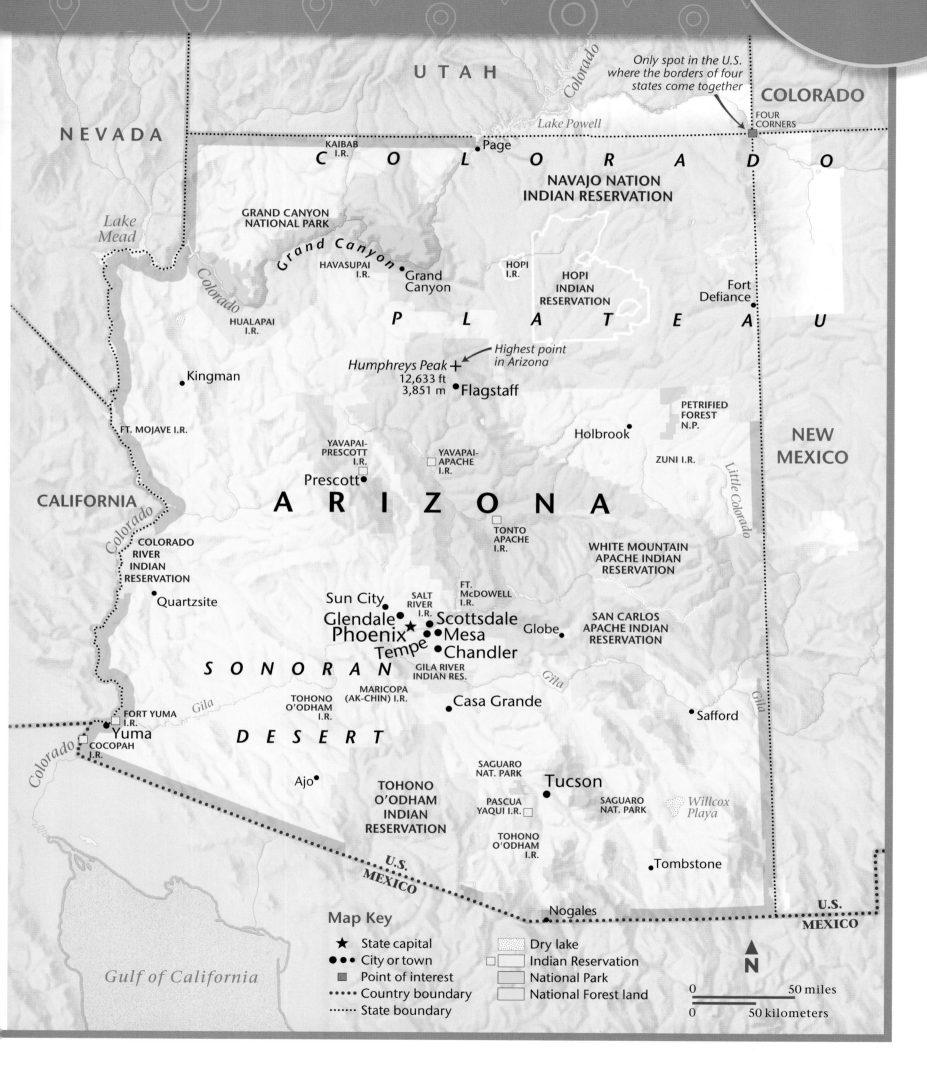

UTAH

COLORADO

NEVADA

Colorado

Lake Powell

Only spot in the U.S. where the borders of four states come together

FOUR CORNERS

Lake Mead

KAIBAB I.R.

● Page

COLORADO

NAVAJO NATION INDIAN RESERVATION

GRAND CANYON NATIONAL PARK

Grand Canyon

Colorado

HAVASUPAI I.R.

● Grand Canyon

HOPI I.R.

HOPI INDIAN RESERVATION

Fort Defiance ●

HUALAPAI I.R.

P L A T E A U

● Kingman

Humphreys Peak 12,633 ft 3,851 m

Highest point in Arizona

● Flagstaff

Little Colorado

PETRIFIED FOREST N.P.

Holbrook ●

NEW MEXICO

FT. MOJAVE I.R.

YAVAPAI-PRESCOTT I.R.

YAVAPAI-APACHE I.R.

ZUNI I.R.

CALIFORNIA

Prescott ●

A R I Z O N A

Colorado

COLORADO RIVER INDIAN RESERVATION

TONTO APACHE I.R.

WHITE MOUNTAIN APACHE INDIAN RESERVATION

● Quartzsite

Sun City ●

SALT RIVER I.R.

FT. McDOWELL I.R.

Glendale ● ★ Scottsdale
Phoenix ● ● Mesa
Tempe ● ● Chandler

Globe ●

SAN CARLOS APACHE INDIAN RESERVATION

S O N O R A N

Gila

GILA RIVER INDIAN RES.

Gila

MARICOPA (AK-CHIN) I.R.

TOHONO O'ODHAM I.R.

● Casa Grande

● Safford

FORT YUMA I.R.

D E S E R T

Yuma ●

COCOPAH I.R.

Colorado

Ajo ●

SAGUARO NAT. PARK

● Tucson

TOHONO O'ODHAM INDIAN RESERVATION

PASCUA YAQUI I.R.

SAGUARO NAT. PARK

Willcox Playa

TOHONO O'ODHAM I.R.

U.S. MEXICO

● Tombstone

U.S. MEXICO

Nogales ●

Gulf of California

Map Key

★ State capital
●●● City or town
■ Point of interest
••• Country boundary
···· State boundary

▦ Dry lake
□ Indian Reservation
▨ National Park
▨ National Forest land

N

| 0 | | 50 miles |
| 0 | | 50 kilometers |

NEW MEXICO

 **LAND & WATER** The Sangre de Cristo Mountains, Carlsbad Caverns, and the Rio Grande are important land and water features of New Mexico.

 STATEHOOD New Mexico became the 47th state in 1912.

PEOPLE & PLACES New Mexico's population is 2,095,428. Santa Fe is the state capital. The largest city is Albuquerque.

FUN FACT Roswell attracts people interested in unidentified flying objects (UFOs). A rancher discovered what he believed to be wreckage of one in 1947.

New Mexico State Flag

Yucca
State Flower

Roadrunner
State Bird

Brightly colored hot-air balloons rise into a blue sky above Albuquerque during the International Balloon Fiesta, the largest such event in the world.

One of the world's oldest cave systems, Carlsbad Caverns, lies beneath the Guadalupe Mountains. The caverns include more than 119 chambers of all sizes.

Chili peppers, seen here in a store in Santa Fe, give Southwestern food a spicy taste. New Mexico is second only to California in the production of chilies.

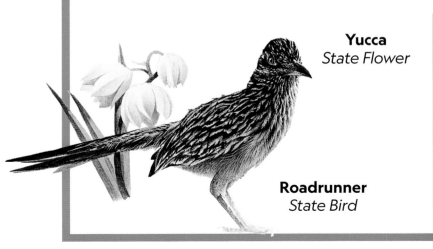

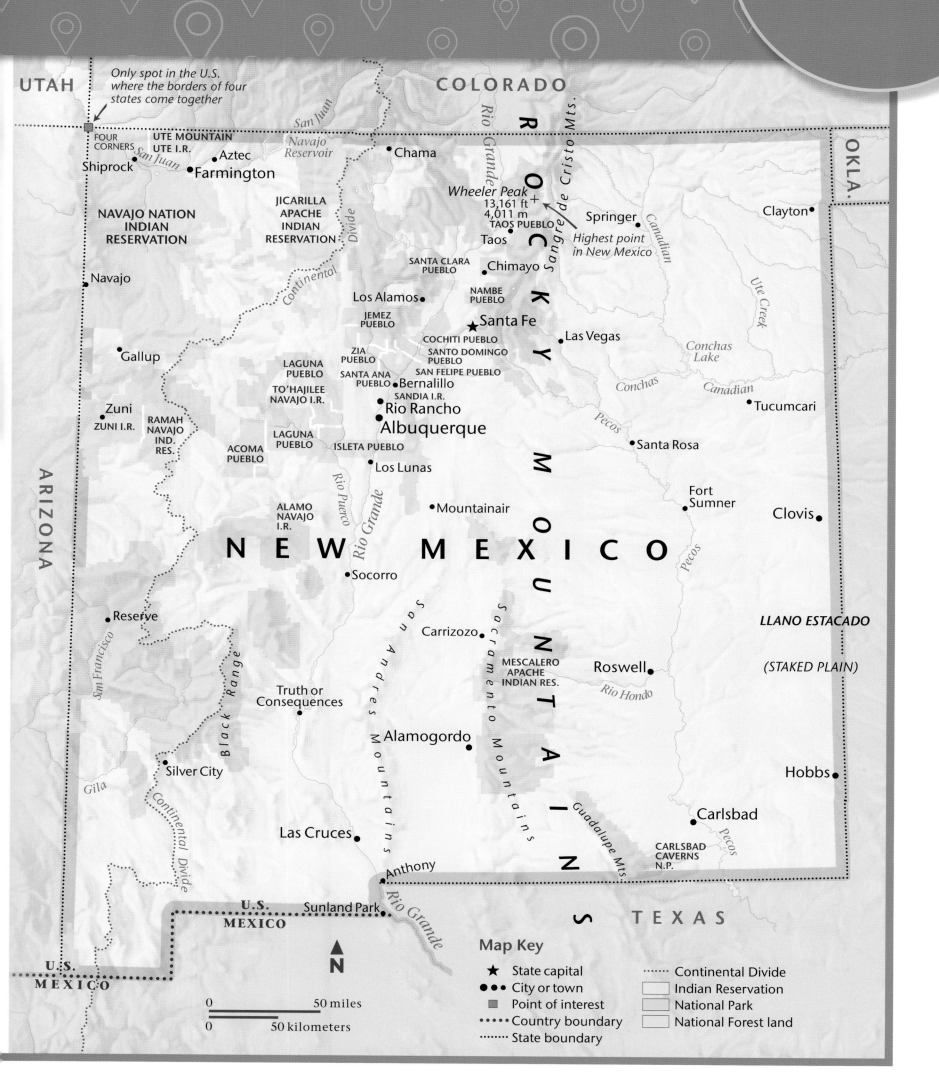

UTAH

COLORADO

OKLA.

ARIZONA

Only spot in the U.S. where the borders of four states come together

FOUR CORNERS

UTE MOUNTAIN UTE I.R.

Aztec

Shiprock

San Juan

Farmington

San Juan

Navajo Reservoir

Chama

Rio Grande

ROCKY

NAVAJO NATION INDIAN RESERVATION

JICARILLA APACHE INDIAN RESERVATION

Continental Divide

Wheeler Peak 13,161 ft 4,011 m

Springer

Clayton

Navajo

TAOS PUEBLO

Taos

Highest point in New Mexico

Sangre de Cristo Mts.

Gallup

SANTA CLARA PUEBLO

Chimayo

Canadian

Los Alamos

NAMBE PUEBLO

Ute Creek

JEMEZ PUEBLO

Santa Fe

Las Vegas

Conchas Lake

Zuni

ZUNI I.R.

RAMAH NAVAJO IND. RES.

LAGUNA PUEBLO

ZIA PUEBLO

SANTA ANA PUEBLO

COCHITI PUEBLO

SANTO DOMINGO PUEBLO

SAN FELIPE PUEBLO

Conchas

Canadian

TO'HAJIILEE NAVAJO I.R.

Bernalillo

SANDIA I.R.

Pecos

Tucumcari

Rio Rancho

ACOMA PUEBLO

LAGUNA PUEBLO

ISLETA PUEBLO

Albuquerque

Santa Rosa

Los Lunas

M

Fort Sumner

ALAMO NAVAJO I.R.

Rio Puerco

Mountainair

O

Clovis

Rio Grande

NEW MEXICO

U

Reserve

Socorro

N

Pecos

LLANO ESTACADO

San Francisco

San Andres Mountains

Carrizozo

Sacramento Mountains

T

(STAKED PLAIN)

Black Range

MESCALERO APACHE INDIAN RES.

Roswell

A

Rio Hondo

Truth or Consequences

I

Silver City

Gila

Alamogordo

N

Hobbs

Continental Divide

Las Cruces

Guadalupe Mts.

Carlsbad

S

CARLSBAD CAVERNS N.P.

Pecos

Anthony

U.S. MEXICO

Sunland Park

Rio Grande

TEXAS

U.S. MEXICO

N

0   50 miles

0   50 kilometers

Map Key

★ State capital

••• City or town

▪ Point of interest

····· Country boundary

····· State boundary

······ Continental Divide

☐ Indian Reservation

☐ National Park

☐ National Forest land

OKLAHOMA

OKLAHOMA

LAND & WATER Black Mesa, the Ouachita Mountains, and the Arkansas River are important land and water features of Oklahoma.

STATEHOOD Oklahoma became the 46th state in 1907.

PEOPLE & PLACES Oklahoma's population is 3,943,079. Oklahoma City is the state capital and the largest city.

FUN FACT Before it became a state, Oklahoma was known as Indian Territory. Today 39 nations, including the Cherokee, Creek, Osage, and Choctaw, have their headquarters in the state.

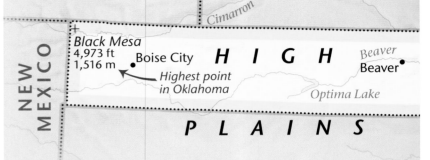

COLORADO

NEW MEXICO

Cimarron

Black Mesa
4,973 ft
1,516 m
Boise City

H I G H

Beaver
Beaver

Highest point in Oklahoma

Optima Lake

P L A I N S

A tornado is a destructive rotating column of air that forms from a thunderstorm. In 1974 five tornadoes struck Oklahoma City in one day.

OKLAHOMA

Oklahoma State Flag

The collared lizard is Oklahoma's state reptile. The lizard is common in the Wichita Mountains and throughout the state.

Scissor-Tailed Flycatcher
State Bird

Rose
State Flower

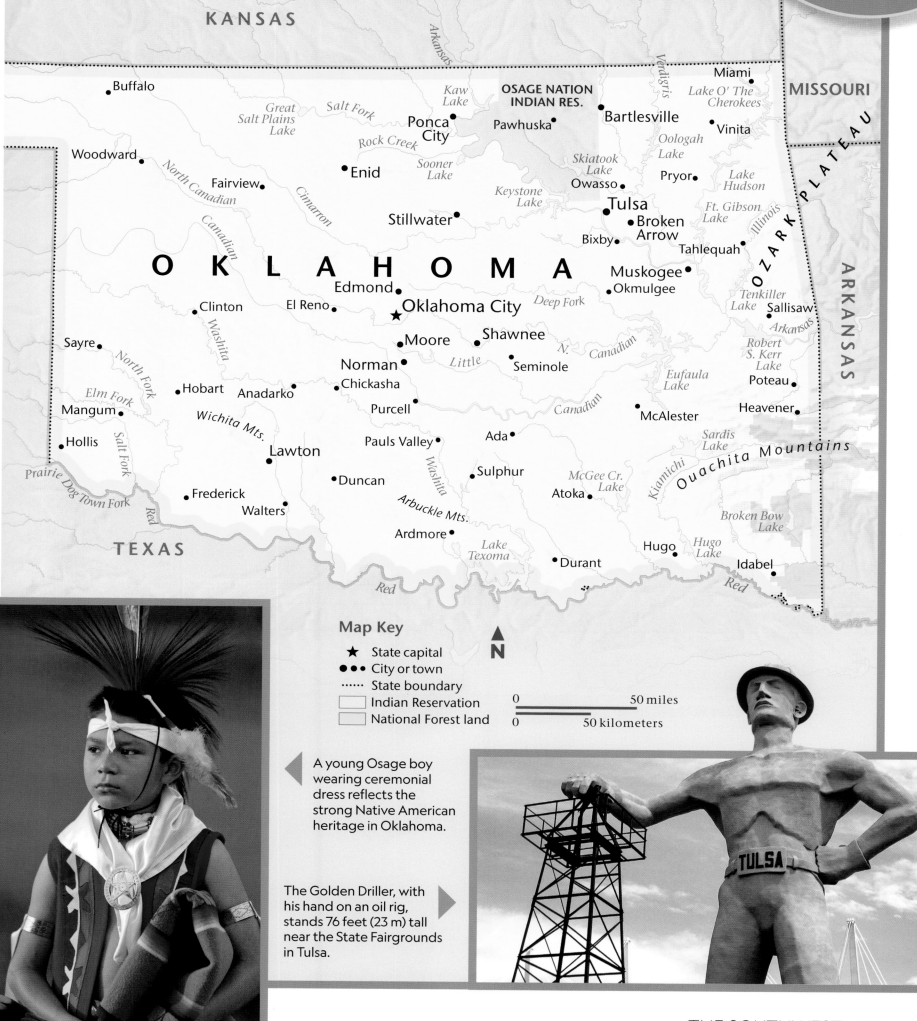

KANSAS

Buffalo

Woodward

Fairview

Great Salt Plains Lake

Salt Fork

Rock Creek

Kaw Lake

Ponca City

Enid

Sooner Lake

Arkansas

Pawhuska

OSAGE NATION INDIAN RES.

Verdigris

Miami

Lake O' The Cherokees

MISSOURI

Bartlesville

Vinita

Oologah Lake

Skiatook Lake

Owasso

Pryor

Lake Hudson

North Canadian

Cimarron

Keystone Lake

Stillwater

Tulsa

Ft. Gibson Lake

Illinois

Broken Arrow

Bixby

Tahlequah

OZARK PLATEAU

Canadian

O K L A H O M A

Edmond

Muskogee

Okmulgee

Tenkiller Lake

Sallisaw

ARKANSAS

Clinton

El Reno

Oklahoma City

Deep Fork

Arkansas

Washita

Moore

Shawnee

N. Canadian

Robert S. Kerr Lake

Sayre

North Fork

Norman

Chickasha

Little

Seminole

Eufaula Lake

Poteau

Elm Fork

Hobart

Anadarko

Purcell

Canadian

Heavener

Mangum

Wichita Mts.

Pauls Valley

Ada

McAlester

Hollis

Salt Fork

Lawton

Washita

Sulphur

McGee Cr. Lake

Sardis Lake

Ouachita Mountains

Prairie Dog Town Fork

Frederick

Walters

Duncan

Arbuckle Mts.

Atoka

Kiamichi

Broken Bow Lake

Red

Ardmore

Lake Texoma

Durant

Hugo

Hugo Lake

Idabel

TEXAS

Red

Red

Map Key

⭐ State capital

●●● City or town

⋯⋯ State boundary

☐ Indian Reservation

☐ National Forest land

N

| 0 | 50 miles |
| 0 | 50 kilometers |

A young Osage boy wearing ceremonial dress reflects the strong Native American heritage in Oklahoma.

The Golden Driller, with his hand on an oil rig, stands 76 feet (23 m) tall near the State Fairgrounds in Tulsa.

TULSA

TEXAS

TEXAS

LAND & WATER The Edwards Plateau, Padre Island National Seashore, and the Rio Grande are important land and water features of Texas.

STATEHOOD Texas became the 28th state in 1845.

PEOPLE & PLACES The population of Texas is 28,701,845. Austin is the state capital. Houston is the largest city.

FUN FACT The Texas Rangers, the country's oldest state law enforcement organization, was established in 1823 to protect settlements in the territory that would become Texas.

The brightly lit Congress Avenue Bridge crosses Town Lake into downtown Austin, where tall buildings rise against the night sky.

Texas leads the United States in oil and natural gas production. A well near Houston pumps oil, called "black gold" because it's worth so much money.

NEW MEXICO

GUADALUPE MTS. N.P.

● El Paso

+ *Guadalupe Peak* 8,751 ft 2,667 m

Highest point in Texas

U.S.
MEXICO

Rio Grande

Davis Mts.

Presidio

Texas State Flag

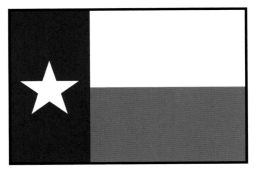

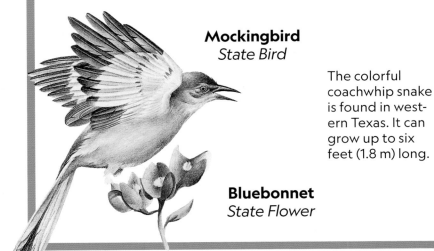

Mockingbird
State Bird

The colorful coachwhip snake is found in western Texas. It can grow up to six feet (1.8 m) long.

Bluebonnet
State Flower

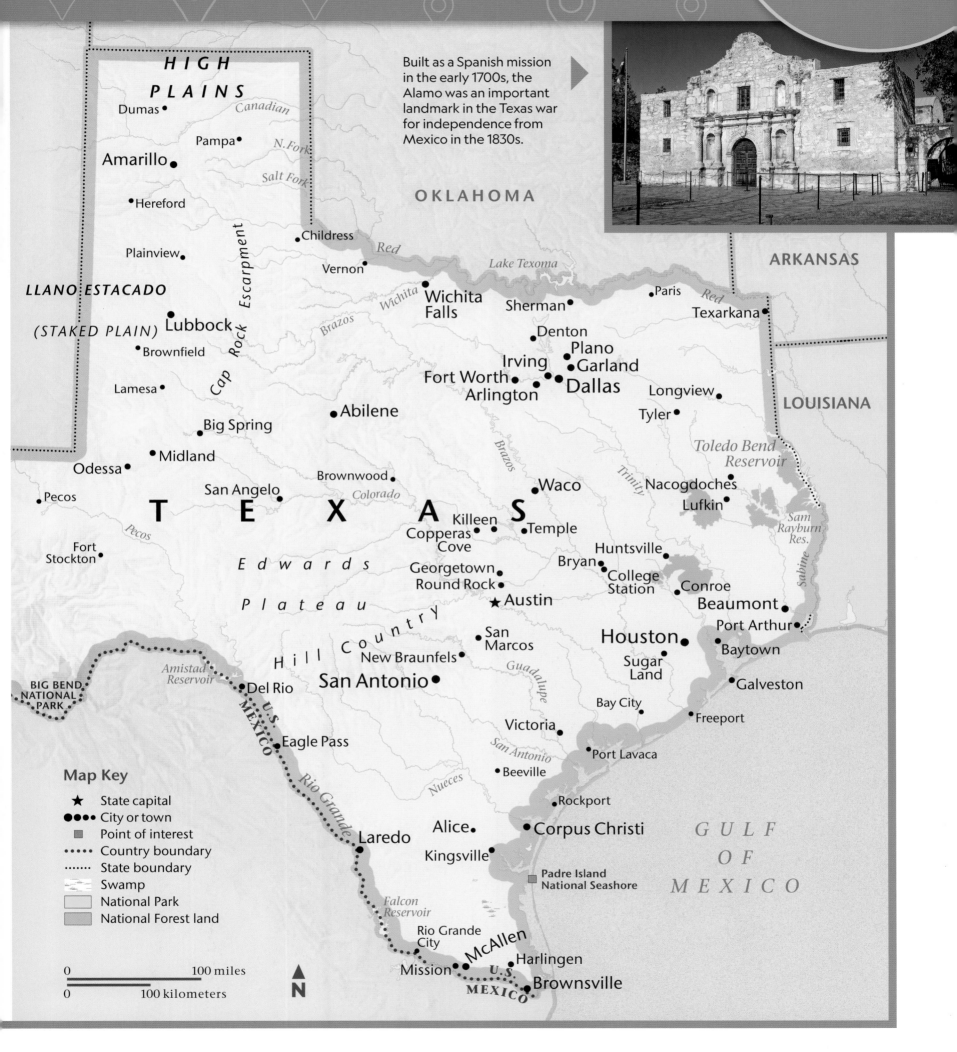

HIGH PLAINS

Dumas •
Pampa •
Amarillo •
• Hereford
Plainview •
• Childress
Vernon •

Canadian
N. Fork
Salt Fork

Built as a Spanish mission in the early 1700s, the Alamo was an important landmark in the Texas war for independence from Mexico in the 1830s.

OKLAHOMA

ARKANSAS

Lake Texoma

Red

Wichita
Brazos

Wichita Falls
Sherman •
• Paris
Red
Texarkana

LLANO ESTACADO

(STAKED PLAIN)

Lubbock •
• Brownfield
Lamesa •
Denton •
Plano •
Irving • Garland •
Fort Worth • Dallas
Arlington

Longview •
Tyler •

LOUISIANA

Cap Rock Escarpment

• Abilene

Brazos

Trinity

Toledo Bend Reservoir

Big Spring •
• Midland
Odessa •
• Pecos
Brownwood •
San Angelo •

Colorado

Waco •
Killeen •
Copperas Cove •
Temple •
Nacogdoches •
Lufkin •

Sam Rayburn Res.

T E X A S

Pecos

Fort Stockton •

Edwards Plateau

Georgetown •
Round Rock •
Huntsville •
Bryan •
College Station •
Conroe •
Beaumont •
Port Arthur •

★ Austin

Sabine

Hill Country

San Marcos •
New Braunfels •
Sugar Land •
Baytown •

Amistad Reservoir

BIG BEND NATIONAL PARK

Del Rio •

San Antonio •

Guadalupe

Houston •

Galveston •

Bay City •
Freeport •

MEXICO
U.S.

Eagle Pass •

Victoria •

San Antonio

Port Lavaca •
• Beeville

Map Key

★ State capital
•••• City or town
■ Point of interest
•••• Country boundary
...... State boundary
Swamp
National Park
National Forest land

Rio Grande

Nueces

Rockport •

Laredo •

Alice •
Kingsville •

Corpus Christi •

G U L F
O F
M E X I C O

Padre Island National Seashore ■

Falcon Reservoir

Rio Grande City •
Mission •
McAllen •
Harlingen •
Brownsville •

U.S.
MEXICO

0 — 100 miles
0 — 100 kilometers

N

THE WEST

The West region makes up almost half the landmass of the United States. The region's varied landscapes range from the frozen heights of Denali in Alaska to the barren desert of Death Valley in California and the lush tropical forests of Hawai'i. More than half the population lives in California, where Los Angeles ranks second only to New York City in number of people. Other parts of the West have few people. Much of the region's land is set aside as parkland and military bases.

Bobcats, named for their short tail, have adapted to environments ranging from forests to deserts and snow-covered mountains.

The snowy peaks of Maroon Bells–Snowmass Wilderness near Aspen, Colorado, rise over 14,000 feet (4,200 m). Mountains—including the Rockies, Tetons, and Sierra Nevada—are important landscape features of the West.

ALASKA

LAND & WATER The Tongass National Forest, Brooks Range, and the Yukon River are important land and water features of Alaska.

STATEHOOD Alaska became the 49th state in 1959.

PEOPLE & PLACES Alaska's population is 737,438. Juneau is the state capital. The largest city is Anchorage.

FUN FACT The most powerful earthquake ever recorded in North America struck Anchorage in 1964. Eighty times more powerful than the 1906 San Francisco earthquake, it measured 9.2 on the Richter scale.

Alaska State Flag

Forget-Me-Not
State Flower

Willow Ptarmigan
State Bird

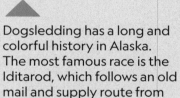

Dogsledding has a long and colorful history in Alaska. The most famous race is the Iditarod, which follows an old mail and supply route from Anchorage to Nome.

CHUKCHI

ASIA

Bering

St. Lawrence I.

St. Matthew I.

Nunivak I.

BERING SEA

St. Paul •
Pribilof Islands

ALEUTIAN ISLANDS
Unimak I.
Unalaska I.
Umnak I. •Unalaska
Yunaska I. *Islands of Four Mountains*

Continuation of the Aleutian Islands on map to the right

PACIFIC OCEAN

Native peoples in Alaska carve totem poles to tell their histories. One place carvers still make totems is Saxman Native Village in Ketchikan.

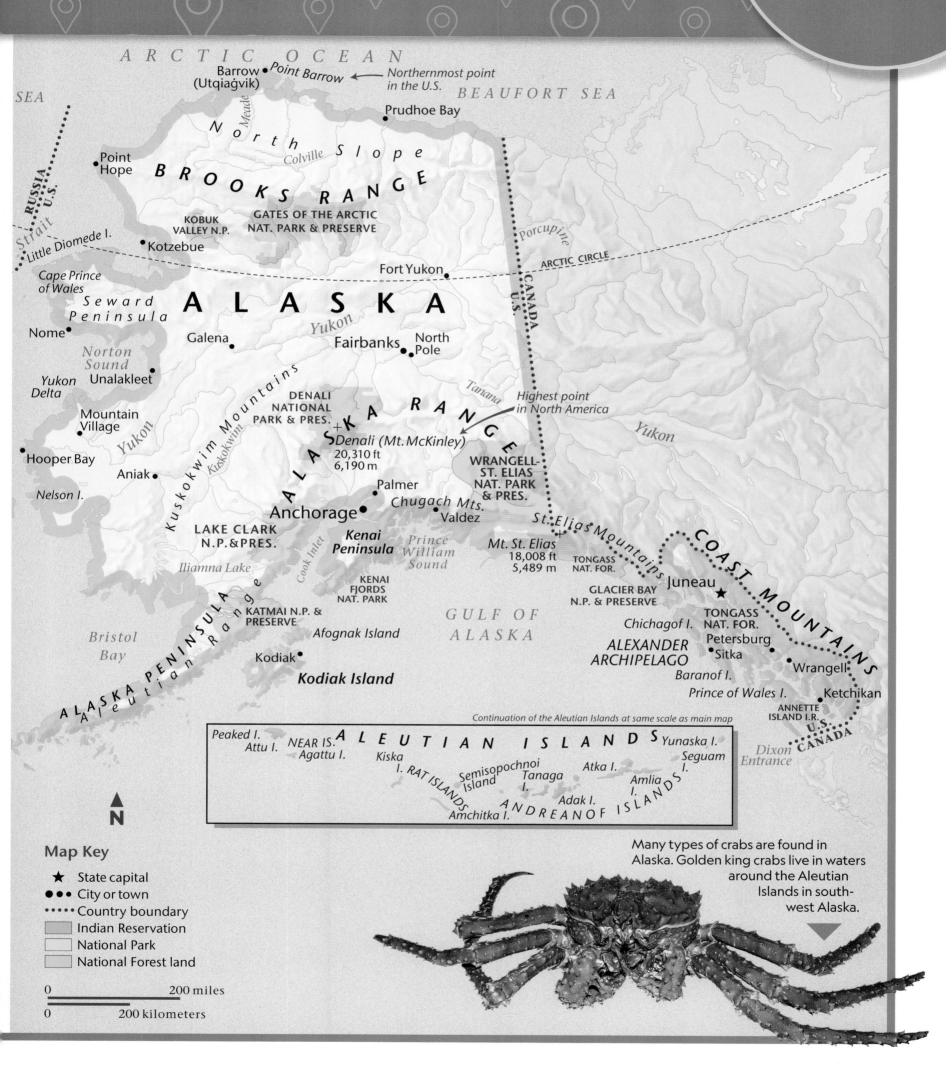

ARCTIC OCEAN

Barrow • Point Barrow ← Northernmost point in the U.S.
(Utqiaġvik)

BEAUFORT SEA

• Prudhoe Bay

SEA

Meade

RUSSIA
U.S.

Strait

Colville

North Slope

B R O O K S   R A N G E

• Point
Hope

GATES OF THE ARCTIC
NAT. PARK & PRESERVE

KOBUK
VALLEY N.P.

Little Diomede I.

Porcupine

• Kotzebue

ARCTIC CIRCLE

Cape Prince
of Wales

Fort Yukon •

CANADA
U.S.

A L A S K A

Seward
Peninsula

Yukon

• Nome

Galena •

Fairbanks •

Norton
Sound

• North
Pole

Yukon
Delta

Unalakleet •

Tanana

Yukon

Mountain
Village •

DENALI
NATIONAL
PARK & PRES.

A L A S K A   R A N G E

Highest point
in North America

Yukon

Kuskokwim

• Hooper Bay

Kuskokwim Mountains

Denali (Mt. McKinley)
20,310 ft
6,190 m

WRANGELL-
ST. ELIAS
NAT. PARK
& PRES.

Aniak •

Palmer •

Nelson I.

Chugach Mts.

St. Elias Mountains

COAST MOUNTAINS

Anchorage •

• Valdez

LAKE CLARK
N.P. & PRES.

Kenai
Peninsula

Prince
William
Sound

Mt. St. Elias
18,008 ft
5,489 m

TONGASS
NAT. FOR.

Iliamna Lake

Cook Inlet

GLACIER BAY
N.P. & PRESERVE

Juneau ★

Ilianna Lake

KENAI
FJORDS
NAT. PARK

GULF OF
ALASKA

TONGASS
NAT. FOR.

ALASKA PENINSULA

Aleutian Range

KATMAI N.P. &
PRESERVE

Chichagof I.

• Petersburg

ALEXANDER
ARCHIPELAGO

• Sitka

Bristol
Bay

Afognak Island

• Wrangell

• Kodiak

Baranof I.

Prince of Wales I.

• Ketchikan

Kodiak Island

ANNETTE
ISLAND I.R.

U.S.
CANADA

Continuation of the Aleutian Islands at same scale as main map

Peaked I.
Attu I.

NEAR IS.

A L E U T I A N   I S L A N D S

Yunaska I.

Dixon
Entrance

Agattu I.

Kiska

I. RAT ISLANDS

Semisopochnoi
Island

Tanaga
I.

Atka I.

Seagum

Amlia
I.

Adak I.

A N D R E A N O F   I S L A N D S

Amchitka I.

N

Map Key

★ State capital
• • • City or town
• • • • Country boundary
▢ Indian Reservation
▢ National Park
▢ National Forest land

0 ——— 200 miles
0 ——— 200 kilometers

Many types of crabs are found in
Alaska. Golden king crabs live in waters
around the Aleutian
Islands in south-
west Alaska.

CALIFORNIA

CALIFORNIA

Stretching more than a mile (1.6 km) across the entrance to San Francisco Bay, the Golden Gate Bridge opened in 1937.

 LAND & WATER The Sierra Nevada, Death Valley, and San Francisco Bay are important land and water features of California.

 STATEHOOD California became the 31st state in 1850.

 PEOPLE & PLACES California's population is 39,557,045. Sacramento is the state capital. The largest city is Los Angeles.

? **FUN FACT** In July 1913, what is now Furnace Creek Ranch in Death Valley experienced a temperature of 134°F (57°C)— the highest temperature ever recorded in the United States.

On a beach near San Simeon two bull elephant seals face off in a loud roaring match in front of sleeping females and pups.

The Tour Thru Tree, near Klamath, is 800 years old and 168 feet (51 m) tall. A tunnel carved through the trunk allows cars to drive through.

California State Flag

Golden Poppy
State Flower

California Quail
State Bird

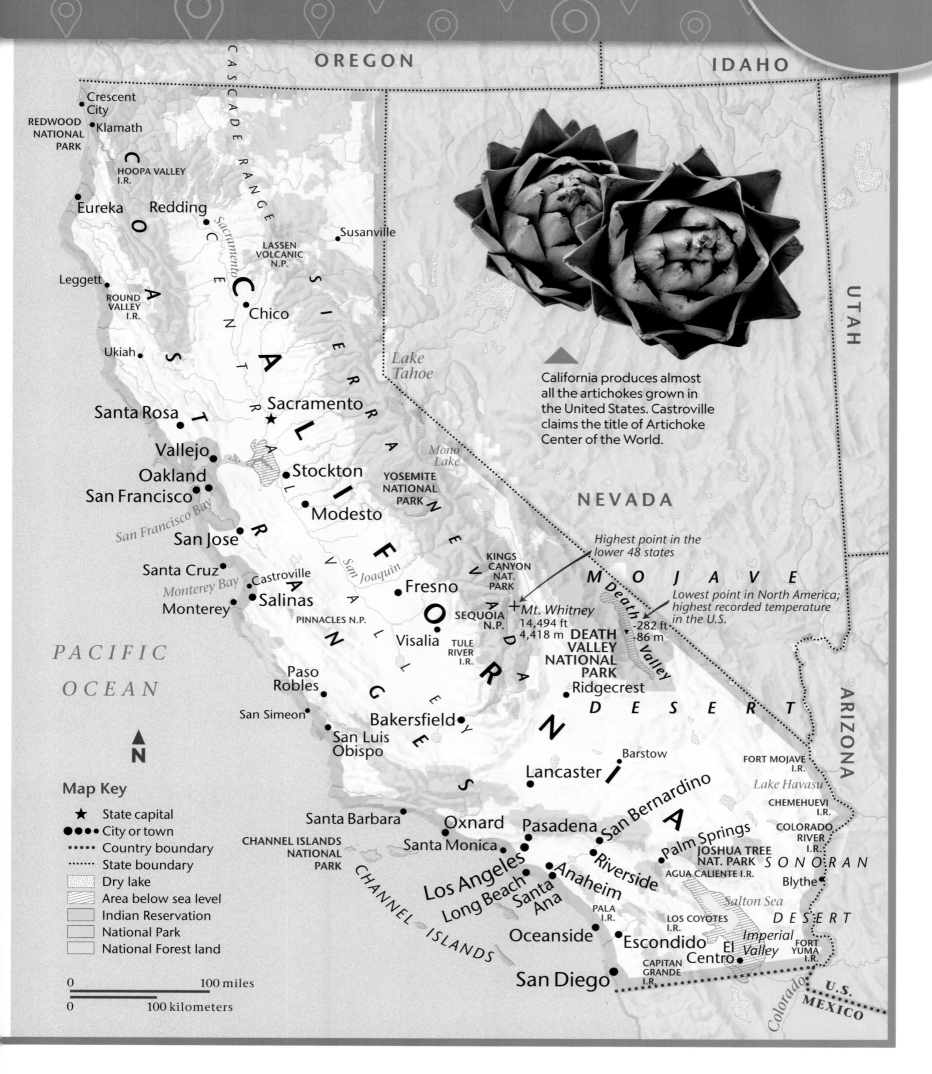

OREGON

IDAHO

Crescent
City
REDWOOD
NATIONAL
PARK
Klamath

CASCADE RANGE

UTAH

HOOPA VALLEY
I.R.

Eureka   Redding

Susanville

LASSEN
VOLCANIC
N.P.

Sacramento

Leggett

ROUND
VALLEY
I.R.

Chico

Ukiah

C A L I F O R N I A

Lake
Tahoe

California produces almost
all the artichokes grown in
the United States. Castroville
claims the title of Artichoke
Center of the World.

Santa Rosa

Vallejo

Oakland

San Francisco

San Francisco Bay

San Jose

Sacramento

Stockton

Modesto

Mono
Lake

YOSEMITE
NATIONAL
PARK

NEVADA

Highest point in the
lower 48 states

Lowest point in North America;
highest recorded temperature
in the U.S.

Santa Cruz

Monterey Bay

Castroville

Salinas

San Joaquin

Fresno

KINGS
CANYON
NAT.
PARK

Monterey

PINNACLES N.P.

Visalia

SEQUOIA
N.P.

TULE
RIVER
I.R.

Mt. Whitney
14,494 ft
4,418 m

DEATH
VALLEY
NATIONAL
PARK

-282 ft
-86 m

Death Valley

M O J A V E

PACIFIC

OCEAN

Paso
Robles

Ridgecrest

D E S E R T

ARIZONA

San Simeon

Bakersfield

San Luis
Obispo

N

Map Key

Lancaster

Barstow

FORT MOJAVE
I.R.

Lake Havasu

CHEMEHUEVI
I.R.

★   State capital

●●●● City or town

Santa Barbara

Oxnard

Pasadena

San Bernardino

COLORADO
RIVER
I.R.

····· Country boundary

········ State boundary

CHANNEL ISLANDS
NATIONAL
PARK

Santa Monica

Los Angeles

Long Beach

Anaheim

Santa
Ana

Riverside

Palm Springs

JOSHUA TREE
NAT. PARK

AGUA CALIENTE I.R.

SONORAN

Blythe

Dry lake

Area below sea level

Indian Reservation

National Park

National Forest land

CHANNEL

ISLANDS

Oceanside

PALA
I.R.

Escondido

CAPITAN
GRANDE
I.R.

LOS COYOTES
I.R.

El
Centro

Salton Sea

Imperial
Valley

D E S E R T

FORT
YUMA
I.R.

0   100 miles

0   100 kilometers

San Diego

Colorado

U.S.
MEXICO

COLORADO

COLORADO

Early native people built more than 600 stone structures into cliff walls that are now part of Mesa Verde National Park.

LAND & WATER The Rocky Mountains, Mount Elbert, and the Colorado River are important land and water features of Colorado.

STATEHOOD Colorado became the 38th state in 1876.

PEOPLE & PLACES Colorado's population is 5,695,564. Denver is the state capital and the largest city.

FUN FACT The 700-foot (210-m)-high sand dunes in Great Sand Dunes National Park and Preserve occupy an area that was covered by an ancient sea more than a million years ago.

Bighorn sheep, known for their large curled horns, live in Rocky Mountain National Park and other mountainous areas of the West.

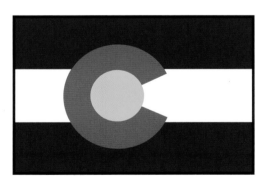

Colorado State Flag

Columbine
State Flower

Lark Bunting
State Bird

Only spot in the U.S. where the borders of four states come together

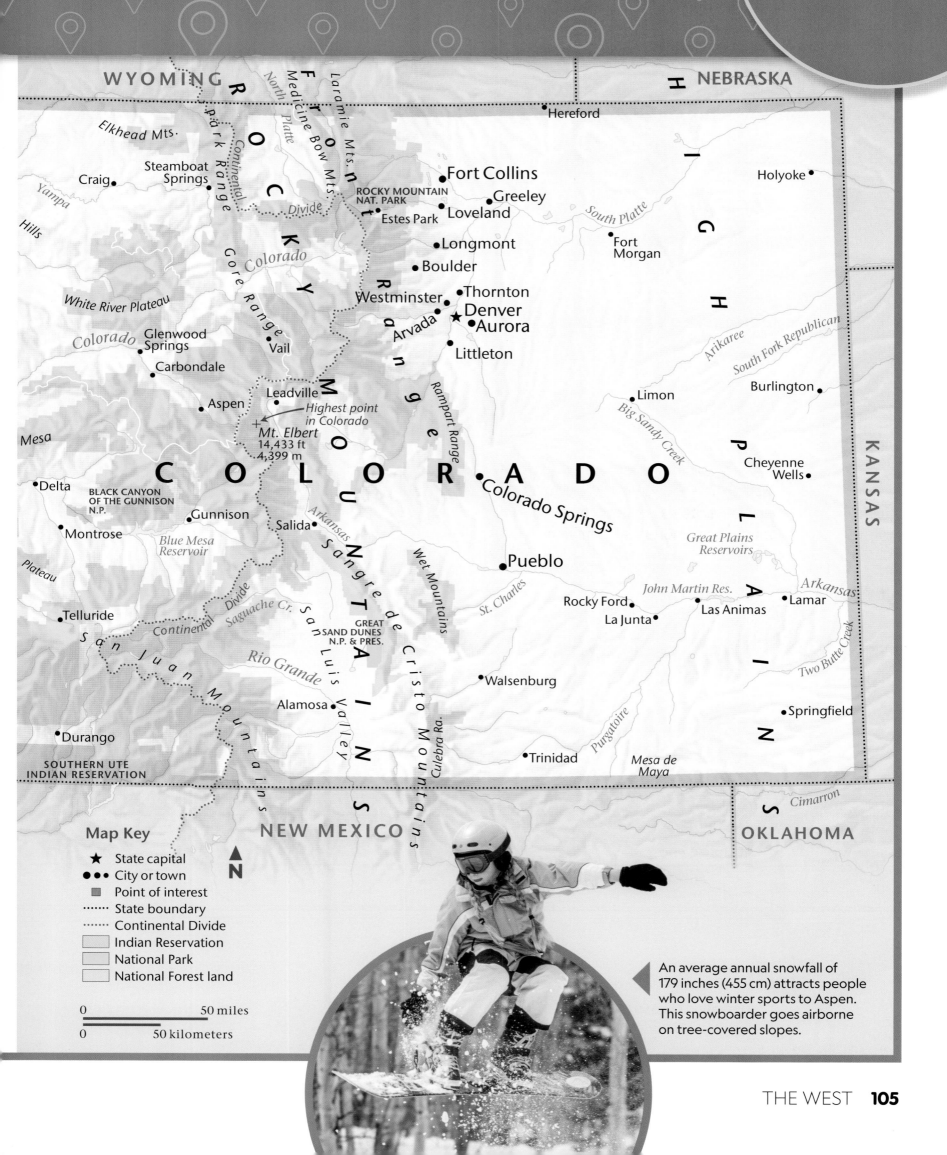

WYOMING

NEBRASKA

Elkhead Mts.

Craig

Steamboat Springs

R O C K Y

Park Range

Continental

North Platte

Medicine Bow Mts.

Laramie Mts.

F r o n t

Hereford

Holyoke

Fort Collins

Greeley

ROCKY MOUNTAIN NAT. PARK

Divide

Estes Park

Loveland

South Platte

Fort Morgan

Yampa

Hills

Colorado

Gore Range

Longmont

Boulder

White River Plateau

R a n g e

Westminster

Thornton

Denver

Arvada

Aurora

Colorado

Glenwood Springs

Vail

Littleton

Arikaree

South Fork Republican

Carbondale

M O U N T A I N S

Aspen

Leadville

Highest point in Colorado

Mt. Elbert 14,433 ft 4,399 m

Rampart Range

Limon

Big Sandy Creek

Burlington

Mesa

C O L O R A D O

Delta

BLACK CANYON OF THE GUNNISON N.P.

Gunnison

Salida

Arkansas

Colorado Springs

Cheyenne Wells

Montrose

Blue Mesa Reservoir

Great Plains Reservoirs

Plateau

Sangre

Wet Mountains

Pueblo

John Martin Res.

Arkansas

Telluride

Continental

Divide

Saguache Cr.

San Luis Valley

de Cristo Mountains

St. Charles

Rocky Ford

La Junta

Las Animas

Lamar

Two Butte Creek

San Juan Mountains

Rio Grande

GREAT SAND DUNES N.P. & PRES.

Walsenburg

Springfield

Durango

Alamosa

Culebra Ra.

Purgatoire

Mesa de Maya

SOUTHERN UTE INDIAN RESERVATION

Trinidad

Cimarron

NEW MEXICO

OKLAHOMA

KANSAS

Map Key

★ State capital
●●● City or town
■ Point of interest
········ State boundary
········ Continental Divide
▢ Indian Reservation
▢ National Park
▢ National Forest land

N

0   50 miles
0   50 kilometers

An average annual snowfall of 179 inches (455 cm) attracts people who love winter sports to Aspen. This snowboarder goes airborne on tree-covered slopes.

HAWAI'I

LAND & WATER
Kilauea crater, Diamond Head, and Pearl Harbor are important land and water features of Hawai'i.

STATEHOOD
Hawai'i became the 50th state in 1959.

PEOPLE & PLACES
Hawai'i's population is 1,420,491. Honolulu is the state capital and the largest city.

FUN FACT
Hawai'i is the fastest growing state in the United States—not in people, but in land. Each of the islands that make up the state was created by lava from erupting volcanoes.

Hawai'i State Flag

Recent eruptions on Kilauea, Hawai'i's most active volcano, have added almost 900 acres (364 ha) of new land to the state.

KAUA'I

Kaulakahi Channel

Lehua

Wai'ale'ale
5,148 ft
1,569 m

Waimea Canyon

Kekaha

Kapa'a

Lihu'e

Kalaheo

Pu'uwai

NI'IHAU

Kaua'i

PACIFIC

A lei, or necklace made of flowers such as orchids, is the traditional gift of greeting or farewell in Hawai'i.

Kure Atoll

Midway Islands

Pearl and Hermes Atoll

Lisianski I.

Laysan I.

Maro Reef

NORTHWESTERN HAWAIIAN

N

0   200 miles

0   200 kilometers

Hibiscus
State Flower

Hawaiian Goose (Nene)
State Bird

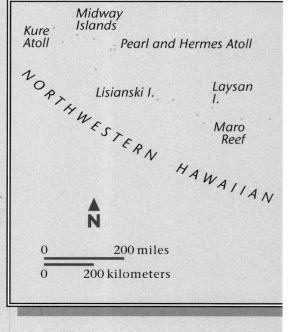

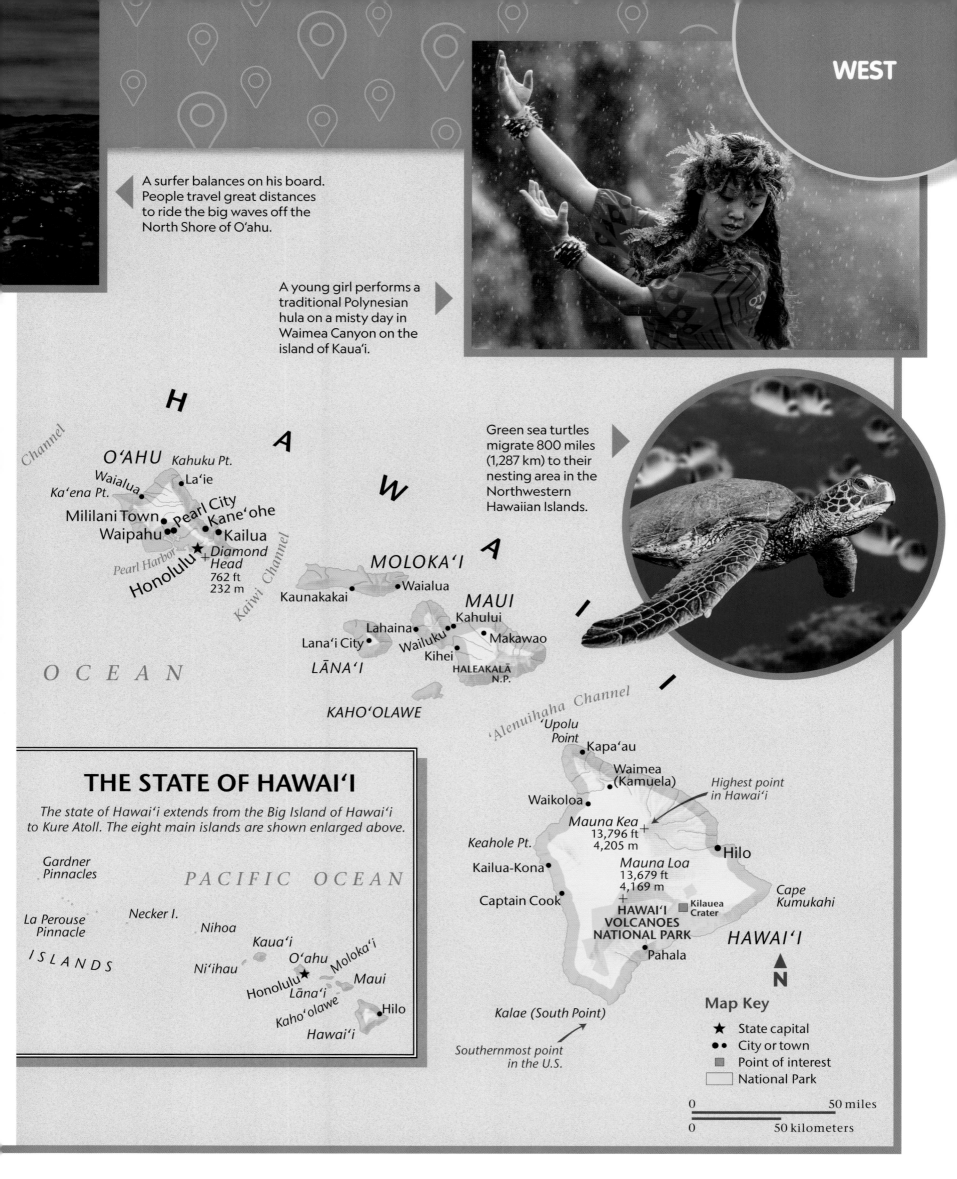

A surfer balances on his board. People travel great distances to ride the big waves off the North Shore of O'ahu.

A young girl performs a traditional Polynesian hula on a misty day in Waimea Canyon on the island of Kaua'i.

Green sea turtles migrate 800 miles (1,287 km) to their nesting area in the Northwestern Hawaiian Islands.

H A W A I I

Channel

O'AHU Kahuku Pt.
Waialua · La'ie
Ka'ena Pt.
Mililani Town · Pearl City · Kane'ohe
Waipahu · · Kailua
Pearl Harbor · Diamond
Honolulu ★ + Head
762 ft
232 m

Kaiwi Channel

MOLOKA'I
· Waialua
Kaunakakai

MAUI
Lahaina · Kahului
Lana'i City · Wailuku · Makawao
· Kihei
LĀNA'I HALEAKALĀ
N.P.

KAHO'OLAWE

O C E A N

'Alenuihaha Channel

'Upolu
Point
· Kapa'au
Waimea
(Kamuela) Highest point
· in Hawai'i
Waikoloa ·
Mauna Kea +
13,796 ft
Keahole Pt. 4,205 m
Mauna Loa
Kailua-Kona · 13,679 ft
4,169 m
Captain Cook · Cape
+ Kumukahi
HAWAI'I ■ Kilauea
VOLCANOES Crater
NATIONAL PARK **HAWAI'I**
· Pahala
N
Kalae (South Point)
↗
Southernmost point
in the U.S.

THE STATE OF HAWAI'I

The state of Hawai'i extends from the Big Island of Hawai'i to Kure Atoll. The eight main islands are shown enlarged above.

Gardner
Pinnacles PACIFIC OCEAN

Necker I.
La Perouse
Pinnacle Nihoa
Kaua'i
I S L A N D S Ni'ihau O'ahu Moloka'i
Honolulu ★ Maui
Lāna'i
Kaho'olawe · Hilo
Hawai'i

Map Key
★ State capital
•• City or town
■ Point of interest
▢ National Park

0   50 miles
0   50 kilometers

IDAHO

LAND & WATER The Bitterroot Range, the Columbia Plateau, and the Snake River are important land and water features of Idaho.

STATEHOOD Idaho became the 43rd state in 1890.

PEOPLE & PLACES Idaho's population is 1,754,208. Boise is the state capital and the largest city.

FUN FACT In preparation for the first mission to the moon, U.S. astronauts visited Craters of the Moon National Monument and Preserve to study its volcanic landscapes and experience its harsh environment.

Idaho State Flag

Syringa (Mock Orange)
State Flower

Mountain Bluebird
State Bird

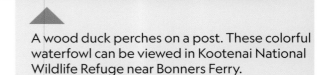

A wood duck perches on a post. These colorful waterfowl can be viewed in Kootenai National Wildlife Refuge near Bonners Ferry.

More than 60 percent of Idaho's land area is forested. Use of this land is overseen by the Forest Products Commission in Boise. Forest products are important to the state's economy.

More than 60 percent of all potatoes grown in Idaho end up as french fries.

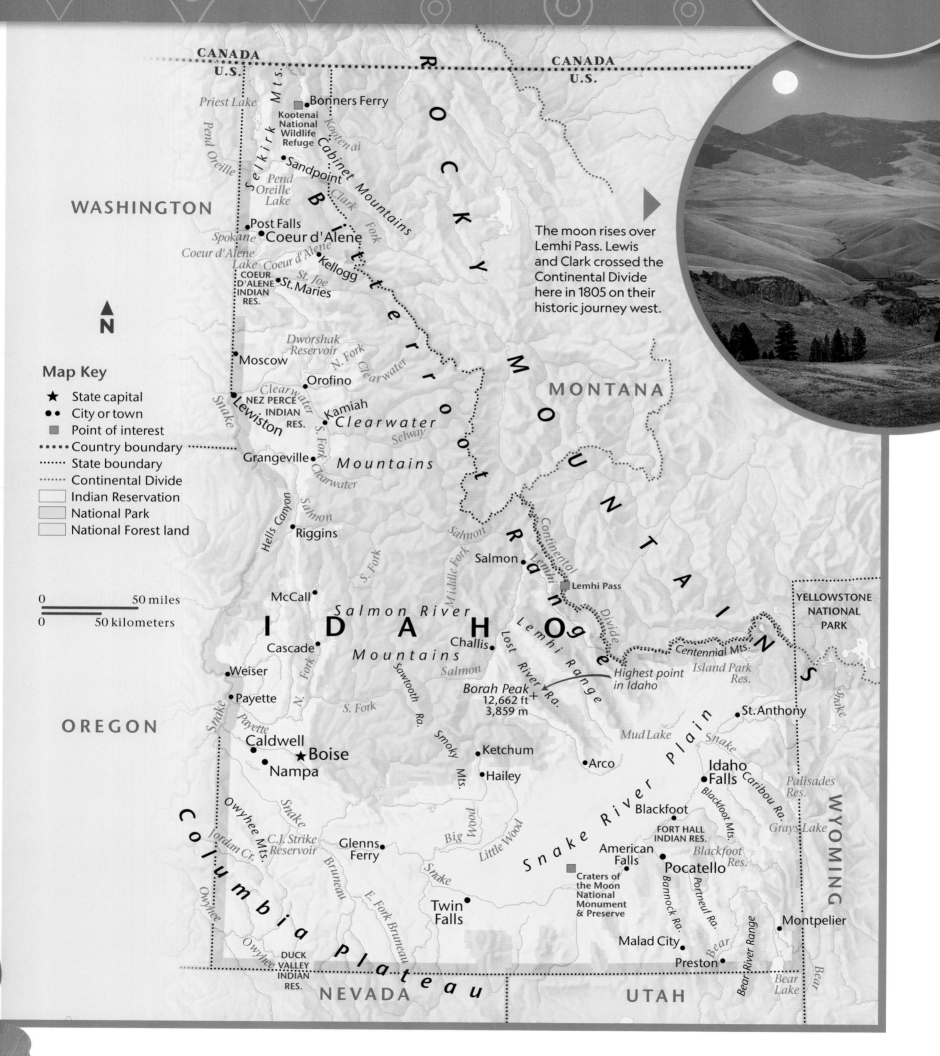

CANADA U.S.

CANADA U.S.

Priest Lake

Bonners Ferry

Kootenai National Wildlife Refuge

R
O
C
K
Y

Kooten ai

Selkirk Mts.

Cabinet Mountains

Pend Oreille

Sandpoint

WASHINGTON

Pend Oreille Lake

Clark Fork

Post Falls

Spokane Coeur d'Alene

Coeur d'Alene Lake

Coeur d'Alene

Kellogg

COEUR D'ALENE INDIAN RES.

St. Maries

St. Joe

B
i
t
t
e
r
r
o
o
t

M
O
U
N
T
A
I
N
S

MONTANA

The moon rises over Lemhi Pass. Lewis and Clark crossed the Continental Divide here in 1805 on their historic journey west.

Dworshak Reservoir

N. Fork

Moscow

Orofino

Clearwater

NEZ PERCE INDIAN RES.

Kamiah

Clearwater

S. Fork Clearwater

Selway

Clearwater Mountains

Lewiston

Snake

Grangeville

Map Key

★ State capital
●• City or town
■ Point of interest
••••• Country boundary
•••••• State boundary
•••••• Continental Divide
▢ Indian Reservation
▢ National Park
▢ National Forest land

Hells Canyon

Salmon

Riggins

S. Fork

Salmon

Salmon

Continental

Lemhi

Lemhi Pass ■

R
a
n
g
e

YELLOWSTONE NATIONAL PARK

Middle Fork

Challis

Lost River Ra.

Lemhi Range

Centennial Mts.

Divide

Island Park Res.

0   50 miles
0   50 kilometers

McCall

Cascade

Salmon River Mountains

Salmon

Highest point in Idaho

I
D
A
H
O

Sawtooth Ra.

Borah Peak
12,662 ft
3,859 m ✛

Snake

Weiser

N. Fork

Payette

S. Fork

Smoky Mts.

Ketchum

Hailey

Little Wood

Arco

Mud Lake

Snake

St. Anthony

OREGON

Payette

Caldwell

★ Boise

Nampa

Snake

Idaho Falls

Snake

Caribou Ra.

Palisades Res.

W
Y
O
M
I
N
G

Owyhee Mts.

Jordan Cr.

C.J. Strike Reservoir

Bruneau

Glenns Ferry

Big Wood

S
n
a
k
e
   R
i
v
e
r
   P
l
a
i
n

Blackfoot

Blackfoot Ra.

Blackfoot Res.

Grays Lake

FORT HALL INDIAN RES.

C
o
l
u
m
b
i
a
   P
l
a
t
e
a
u

Owyhee

Owyhee

Snake

E. Fork Bruneau

Twin Falls

■ Craters of the Moon National Monument & Preserve

American Falls

Pocatello

Bannock Ra.

Portneuf Ra.

Montpelier

Bear

Bear River Range

Bear

DUCK VALLEY INDIAN RES.

Malad City

Preston

Bear Lake

NEVADA

UTAH

MONTANA

LAND & WATER The Rocky Mountains, the Great Plains, and the Yellowstone River are important land and water features of Montana.

STATEHOOD Montana became the 41st state in 1889.

PEOPLE & PLACES Montana's population is 1,062,305. Helena is the state capital. The largest city is Billings.

FUN FACT Montana is the only state with river systems that empty southeast into the Gulf of Mexico, north into Canada's Hudson Bay, and west into the Pacific Ocean.

Montana State Flag

Bitterroot
State Flower

Western Meadowlark
State Bird

Skiers ride a chairlift up a snowy mountain slope in Whitefish.

Rugged peaks of the northern Rocky Mountains are reflected in the still surface of a mountain lake in Glacier National Park.

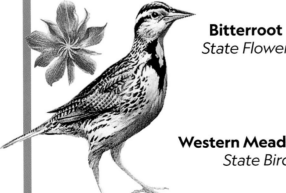

CANADA
U.S.

Lake Koocanusa
Eureka
GLACIER NATIONAL PARK
BLACKFEET INDIAN RES.
N. Fork
Flathead
Kootenai
Salish Mountains
ROCKY
Continental Divide
Browning
Cabinet Mountains
Libby
Whitefish
Kalispell
Flathead Lake
Clark Fork
Thompson Falls
FLATHEAD INDIAN RES.
Polson
S. Fork Flathead
Moiese
Flathead
National Bison Range
MOUNTAIN
Missoula
Clark Fork
M
IDAHO
Deer Lodge
Anaconda
Butte
Dillon
Bitterroot Range
Red Rock
Continental

CANADA
U.S.

CANADA
U.S.

Cut Bank

Marias

Milk   Chinook

Havre

ROCKY BOYS
I.R.

FORT
BELKNAP
INDIAN
RESERVATION

Malta

Milk

Scobey   Plentywood

FORT PECK
INDIAN
RESERVATION

G R E A T

Teton

Fort Benton

Missouri

Glasgow

Wolf Point

Missouri

Sidney

Great Falls

Fort Peck Lake

Circle

Yellowstone

Jordan

Glendive

Wibaux

M   O   N   T   A   N   A

Lewistown

Terry

P

L

★Helena

Canyon Ferry L.

Townsend

Missouri

Roundup

Musselshell

Miles City

Baker

A

Yellowstone

Forsyth

I

Jefferson

Big Timber

Billings

Bighorn

Colstrip

Tongue

N

Madison

Gallatin

Bozeman

Columbus

Hardin

Crow Agency

CROW INDIAN
RESERVATION

NORTHERN
CHEYENNE
I.R.

Powder

Little Missouri

Broadus

S

T

Virginia City

Granite Peak
12,799 ft
3,901 m
+

Clarks Fk.

*Highest point
in Montana*

A

I

Yellowstone

Absaroka Range

Red Lodge

Bighorn

WYOMING

Mountains

N

West
Yellowstone

YELLOWSTONE
NATIONAL
PARK

Divide

S

NORTH DAKOTA

SOUTH DAKOTA

N

Montana offers many opportunities to explore the natural environment. Here a young girl rides her horse through a grassy meadow.

American bison are protected in the National Bison Range, a wildlife refuge near Moiese.

Map Key

★ State capital
•• City or town
■ Point of interest
•••• Country boundary
•••• State boundary
•••• Continental Divide
▢ Indian Reservation
▢ National Park
▢ National Forest land

0   50 miles
0   50 kilometers

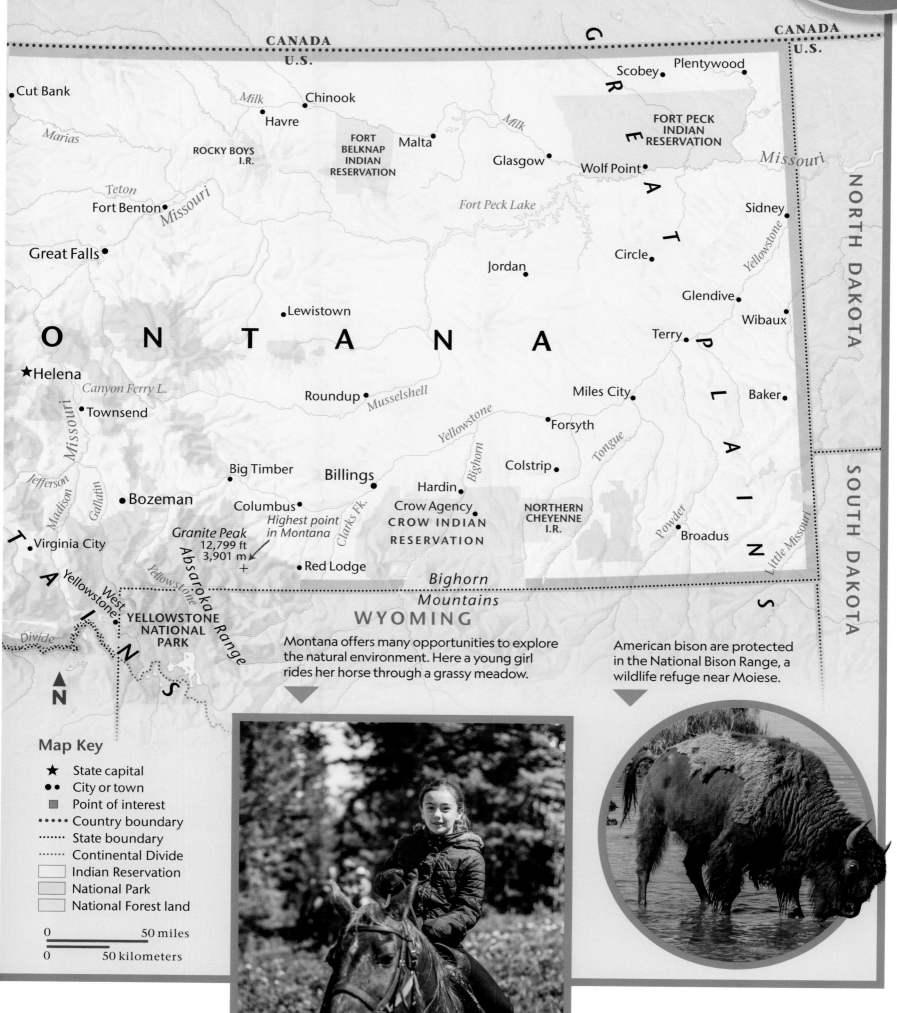

NEVADA

NEVADA

LAND & WATER The Great Basin, the Mojave Desert, and Lake Mead are important land and water features of Nevada.

STATEHOOD Nevada became the 36th state in 1864.

PEOPLE & PLACES Nevada's population is 3,034,392. Carson City is the state capital. The largest city is Las Vegas.

FUN FACT Kangaroo rats, which live in the Mojave Desert and other arid areas of the West, are small, seed-eating rodents that can survive with little or no water.

Nevada State Flag

Mountain Bluebird
State Bird

Sagebrush
State Flower

The Luxor re-creates a scene from ancient Egypt. It is one of the many lavish hotels that attract millions of tourists to Las Vegas.

Paiute people, dressed in ceremonial clothing, live on the Pyramid Lake Reservation near Reno. Their economy centers on recreational activities such as fishing and camping.

The desert environment of Nevada includes many plants that tolerate very dry conditions. The setting sun highlights mountains in the distance.

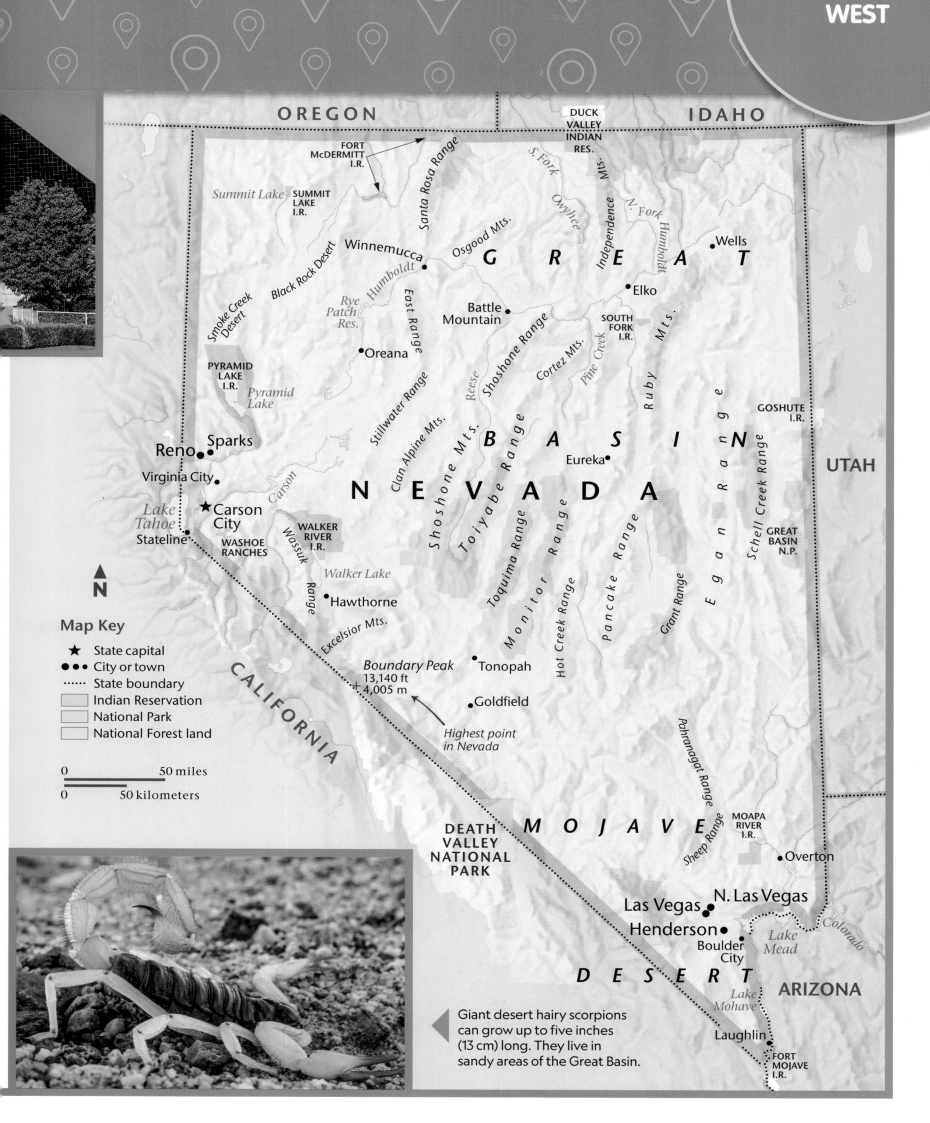

OREGON

IDAHO

DUCK
VALLEY
INDIAN
RES.

FORT
McDERMITT
I.R.

Santa Rosa Range

S. Fork Owyhee

N. Fork

Independence Mts.

Humboldt

Wells

Summit Lake

SUMMIT
LAKE
I.R.

Winnemucca

Osgood Mts.

G R E A T

Black Rock Desert

Smoke Creek Desert

Humboldt

Rye Patch Res.

Battle
Mountain

Elko

SOUTH
FORK
I.R.

East Range

Oreana

PYRAMID
LAKE
I.R.

Pyramid Lake

Stillwater Range

Reese

Shoshone Range

Cortez Mts.

Pine Creek

Ruby Mts.

GOSHUTE
I.R.

B A S I N

UTAH

Reno

Sparks

Carson

N E V A D A

Clan Alpine Mts.

Shoshone Mts.

Toiyabe Range

Eureka

Schell Creek Range

Virginia City

Lake Tahoe

★ Carson
City

WALKER
RIVER
I.R.

Egan Range

GREAT
BASIN
N.P.

Stateline

WASHOE
RANCHES

Wassuk Range

Toquima Range

Monitor Range

Hot Creek Range

Pancake Range

Grant Range

N

Walker Lake

Hawthorne

Map Key

★ State capital

●●● City or town

‥‥‥ State boundary

Indian Reservation

National Park

National Forest land

Excelsior Mts.

Boundary Peak
13,140 ft
+ 4,005 m

Tonopah

Goldfield

*Highest point
in Nevada*

Pahranagat Range

0   50 miles

0   50 kilometers

C A L I F O R N I A

DEATH
VALLEY
NATIONAL
PARK

M O J A V E

MOAPA
RIVER
I.R.

Sheep Range

Overton

N. Las Vegas

Las Vegas

Henderson

Boulder
City

Lake Mead

Colorado

D E S E R T

ARIZONA

Lake Mohave

Laughlin

FORT
MOJAVE
I.R.

Giant desert hairy scorpions
can grow up to five inches
(13 cm) long. They live in
sandy areas of the Great Basin.

OREGON

The 125-foot (38-m) Astoria Column near the mouth of the Columbia River is covered with scenes of historic events.

LAND & WATER The Cascade Range, Mount Hood, and the Columbia River are important land and water features of Oregon.

STATEHOOD Oregon became the 33rd state in 1859.

PEOPLE & PLACES Oregon's population is 4,190,713. Salem is the state capital. The largest city is Portland.

FUN FACT Crater Lake in the Cascade Range takes its name from the crater, or gigantic hole, created when a volcanic eruption almost 8,000 years ago caused the top of a mountain to collapse.

The cool, moist climate of the Willamette River Valley is well suited for growing certain varieties of grapes.

Rocky outcrops called sea stacks line Oregon's Pacific coast. They are the remains of a former coastline that has been eroded by waves.

STATE OF OREGON

1859

Oregon State Flag

Oregon Grape
State Flower

Western Meadowlark
State Bird

Map labels: PACIFIC OCEAN, Astoria, Trask, Tillamook, Newport, RANGE, Umpqua, Coos Bay, North Bend, Coos Bay, Coos, Roseburg, Cape Blanco, Gold Beach, Grants Pass, COAST, Illinois, Brookings

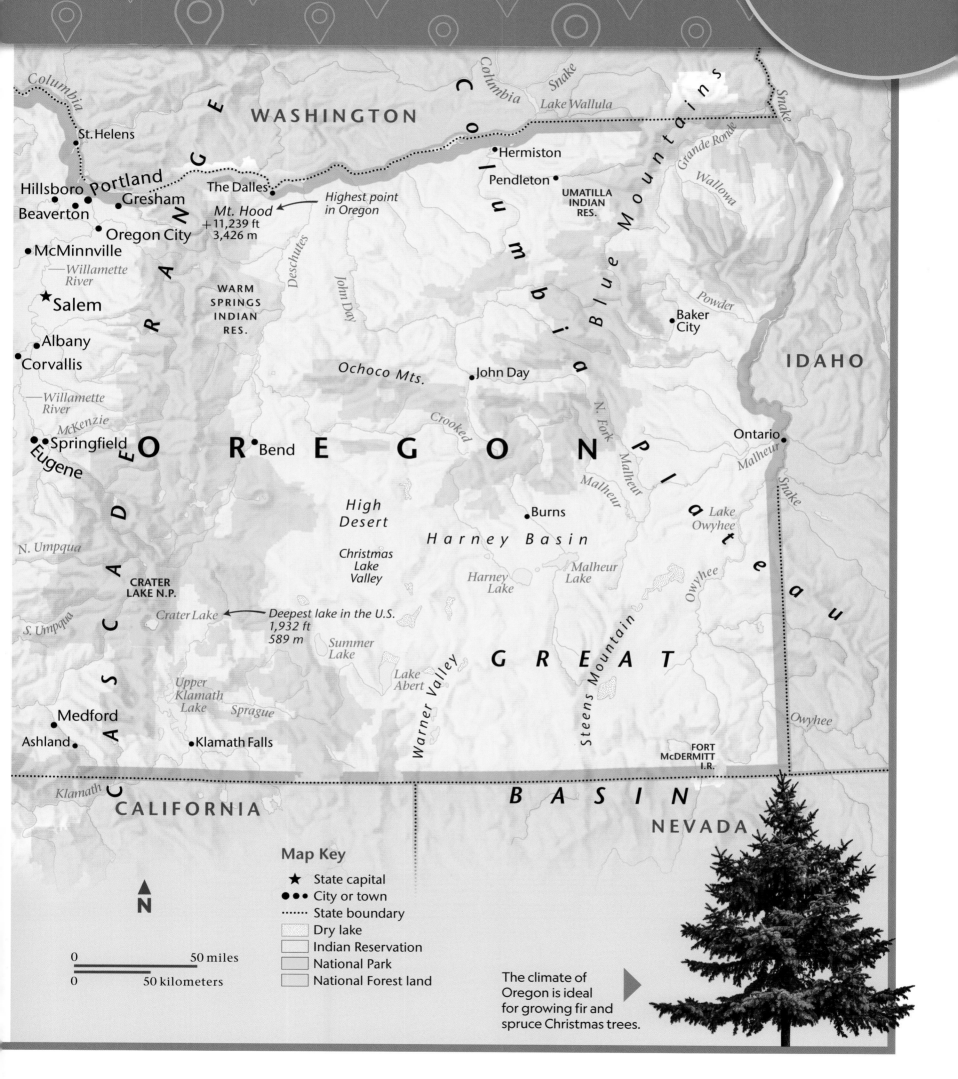

Columbia

WASHINGTON

St. Helens

Hillsboro Portland
Gresham
Beaverton
Oregon City
McMinnville

Willamette River

★ **Salem**

Albany
Corvallis

Willamette River

McKenzie

Springfield
Eugene

N. Umpqua

CRATER LAKE N.P.

S. Umpqua

The Dalles

Mt. Hood Highest point
+11,239 ft in Oregon
3,426 m

WARM SPRINGS INDIAN RES.

Deschutes

John Day

Ochoco Mts.

R Bend

E G O N

Crooked

High Desert

Christmas Lake Valley

Columbia *Snake*

Lake Wallula   *Snake*

Hermiston

Pendleton

UMATILLA INDIAN RES.

Blue Mountains

Grande Ronde

Wallowa

Powder

Baker City

IDAHO

John Day

N. Fork

Malheur

Ontario

Malheur

Burns

Harney Basin

Malheur

Owyhee

Lake Owyhee

Plateau

Snake

Crater Lake ← Deepest lake in the U.S.
1,932 ft
589 m

Summer Lake

Upper Klamath Lake

Sprague

Medford
Ashland

Klamath Falls

Klamath

CALIFORNIA

Harney Lake

Malheur Lake

Lake Abert

Warner Valley

G R E A T

Steens Mountain

Owyhee

FORT McDERMITT I.R.

B A S I N

NEVADA

Map Key

↑ N

★ State capital
••• City or town
⋯⋯ State boundary
▨ Dry lake
▫ Indian Reservation
▨ National Park
▫ National Forest land

0 ————— 50 miles
0 ————— 50 kilometers

The climate of Oregon is ideal for growing fir and spruce Christmas trees.

UTAH

LAND & WATER
The Great Basin, the Uinta Mountains, and Great Salt Lake are important land and water features of Utah.

STATEHOOD Utah became the 45th state in 1896.

PEOPLE & PLACES Utah's population is 3,161,105. Salt Lake City is the state capital and the largest city.

FUN FACT Great Salt Lake is the largest natural lake west of the Mississippi River. At its lowest water levels, the lake is as much as eight times saltier than the ocean.

Utah State Flag

Sego Lily
State Flower

California Gull
State Bird

Water sports such as tubing are popular activities in Glen Canyon National Recreation Area.

A newly married couple stands in front of the Temple in Salt Lake City, where Mormons gather for religious ceremonies.

Delicate Arch in Arches National Park is one of more than 2,000 arches that have been eroded by the natural forces of wind and water over millions of years.

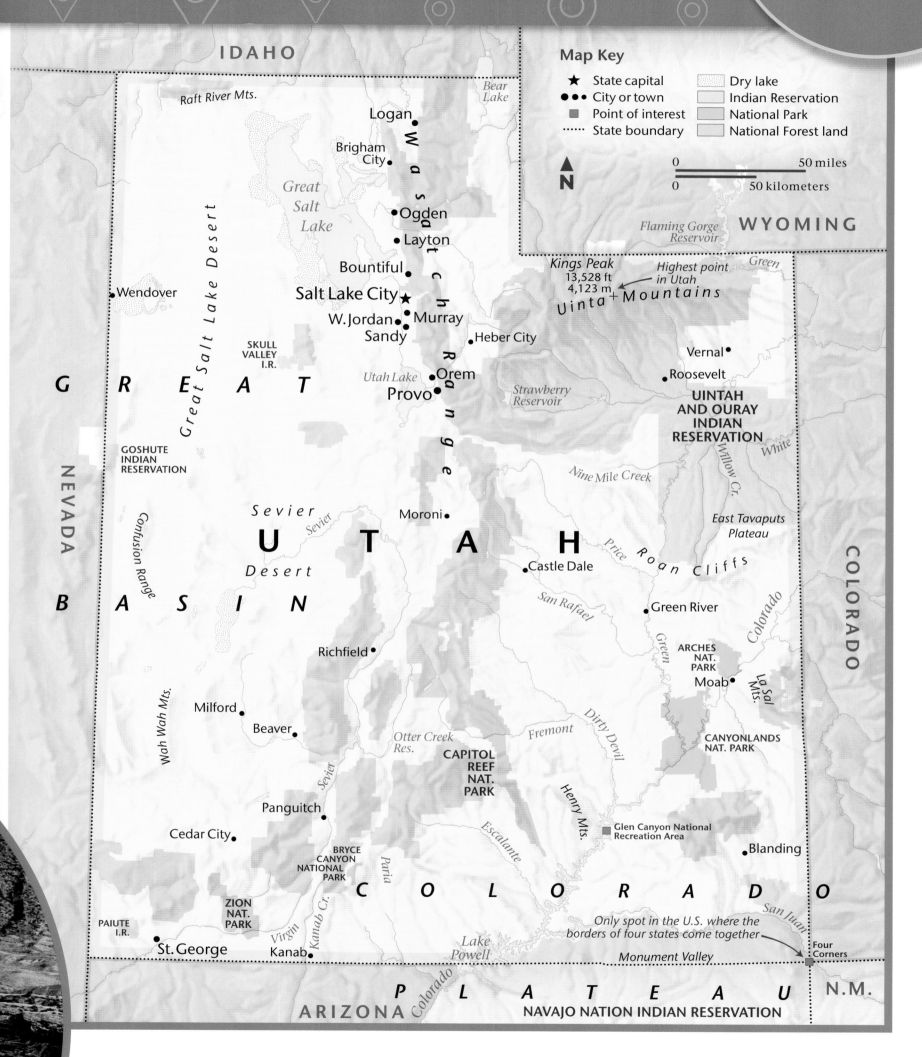

IDAHO

Raft River Mts.

Logan

Brigham City

Great Salt Lake

Bear Lake

Map Key

★ State capital
●●● City or town
■ Point of interest
⋯⋯ State boundary

Dry lake
Indian Reservation
National Park
National Forest land

N

0   50 miles
0   50 kilometers

WYOMING

Flaming Gorge Reservoir

Ogden

Layton

Bountiful

Salt Lake City ★

W. Jordan   Murray
Sandy

Heber City

Wendover

SKULL VALLEY I.R.

Wasatch Range

Kings Peak
13,528 ft
4,123 m

Highest point in Utah

Uinta Mountains

Green

GOSHUTE INDIAN RESERVATION

Great Salt Lake Desert

Utah Lake
Orem
Provo

Strawberry Reservoir

Vernal

Roosevelt

UINTAH AND OURAY INDIAN RESERVATION

White

Willow Cr.

G R E A T

Sevier

Sevier

Nine Mile Creek

East Tavaputs Plateau

NEVADA

Confusion Range

U T A H

Moroni

Price

Roan Cliffs

Colorado

COLORADO

B A S I N

Desert

Castle Dale

San Rafael

Green River

ARCHES NAT. PARK

Richfield

Wah Wah Mts.

Milford

Beaver

Otter Creek Res.

CAPITOL REEF NAT. PARK

Fremont

Dirty Devil

Green

Moab

La Sal Mts.

CANYONLANDS NAT. PARK

Sevier

Panguitch

Henry Mts.

Escalante

Glen Canyon National Recreation Area

Blanding

Cedar City

BRYCE CANYON NATIONAL PARK

Paria

Kanab Cr.

C O L O R A D O

San Juan

PAIUTE I.R.

ZION NAT. PARK

Virgin

St. George

Kanab

Lake Powell

Only spot in the U.S. where the borders of four states come together

Monument Valley

Four Corners

N.M.

P L A T E A U

ARIZONA   Colorado   NAVAJO NATION INDIAN RESERVATION

WASHINGTON

LAND & WATER
The Olympic Mountains, the Palouse Hills, and Puget Sound are important land and water features of Washington.

STATEHOOD
Washington became the 42nd state in 1889.

PEOPLE & PLACES
Washington's population is 7,535,591. Olympia is the state capital. The largest city is Seattle.

FUN FACT
Mount Rainier, a dormant volcano, last erupted in 1969. Another nearby volcano, Mount St. Helens, erupted in 1980. Winds carried ash from the eruption as far away as Maine.

Washington State Flag

Coast Rhododendron
State Flower

American Goldfinch
State Bird

A Roosevelt elk grazes in the temperate rainforest of Olympic National Forest. Adult males weigh up to 1,000 pounds (454 kg).

The skyline of Seattle is easily identified by its Space Needle tower. The city is an important West Coast port.

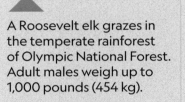

Vancouver Island

Cape Flattery
Strait of Juan de Fuca
MAKAH I.R.
Port Angeles

PACIFIC OCEAN

Olympic Mountains
OLYMPIC NAT. PARK

QUINAULT INDIAN RES.

Grays Harbor
Willapa Bay

COAST RANGES

Cape Disappointment
Columbia

Strait

N

0 ——— 50 miles
0 ——— 50 kilometers

Map Key
★ State capital
●●● City or town
⋯⋯ State boundary
••• Country boundary
▨ Glacier
▢ Indian Reservation
▢ National Park
▢ National Forest land

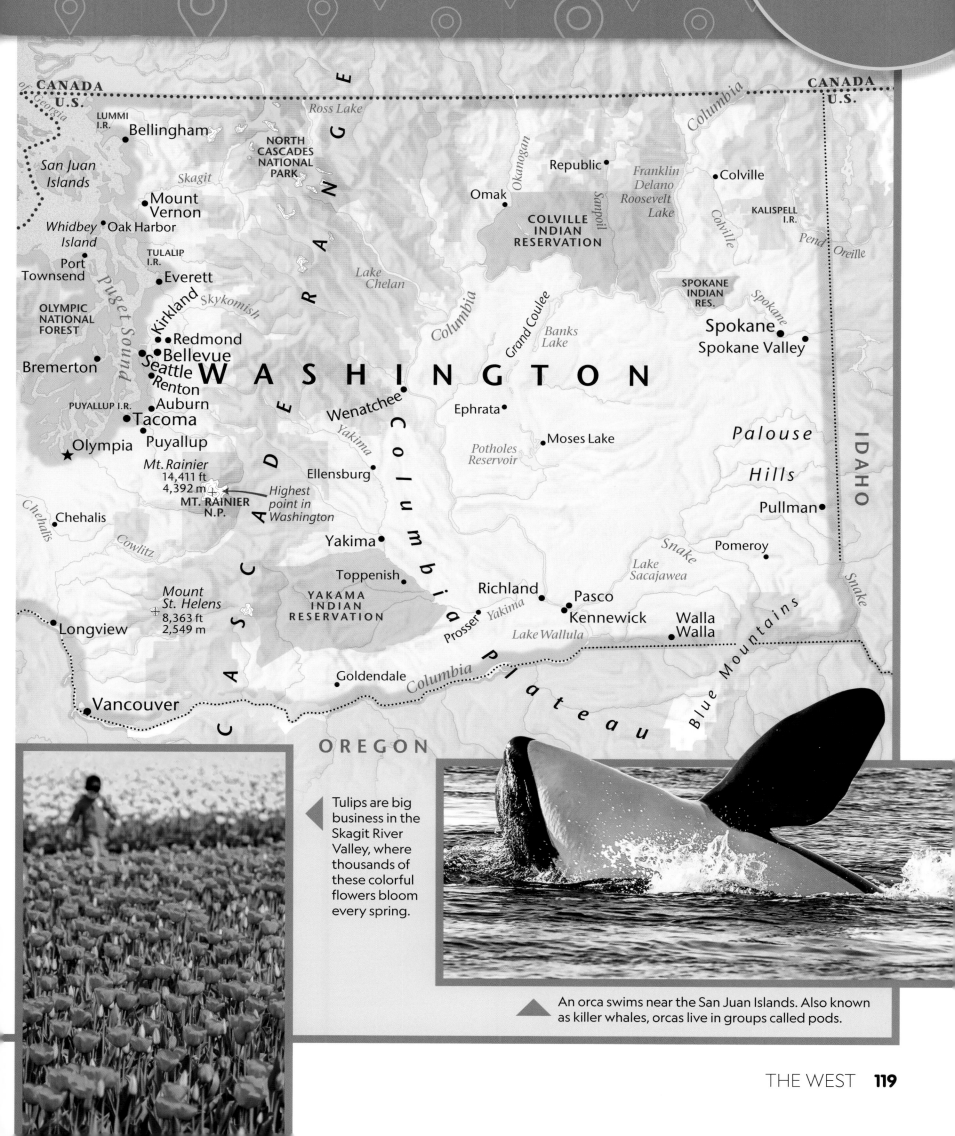

CANADA
U.S.
of Georgia

CANADA
U.S.

LUMMI
I.R.

Bellingham

Ross Lake

NORTH
CASCADES
NATIONAL
PARK

Columbia

*San Juan
Islands*

Skagit

Republic

*Franklin
Delano
Roosevelt
Lake*

Colville

Mount
Vernon

Omak

Okanogan

Sampoil

KALISPELL
I.R.

*Whidbey
Island*

Oak Harbor

COLVILLE
INDIAN
RESERVATION

Colville

Port
Townsend

TULALIP
I.R.

*Lake
Chelan*

Pend

Oreille

OLYMPIC
NATIONAL
FOREST

Everett

Skykomish

SPOKANE
INDIAN
RES.

Spokane

Kirkland

Columbia

Grand Coulee

*Banks
Lake*

Spokane

Redmond

Spokane Valley

Bremerton

Puget Sound

Bellevue

Seattle

W A S H I N G T O N

Renton

Ephrata

Palouse

PUYALLUP I.R.

Auburn

Wenatchee

Yakima

Moses Lake

*Potholes
Reservoir*

Hills

Tacoma

Olympia ★

Puyallup

Pullman

Mt. Rainier
14,411 ft
4,392 m

Columbia

Ellensburg

Chehalis

Chehalis

MT. RAINIER
N.P.

*Highest
point in
Washington*

Yakima

Snake

Pomeroy

*Lake
Sacajawea*

Cowlitz

Toppenish

Richland

Pasco

Mount
St. Helens
8,363 ft
2,549 m

YAKAMA
INDIAN
RESERVATION

Yakima

Kennewick

Walla
Walla

Snake

Longview

Prosser

Lake Wallula

C A S C A D E   **R A N G E**

C o l u m b i a

I D A H O

Vancouver

Goldendale

Columbia   *Plateau*

Blue Mountains

O R E G O N

Tulips are big
business in the
Skagit River
Valley, where
thousands of
these colorful
flowers bloom
every spring.

An orca swims near the San Juan Islands. Also known
as killer whales, orcas live in groups called pods.

WYOMING

WYOMING

LAND & WATER
The Rocky Mountains, Yellowstone National Park, and the Green River are important land and water features of Wyoming.

STATEHOOD
Wyoming became the 44th state in 1890.

PEOPLE & PLACES
Wyoming's population is 577,737. Cheyenne is the state capital and the largest city.

FUN FACT
Wyoming is called the Equality State because it was the first state to give white women the right to vote, granted in 1869 when Wyoming was still a territory.

Wyoming State Flag

Indian Paintbrush
State Flower

Western Meadowlark
State Bird

Steam and water from Old Faithful Geyser in Yellowstone National Park erupt more than 100 feet (30 m) into the air.

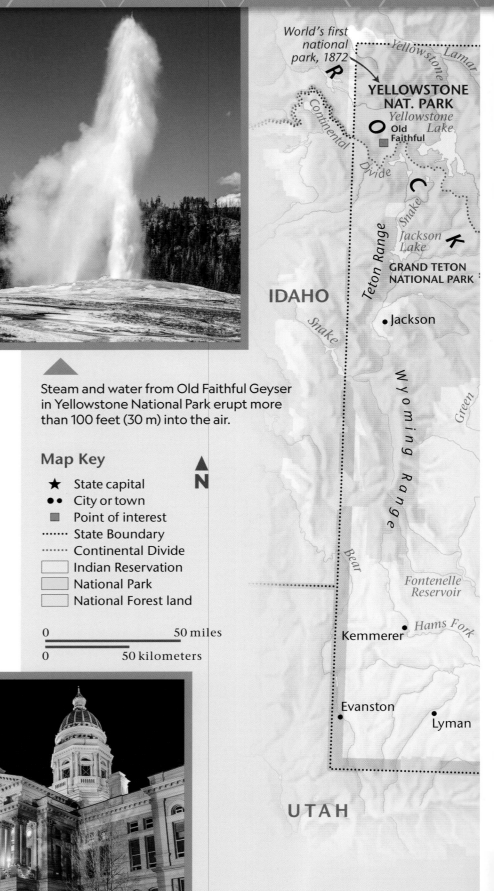

World's first national park, 1872

YELLOWSTONE NAT. PARK
Yellowstone Lake
Old Faithful

GRAND TETON NATIONAL PARK

IDAHO

Teton Range

Jackson Lake

Snake

• Jackson

Continental Divide

Wyoming Range

Green

Bear

Fontenelle Reservoir

Kemmerer • Hams Fork

• Evanston

Lyman

UTAH

Map Key
★ State capital
•• City or town
■ Point of interest
······ State Boundary
······ Continental Divide
☐ Indian Reservation
☐ National Park
☐ National Forest land

N

0   50 miles
0   50 kilometers

The Wyoming state capitol building in Cheyenne was completed in 1890. It is now a national historic landmark.

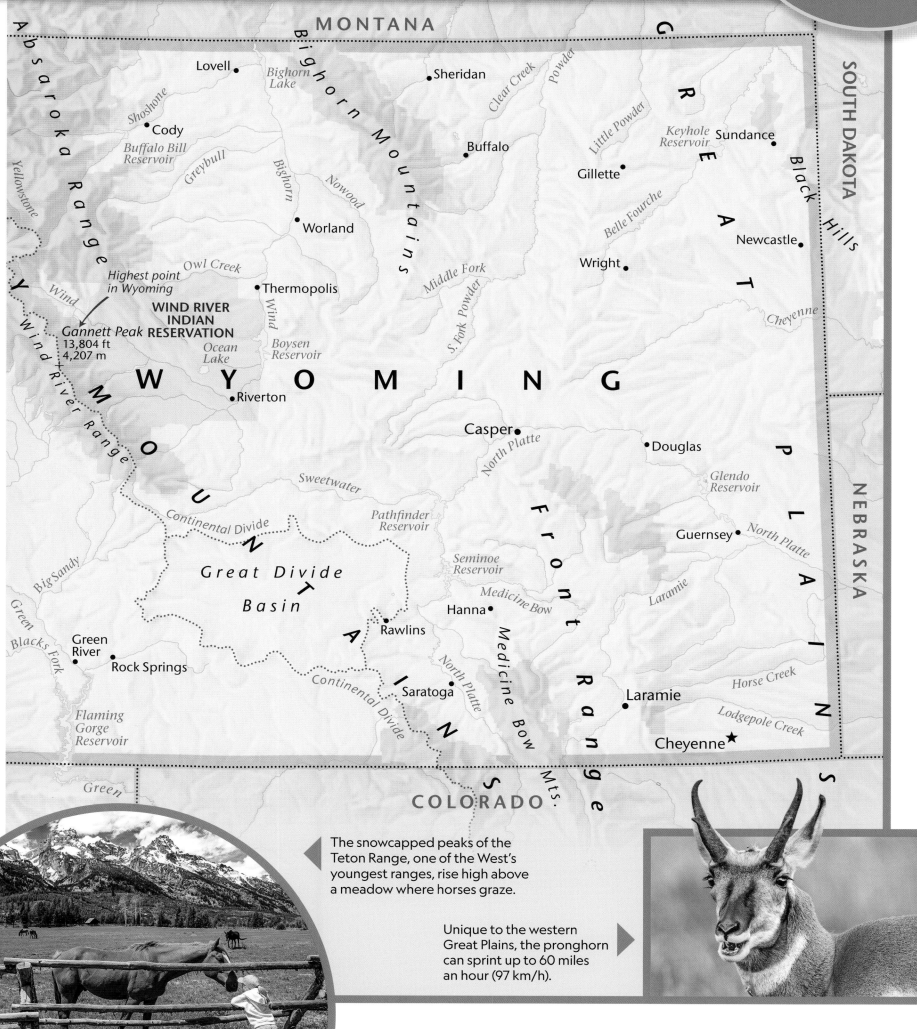

MONTANA

SOUTH DAKOTA

Lovell
Sheridan
Bighorn Lake
Clear Creek
Powder

Shoshone
Cody
Buffalo
Little Powder
Keyhole Reservoir
Sundance

Buffalo Bill Reservoir
Greybull
Gillette
Belle Fourche
Black Hills

Bighorn
Nowood
Newcastle

Worland
Wright

Absaroka Range

Yellowstone

Owl Creek
Middle Fork
Cheyenne

Wind
Highest point in Wyoming
Thermopolis
S. Fork Powder

WIND RIVER INDIAN RESERVATION
Gannett Peak
13,804 ft
4,207 m
Wind
Boysen Reservoir

Wind River Range

Ocean Lake

W Y O M I N G

Riverton

Casper
Douglas

North Platte
Glendo Reservoir

Sweetwater

Continental Divide
Pathfinder Reservoir

Guernsey
North Platte

Great Divide Basin
Seminoe Reservoir

Front Range

Medicine Bow
Laramie

Big Sandy
Hanna

Green

Blacks Fork
Green River
Rawlins

Medicine Bow

Rock Springs
Continental Divide
Saratoga
North Platte
Horse Creek

Laramie

Flaming Gorge Reservoir
Lodgepole Creek

Cheyenne ★

Green
Mts.
COLORADO

NEBRASKA

GREAT PLAINS

M O U N T A I N S

Bighorn Mountains

The snowcapped peaks of the Teton Range, one of the West's youngest ranges, rise high above a meadow where horses graze.

Unique to the western Great Plains, the pronghorn can sprint up to 60 miles an hour (97 km/h).

U.S. TERRITORIES

Across Two Seas

Listed below are the five largest* of the 14 U.S. territories (areas that belong to the U.S. but that are not states), along with their flags and key information. Two are in the Caribbean Sea; three are in the Pacific Ocean. Can you find the other nine U.S. territories on the map?

U.S. CARIBBEAN TERRITORIES

PUERTO RICO
Area: 3,508 sq mi (9,086 sq km)
Population: 3,294,626
Capital: San Juan
Languages: Spanish, English

U.S. VIRGIN ISLANDS
Area: 149 sq mi (386 sq km)
Population: 106,977
Capital: Charlotte Amalie
Languages: English, Spanish or Spanish Creole, French or French Creole

U.S. PACIFIC TERRITORIES

AMERICAN SAMOA
Area: 77 sq mi (199 sq km)
Population: 50,826
Capital: Pago Pago
Languages: Samoan, English

NORTHERN MARIANA ISLANDS
Area: 184 sq mi (477 sq km)
Population: 51,994
Capital: Capital Hill
Languages: Philippine languages, Chamorro, English

GUAM
Area: 217 sq mi (561 sq km)
Population: 167,772
Capital: Hagåtña (Agana)
Languages: English, Filipino, Chamorro

OTHER U.S. TERRITORIES
Baker Island, Howland Island, Jarvis Island, Johnston Atoll, Kingman Reef, Midway Islands, Navassa Island, Palmyra Atoll, Wake Island

*Close-up views of the five largest territories are highlighted in enlarged inset maps labeled with a letter. You can see where each territory is by looking for its corresponding letter on the main map.

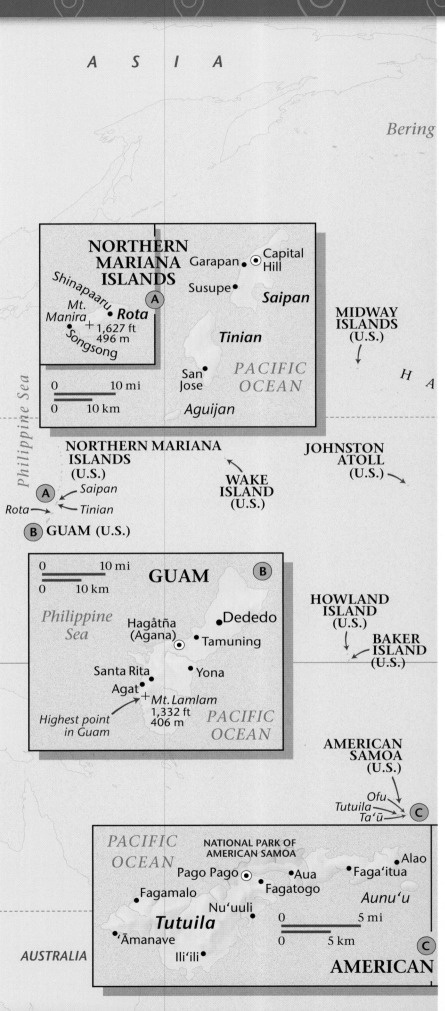

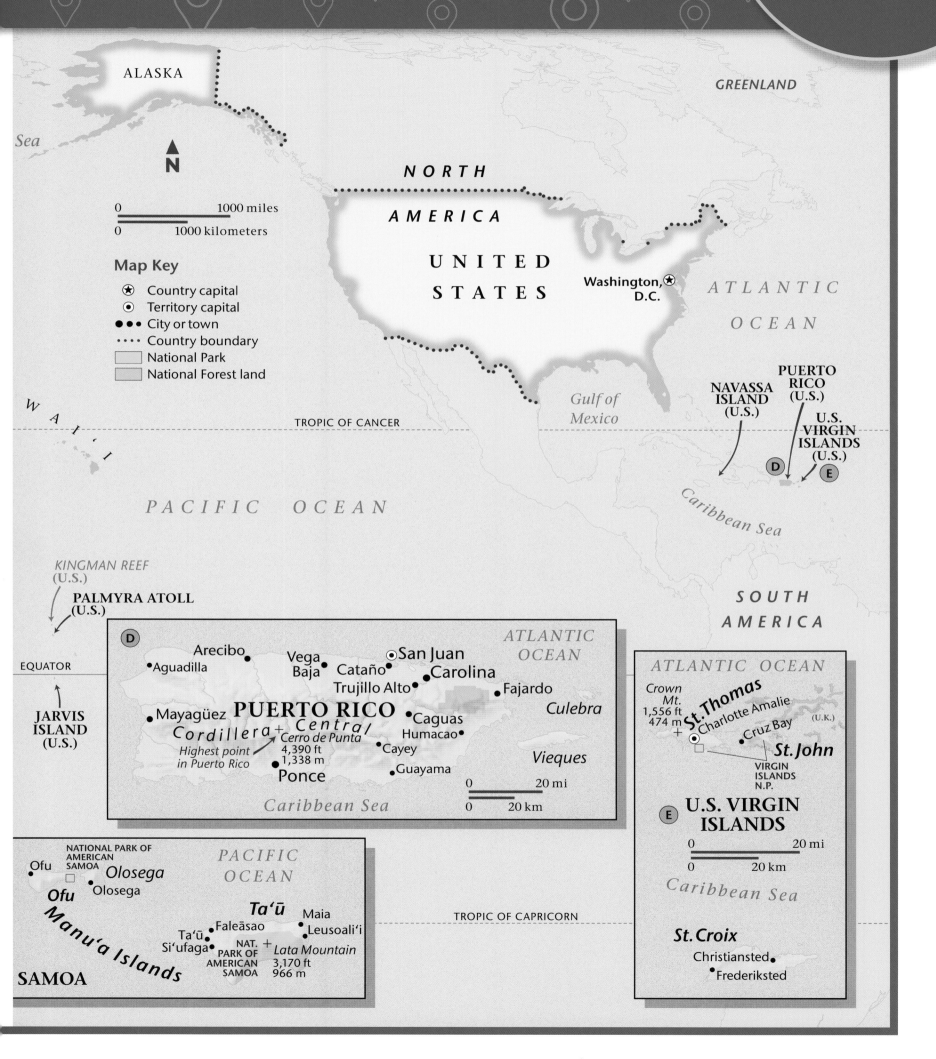

Map Key

- ★ Country capital
- ⊙ Territory capital
- ● City or town
- ⋯ Country boundary
- ▢ National Park
- ▢ National Forest land

ALASKA

GREENLAND

N

0 ——— 1000 miles
0 ——— 1000 kilometers

NORTH

AMERICA

UNITED
STATES

Washington, ⊛
D.C.

ATLANTIC

OCEAN

HAWAI'I

TROPIC OF CANCER

Gulf of
Mexico

NAVASSA
ISLAND
(U.S.)

PUERTO
RICO
(U.S.)

U.S.
VIRGIN
ISLANDS
(U.S.)

D   E

PACIFIC   OCEAN

Caribbean Sea

KINGMAN REEF
(U.S.)

PALMYRA ATOLL
(U.S.)

SOUTH

AMERICA

EQUATOR

JARVIS
ISLAND
(U.S.)

Puerto Rico inset (D)

ATLANTIC
OCEAN

- Aguadilla
- Arecibo
- Vega Baja
- Cataño
- ⊙ San Juan
- Carolina
- Trujillo Alto
- Fajardo
- Culebra
- Mayagüez
- **PUERTO RICO**
- *Central*
- *Cordillera* + Cerro de Punta
- Caguas
- Humacao
- Highest point in Puerto Rico 4,390 ft 1,338 m
- Cayey
- Vieques
- Ponce
- Guayama

Caribbean Sea

0 ——— 20 mi
0 ——— 20 km

U.S. Virgin Islands inset (E)

ATLANTIC OCEAN

Crown Mt.
1,556 ft
474 m +
St. Thomas
Charlotte Amalie
(U.K.)
Cruz Bay
▢
St. John
VIRGIN
ISLANDS
N.P.

E **U.S. VIRGIN
ISLANDS**

0 ——— 20 mi
0 ——— 20 km

Caribbean Sea

St. Croix
Christiansted
Frederiksted

American Samoa inset

- Ofu
- NATIONAL PARK OF AMERICAN SAMOA
- *Olosega*
- Olosega
- **Ofu**

PACIFIC
OCEAN

- *Ta'ū*
- Maia
- Ta'ū
- Faleāsao
- Leusoali'i
- Si'ufaga
- NAT. PARK OF AMERICAN SAMOA
- + Lata Mountain 3,170 ft 966 m

Manu'a Islands

SAMOA

TROPIC OF CAPRICORN

The United States at a Glance

Land

Five Largest States by Area

1. Alaska: 665,384 sq mi (1,723,337 sq km)
2. Texas: 268,596 sq mi (695,660 sq km)
3. California: 163,694 sq mi (423,966 sq km)
4. Montana: 147,040 sq mi (380,832 sq km)
5. New Mexico: 121,590 sq mi (314,917 sq km)

Water

Primary Water Bodies Bordering the U.S.

1. Pacific Ocean: 69,000,000 sq mi (178,800,000 sq km)
2. Atlantic Ocean: 35,400,000 sq mi (91,700,000 sq km)
3. Arctic Ocean: 5,600,000 sq mi (14,700,000 sq km)
4. Gulf of Mexico: 591,500 sq mi (1,532,000 sq km)

Highest, Longest, Largest

The numbers below show locations on the map.

❶ Highest Mountain
Denali (Mount McKinley), in Alaska:
20,310 ft (6,190 m)

❷ Longest River System
Mississippi–Missouri: 3,710 mi
(5,971 km)

❸ Largest Freshwater Lake
(entirely in the U.S.)
Lake Michigan:
22,300 sq mi (57,800 sq km)

❹ Largest Saltwater Lake
Great Salt Lake, in Utah:
1,700 sq mi (4,403 sq km)

❺ Northernmost Point
Point Barrow, Alaska

❻ Southernmost Point
Kalae, Hawai'i

❼ Easternmost Point
Sail Rock, West Quoddy Head, Maine

❽ Westernmost Point
Peaked Island, Alaska

People

In 2018 more than 327 million people lived in the United States. Of these, more than 44 million were born in another country. The largest foreign-born group came from Mexico, followed by India, the Philippines, and China. By 2060 it is projected that the country's population will be greater than 400 million, with almost 70 million being foreign-born.

Five Largest States by Number of People (2018)

1. California: 39,557,045 people
2. Texas: 28,701,845 people
3. Florida: 21,299,325 people
4. New York: 19,542,209 people
5. Pennsylvania: 12,807,060 people

Five Largest Cities* by Number of People (2018)

1. New York, NY: 8,398,748 people
2. Los Angeles, CA: 3,990,456 people
3. Chicago, IL: 2,705,994 people
4. Houston, TX: 2,325,502 people
5. Phoenix, AZ: 1,660,272 people

*Figures are for city proper, not metropolitan area.

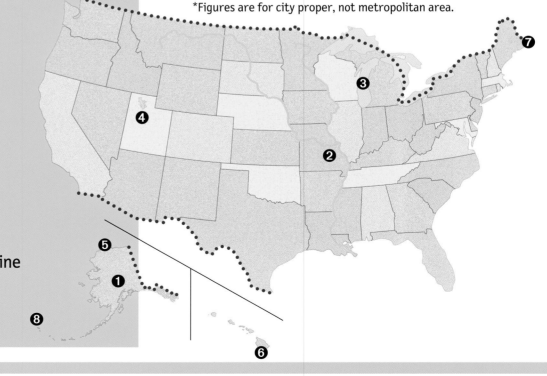

Glossary

Barrier island: a long sandy island that runs parallel to a shore

Boundary: a line on a map that separates one political or mapped area from another; physical features (such as mountains and rivers) or latitude and longitude lines sometimes serve as boundaries

Capital: a place where a country or state government is located

Central America: a region of North America (including Guatemala, Belize, Honduras, El Salvador, Nicaragua, Costa Rica, and Panama) that lies south of Mexico, joining the continents of North and South America

Coniferous forest: needleleaf trees that bear seeds in cones

Container ships: large ships that carry goods in truck-size metal containers among world ports

Contiguous U.S.: the lower 48 states, which are joined together; excludes Alaska and Hawai'i

Continental U.S.: the 49 states located on the continent of North America; excludes Hawai'i

Continental Divide: In the U.S., the natural boundary separating waters flowing into the Atlantic Ocean and Gulf of Mexico from those flowing into the Pacific Ocean

Creole: a blended language evolved from contact between two or more unrelated languages

Deciduous forest: trees, such as oak, maple, and beech, that lose their leaves in the cold season

Delmarva Peninsula: an East Coast peninsula named for the states it includes: Delaware, Maryland, and Virginia

Desert: a region with either hot or cold temperatures that receives 10 inches (25 cm) or less of precipitation a year

Dormant volcano: a volcano that is currently inactive but that may erupt at some time in the future

Erosion: the process by which wind, water, or ice carries away rocks, soil, and other weathered material on Earth's surface

Estuary: the wide part of a river near a sea, where freshwater and saltwater mix

Exports: products made in one place and sent to another to be sold

Foothills: a region of lower hills at the base of a mountain

Fossil: an impression left by the remains of ancient animals or plants that has been preserved in rock or tree sap

Grassland: large areas of mainly flat land covered with grasses

High Plains: flat or gently rolling land above 2,000 feet (600 m); semiarid region east of the Rocky Mountains

Indian reservation: land set aside by the U.S. government for Native Americans to live on and govern

Louisiana Purchase: land purchased from France in 1803 that stretched from the Mississippi River to the Rocky Mountains, and from the Gulf of Mexico to Canada, doubling the size of the country at that time

Mormon: a person who belongs to the Church of Jesus Christ of Latter-day Saints; a religion founded in the U.S. in 1830 by Joseph Smith, Jr.

Mouth: a place where a river empties into an ocean or other large body of water

Peninsula: a large piece of land that sticks out into the water

Sedimentary: a kind of rock, such as sandstone, made of small, compressed particles

Shakers: members of a religious group who did not marry and lived in communal societies

Sunbelt: a region of the southern and western U.S. experiencing rapid economic growth and population increase due to people moving to the region

Temperate rainforest: forests found along the Pacific coast of North America where there is a cool, moist climate and where rainfall is abundant

Tropical rainforest: forests near the Equator that have at least 80 inches (200 cm) of rain each year and an average yearly temperature of 77°F (25°C)

Tundra: a region at high latitudes or high elevations that has cold temperatures, low vegetation, and a short growing season

Wetland: land that is covered with or soaked by water; includes swamps, marshes, and bogs

Two-Letter Postal Codes

ALABAMA	AL	LOUISIANA	LA	OKLAHOMA	OK
ALASKA	AK	MAINE	ME	OREGON	OR
ARIZONA	AZ	MARYLAND	MD	PENNSYLVANIA	PA
ARKANSAS	AR	MASSACHUSETTS	MA	RHODE ISLAND	RI
CALIFORNIA	CA	MICHIGAN	MI	SOUTH CAROLINA	SC
COLORADO	CO	MINNESOTA	MN	SOUTH DAKOTA	SD
CONNECTICUT	CT	MISSISSIPPI	MS	TENNESSEE	TN
DELAWARE	DE	MISSOURI	MO	TEXAS	TX
DISTRICT OF COLUMBIA	DC	MONTANA	MT	UTAH	UT
FLORIDA	FL	NEBRASKA	NE	VERMONT	VT
GEORGIA	GA	NEVADA	NV	VIRGINIA	VA
HAWAI'I	HI	NEW HAMPSHIRE	NH	WASHINGTON	WA
IDAHO	ID	NEW JERSEY	NJ	WEST VIRGINIA	WV
ILLINOIS	IL	NEW MEXICO	NM	WISCONSIN	WI
INDIANA	IN	NEW YORK	NY	WYOMING	WY
IOWA	IA	NORTH CAROLINA	NC		
KANSAS	KS	NORTH DAKOTA	ND		
KENTUCKY	KY	OHIO	OH		

Metric Conversions Found in This Atlas

CONVERSIONS TO METRIC MEASUREMENTS

WHEN YOU KNOW	MULTIPLY BY	TO FIND
INCHES (IN)	2.54	CENTIMETERS (CM)
FEET (FT)	0.30	METERS (M)
MILES (MI)	1.61	KILOMETERS (KM)
SQUARE MILES (SQ MI)	2.59	SQUARE KILOMETERS (SQ KM)
POUNDS (LB)	0.45	KILOGRAMS (KG)

CONVERSIONS FROM METRIC MEASUREMENTS

WHEN YOU KNOW	MULTIPLY BY	TO FIND
CENTIMETERS (CM)	0.39	INCHES (IN)
METERS (M)	3.28	FEET (FT)
KILOMETERS (KM)	0.62	MILES (MI)
SQUARE KILOMETERS (SQ KM)	0.39	SQUARE MILES (SQ MI)
KILOGRAMS (KG)	2.20	POUNDS (LB)

Index

Pictures and the text that describes them have their page numbers printed in **bold** type.

Photo Credits

Art for state flowers and state birds by Robert E. Hynes.

COVER
Front cover: (Statue of Liberty), Amy Harris/Dreamstime; (Earth), ixpert/Shutterstock; (fireworks), yayasya/Adobe Stock; (Mt. Rushmore), EyeWire Images; (baseball), Dan Thornberg/Shutterstock; (sign), photoDISC; (eagle), EyeWire Images; Back cover: (orca), Sandy Buckley/Shutterstock; (snowboarder), Noah Clayton/Getty Images; (bear), Tony Campbell/Shutterstock; (volcano), Jim Sugar/Getty Images; (beach), Mike Brake/Shutterstock; (rocket), NASA; Front flap: (horse), Zuzule/Shutterstock

FRONT MATTER
6 (UP), Charles Krebs/Getty Images; 6 (CTR), Mike Brake/Shutterstock; 6 (LO LE), Enrique Ramos/Shutterstock; 6 (LO RT), James Randklev/Getty Images; 7, Olivier Le Queinec/Shutterstock; 8 (UP), Billy Hustace/Getty Images; 8 (LO), gurineb/Getty Images; 9 (LE), Mark R/Shutterstock; 9 (RT), dibrova/Shutterstock; 10 (UP), photoDISC; 10 (CTR), photoDISC; 11 (UP), Taylor S. Kennedy/National Geographic Image Collection; 11 (LO), Jahi Chikwendiu/The Washington Post via Getty Images

THE NORTHEAST
12, gnagel/Getty Images; 12-13, Skip Brown/National Geographic Image Collection; 14 (UP), Shawn Pecor/Shutterstock; 14 (LO RT), Donald Gargano/Shutterstock; 15, Joel Sartore/National Geographic Image Collection; 16 (UP), Jake Rajs/Getty Images; 16 (CTR), Kevin Fleming/Getty Images; 16-17 (LO RT), aimintang/Getty Images; 17, Catherine Lane/iStockphoto; 18 (UP), photoDISC; 18 (CTR), Mikael Damkier/Shutterstock; 18 (LO RT), Jeff Schultes/Shutterstock; 19, Noah Strycker/Shutterstock; 20 (UP), Emory Kristof/National Geographic Image Collection; 20 (LO RT), Veni/iStockphoto; 21 (UP), Justine Gecewicz/iStockphoto; 21 (LO), James L. Stanfield/National Geographic Image Collection; 22 (UP), Christopher Penler/Shutterstock; 22 (LO RT), Lijuan Guo/Shutterstock; 23 (LE), CO Leong/Shutterstock; 23 (RT), Brett Atkins/Shutterstock; 24 (UP), Paula Stephens/Shutterstock; 24 (CTR), Marcel Jancovic/Shutterstock; 24 (LO RT), George & Judy Manna/Getty Images; 25, Tony Campbell/Shutterstock; 26 (UP), Dave Raboin/iStockphoto; 26 (CTR), CaseyMartin/Shutterstock; 26 (LO RT), Eloi_Omella/Getty Images; 27 (UP), Andrew F. Kazmierski/Shutterstock; 27 (LO), Sheldon Kralstein/iStockphoto; 28 (UP), Cathleen Abers-Kimball/iStockphoto; 28 (LO RT), Richard Levine/Alamy Stock Photo; 29, Glenn Taylor/iStockphoto; 30 (RT), blackwaterimages/iStockphoto; 31 (LE), Jeremy Edwards/iStockphoto; 31 (RT), Racheal Grazias/Shutterstock; 32 (UP), SmarterMedium/Shutterstock; 32 (CTR), Mona Makela/Shutterstock; 32 (LO RT), Joy Brown/Shutterstock; 33, Robert Kelsey/Shutterstock; 34 (UP), Thomas M Perkins/Shutterstock; 34 (LO RT), sianc/Shutterstock; 35 (UP), Albe84/Adobe Stock; 35 (LO), rebvt/Shutterstock

THE SOUTHEAST
36, Adria Photography/Getty Images; 36-37, Maria Stenzel/National Geographic Image Collection; 38 (UP), Darryl Vest/Shutterstock; 38 (CTR), Kevin Fleming/Corbis/VCG/Getty Images; 38 (LO RT), Wayne James/Shutterstock; 39, Ronnie Howard/Shutterstock; 40 (UP), courtesy of the Museum of Discovery; 40 (LO RT), Bill Barksdale/Getty Images; 41, Travel Bug/Shutterstock; 42 (UP), Wayne Johnson/iStockphoto; 42 (LO RT), NASA; 43 (UP), Varina and Jay Patel/iStockphoto; 43 (LO), Valentyn Volkov/Shutterstock; 44 (UP), jackweichen/Shutterstock; 44 (CTR), Antonio V. Oquias/Shutterstock; 44 (LO RT), Brian Lasenby/Shutterstock; 45, Andrew F. Kazmierski/Shutterstock; 46 (UP), Leon Ritter/Shutterstock; 46 (CTR), Craig Wactor/Shutterstock; 46 (LO RT), Anne Kitzman/Shutterstock; 47, Neale Cousland/Shutterstock; 48 (UP), f11photo/Getty Images; 48 (CTR), J. Helgason/Shutterstock; 48 (LO RT), Bob Sacha/Getty Images; 49 (LE), Stephen Helstowski/Shutterstock; 49 (RT), Kathryn Bell/Shutterstock; 50 (UP), Vilmos Varga/Shutterstock; 50 (CTR), Daniela Duncan/Getty Images; 50 (LO RT), Robert Francis/Alamy Stock Photo; 51, Mike Flippo/Shutterstock; 52 (CTR), Leah-Anne Thompson/Shutterstock; 52 (RT), Alex Krassel/Shutterstock; 53 (LE), Rob Byron/Shutterstock; 53 (RT), Brad Whitsitt/Shutterstock; 54 (RT), Rafael Ramirez Lee/Shutterstock; 55 (UP), Zach Holmes/Alamy Stock Photo; 55 (LO), Richard Ellis/Alamy Stock Photo; 56 (UP), Envision/Getty Images; 56 (LO RT), Bryan Busovicki/Shutterstock; 57 (LE), Wayne James/Shutterstock; 57 (RT), Creative Jen Designs/Shutterstock; 58 (UP), Darren K. Fisher/Shutterstock; 58 (LO RT), Travel Bug/Shutterstock; 59 (LE), Graham S. Klotz/Shutterstock; 59 (RT), Adam Kenneth Campbell/Shutterstock; 60 (UP), Robert Pernell/Shutterstock; 60 (CTR), Ken Inness/Shutterstock; 60 (LO RT), Mary Terriberry/Shutterstock; 61, Adam Kenneth Campbell/Shutterstock

THE MIDWEST
62, Holly Hildreth/Getty Images; 62-63, Jim Brandenburg/Minden Pictures; 64 (UP), Raymond Boyd/Getty Images; 64 (CTR), Tim Boyle/Getty Images; 64 (LO RT), Jenny Solomon/Shutterstock; 65, Kim Karpeles/Alamy Stock Photo; 66 (UP LE), James Steidl/Shutterstock; 66 (UP RT), Todd Taulman/Shutterstock; 66 (CTR), John J. Klaiber Jr/Shutterstock; 66 (LO RT), Melissa Farlow/National Geographic Image Collection; 68 (UP), jokter/Shutterstock; 68 (LO RT), Madeleine Openshaw/Shutterstock; 69 (LE), Steve Schneider/iStockphoto; 69 (RT), Andre Jenny/Alamy Stock Photo; 70 (UP), aceshot1/Shutterstock; 70 (LO RT), Rusty Dodson/Shutterstock; 71, Matthew/Adobe Stock; 72 (UP), Gary Paul Lewis/Shutterstock; 72 (CTR), Rachel L. Sellers/Shutterstock; 72 (LO RT), John Brueske/Shutterstock; 73, Cornelia Schaible/iStockphoto; 74 (UP), LazyFocus/Shutterstock; 74 (CTR), V J Matthew/Shutterstock; 74 (LO RT), Geoffrey Kuchera/Shutterstock; 75, Phil Schermeister/Corbis/VCG/Getty Images; 76 (UP), Neil Phillip Mey/Shutterstock; 76 (LO RT), Jose Gil/Shutterstock; 77 (LE), Bill Grant/Alamy Stock Photo; 77 (RT), Rusty Dodson/Shutterstock; 78 (UP), Bates Littlehales/National Geographic Image Collection; 78 (LO RT), H. Abernathy/ClassicStock/Getty Images; 79 (UP), Joel Sartore/National Geographic Image Collection; 79 (LO), marekuliasz/Shutterstock; 80 (UP), Randy Olson/National Geographic Image Collection; 80 (CTR), Ian C. Martin/National Geographic Image Collection; 80 (LO RT), CarbonBrain/Getty Images; 81, Pierrette Guertin/iStockphoto; 82 (UP), aceshot1/Shutterstock; 82 (CTR), Alex Neauville/Shutterstock; 82 (LO RT), James Marvin Phelps/Shutterstock; 83, Weldon Schloneger/Shutterstock; 84 (UP), Werner Bollmann/Getty Images; 84 (CTR), NaughtyNut/Shutterstock; 84 (LO RT), Ira Block/National Geographic Image Collection; 85, Aaron Huey/National Geographic Image Collection; 86 (UP LE), Brad Thompson/Shutterstock; 86 (UP RT), Steve Raymer/National Geographic Image Collection; 86 (CTR), Volkman K. Wentzel/National Geographic Image Collection; 86 (LO RT), Alvis Upitis/Getty Images; 87, Layne Kennedy/Getty Images

THE SOUTHWEST
88, DonLand/Shutterstock; 88-89, Jack Dykinga/National Geographic Image Collection; 90 (UP), Michael Nichols/National Geographic Image Collection; 90 (CTR), zschnepf/Shutterstock; 90 (LO RT), David Edwards/National Geographic Image Collection; 92 (UP), italianestro/Shutterstock; 92 (CTR), Mariusz S. Jurgielewicz/Shutterstock; 92 (LO RT), Ralph Lee Hopkins/National Geographic Image Collection; 94 (UP), Clint Spencer/iStockphoto; 94 (LO RT), MWaits/Shutterstock; 95 (LE), Steven Clevenger/Corbis via Getty Images; 95 (RT), Phil Anthony/Shutterstock; 96 (UP), Ben Conlan/iStockphoto; 96 (CTR), Mira/Alamy Stock Photo; 96 (LO RT), Rusty Dodson/Shutterstock; 97, CrackerClips/Getty Images

THE WEST
98, Barrett Hedges/National Geographic Image Collection; 98-99, Gordon Wiltsie/National Geographic Image Collection; 100 (UP), Benoit Rousseau/iStockphoto; 100 (LO RT), alysta/Shutterstock; 101, Michael Pemberton/Shutterstock; 102 (UP), Stas Volik/Shutterstock; 102 (CTR), PhotoviewPlus/Getty Images; 102 (LO RT), Frank Siteman/Shutterstock; 103, Elke Dennis/Shutterstock; 104 (UP), photoDISC; 104 (LO RT), Larsek/Shutterstock; 105, John P Kelly/Getty Images; 106 (UP), Jarvis Gray/Shutterstock; 106 (CTR), Jim Sugar/Getty Images; 106 (LO RT), Punchalit Chotiksatian/Shutterstock; 107 (UP), Steve Raymer/National Geographic Image Collection; 107 (LO), Jeff Hunter/Getty Images; 108 (UP), Bryan Brazil/Shutterstock; 108 (CTR), Raymond Gehman/National Geographic Image Collection; 108 (LO RT), David P. Smith/Shutterstock; 109, Dick Durrance II/National Geographic Image Collection; 110 (UP), Noah Clayton/Getty Images; 110 (LO RT), Doug Lemke/Shutterstock; 111 (LE), Dana Neibert/Getty Images; 111 (RT), Jerry Sharp/Shutterstock; 112 (UP), Andrew Zarivny/Shutterstock; 112 (CTR), W. Robert Moore/National Geographic Image Collection; 112 (LO RT), Sam Abel/National Geographic Image Collection; 113, Scott T. Smith/Alamy Stock Photo; 114 (UP), Jen Lynn Arnold/Shutterstock; 114 (CTR), Rachell Coe/Shutterstock; 114 (LO RT), Peter Kunasz/Shutterstock; 115, Lotus_studio/Shutterstock; 116 (UP), Grafton Marshall Smith/Corbis; 116 (CTR), Nelson Sirlin/Shutterstock; 116 (LO RT), PhotoDISC; 118 (UP), Natalia Bratslavsky/Shutterstock; 118 (LO RT), Luis Salazar/Shutterstock; 119 (LE), oksana.perkins/Shutterstock; 119 (RT), Sandy Buckley/Shutterstock; 120 (UP), Videowokart/Shutterstock; 120 (LO RT), Henryk Sadura/Shutterstock; 121 (LE), Peter Kunasz/Shutterstock; 121 (RT), Nancy Bauer/Shutterstock

First edition copyright © 2009 National Geographic Society
Second edition copyright © 2016 National Geographic Partners, LLC
Third edition copyright © 2020 National Geographic Partners, LLC

Since 1888, the National Geographic Society has funded more than 12,000 research, exploration, and preservation projects around the world. The Society receives funds from National Geographic Partners, LLC, funded in part by your purchase. A portion of the proceeds from this book supports this vital work. To learn more, visit natgeo.com/info.

For more information, visit nationalgeographic.com, call 1-877-873-6846, or write to the following address:

National Geographic Partners
1145 17th Street N.W.
Washington, DC 20036-4688 U.S.A.

Visit us online at nationalgeographic.com/books

For librarians and teachers: nationalgeographic.com/books/librarians-and-educators

More for kids from National Geographic: natgeokids.com

National Geographic Kids magazine inspires children to explore their world with fun yet educational articles on animals, science, nature, and more. Using fresh storytelling and amazing photography, *Nat Geo Kids* shows kids ages 6 to 14 the fascinating truth about the world—and why they should care. **kids.nationalgeographic.com/subscribe**

For rights or permissions inquiries, please contact National Geographic Books Subsidiary Rights: bookrights@natgeo.com

Designed by Kathryn Robbins

National Geographic supports K–12 educators with ELA Common Core Resources. Visit natgeoed.org/commoncore for more information.

Trade paperback ISBN: 978-1-4263-3825-0
Hardcover ISBN: 978-1-4263-3824-3
Reinforced library binding ISBN: 978-1-4263-3826-7

The publisher would like to thank everyone who worked to make this book come together: Martha Sharma, geographer/writer/researcher; Suzanne Fonda, project manager; Angela Modany, associate editor; Ruthie Thompson, production designer; Hilary Andrews, associate photo editor; Mike McNey, map production; Maureen J. Flynn, map edit; Joan Gossett, production editor; and Gus Tello and Anne LeongSon, design production assistants.

Printed in Malaysia
20/IVM/1

There's always more ...
TO EXPLORE!

National Geographic Kids has the perfect atlas for kids of every age, from preschool through high school—all with the latest age-appropriate facts, maps, images, and more.

The atlas series is designed to grow as kids grow, adding more depth and relevant material at every level to help them stay curious about the world and to succeed at school and in life!

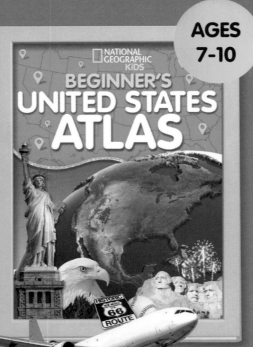

AGES 7-10

NATIONAL GEOGRAPHIC KIDS
BEGINNER'S
UNITED STATES
ATLAS

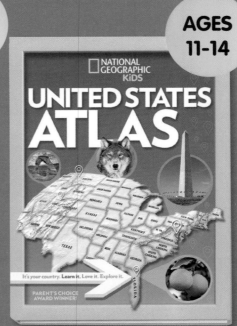

AGES 11-14

NATIONAL GEOGRAPHIC KIDS
UNITED STATES
ATLAS

It's your country. **Learn it. Love it. Explore it.**
PARENT'S CHOICE AWARD WINNER!